Australian Signpost MATHS

6

Mentals

Alan McSeveny Rachel McSeveny

Pearson Australia
(a division of Pearson Australia Group Pty Ltd)
707 Collins Street, Melbourne, Victoria 3008
PO Box 23360, Melbourne, Victoria 8012
www.pearson.com.au

First published 2018 by Pearson Australia
2025 2024 2023 2022
10 9 8 7 6 5 4 3 2 1

Content and Learning Specialist: Sophie Matta
Project Manager: Shelly Wang
Production Manager: Elizabeth Gosman
Editor: Louise Powell
Designers: Anne Donald & Jennifer Johnston
Cover Designer: Jennifer Johnston
Rights & Permissions Editor: Samantha Russell-Tulip
Senior Publishing Services Analyst: Rob Currulli
Cover art: Michael Barter
Cover background: rf_vector/Shutterstock.com
Illustrators: Michael Barter, Wendy Gorton, John Winter

Printed in Malaysia (CTP-VVP)

ISBN 978 1 4886 2192 5

Pearson Australia Group Pty Ltd ABN 40 004 245 943

Introduction

Using the Mentals Books

Each unit of a Mentals Book is programed to review Student Book content from the previous two weeks (based on the Suggested Program in the Teacher's Book). For example, Unit 15 of the Mentals Book can be set as homework to review weeks 13 and 14 of the Student Book while week 15 is being taught.

Presentation

- The content of the strands Number and Algebra, Measurement and Geometry, and Statistics and Probability is covered thoroughly.
- Essential skills are explained.
- Language, problem solving, graphs and tables are given a high profile.
- Mathematics is applied to real-life situations wherever possible.
- The **Arithmetic Card** (page 5) is an exciting teaching tool for practising basic number skills.
- **ID Cards** (pages 6–9) review the terms essential to success in the course.
- **Measurement examples and standards** (page 84 and inside back cover) are provided so that students can estimate effectively.

Mixed-topic Questions

The units present questions in a mixed-topic format.

- This is essential for thorough understanding and continuous review.
- In real life, similar questions don't often occur together.
- It allows the teacher to discover weaknesses that could otherwise pass unnoticed.
- It provides a real test of understanding.

Graded Questions

- Column 1: easier
- Columns 2 and 3: harder
- Column 4: Extension and Challenge

Motivation

- Cartoons make mathematics more appealing.
- There are two lizards hidden on each page for students to find.

Extra Activities

- Problem-solving **strategies** are introduced in a carefully planned sequence throughout the series.

- Important concepts from **Number and Algebra** and **Measurement and Geometry** are explored.

- **Measurement** concepts and activities are introduced and investigated.

- **Statistics and Probability** concepts (Data and Chance) are presented for revision and extension.

- A **tables** program for each of the four operations is included.
- It is important for students to try to learn addition and multiplication tables by heart.

Contents

Teaching Ideas Using Headers

Unit	Content	Extra Activity	Unit	Content	Extra Activity
1:1/2 **1:3/4**	+ 3, + 5 Personal measures	+ Tables Measure	**20:1/2** **20:3/4**	÷ 9, ÷ 9 Profit and loss	÷ Tables Concept
2:1/2 **2:3/4**	− 2, − 4 Language	− Tables ID Card D	**21:1/2** **21:3/4**	Problem solving Height	Strategy Time Concept
3:1/2 **3:3/4**	× 10, × 5 Rounding (nearest 5c)	× Tables Concept	**22:1/2** **22:3/4**	Language Problem solving	ID Card C Strategy Time
4:1/2 **4:3/4**	× 2, × 4 Square numbers	× Tables Concept	**23:1/2** **23:3/4**	÷ 7, ÷ 8 Crossnumber puzzle	÷ Tables Concept
5:1/2 **5:3/4**	+ 4, + 6 Travel graph	+ Tables Concept	**24:1/2** **24:3/4**	÷ 4 Problem solving	÷ Tables Strategy Time
6:1/2 **6:3/4**	− 3, − 7 Order of operations	− Tables Concept	**25:1/2** **25:3/4**	÷ 6 Fractions	÷ Tables Concept
7:1/2 **7:3/4**	Order of operations Language	Concept ID Card B	**26:1/2** **26:3/4**	Mass Tally	Measure Chance
8:1/2 **8:3/4**	Percentages Equivalent fractions	Concept Concept	**27:1/2** **27:3/4**	Language Fractions	ID Card A Concept
9:1/2 **9:3/4**	Multiplication Distance	× Tables Measure	**28:1/2** **28:3/4**	÷ 8 Fractions to decimals	÷ Tables Concept
10:1/2 **10:3/4**	× 3, × 6 Problem solving	× Tables Strategy Time	**29:1/2** **29:3/4**	÷ 7 Problem solving	÷ Tables Strategy Time
11:1/2 **11:3/4**	÷ 5, ÷ 10 Problem solving	÷ Tables Strategy Time	**30:1/2** **30:3/4**	× 8, × 6 Codes	× Tables Concept
12:1/2 **12:3/4**	Language Averages	ID Card A Concept	**31:1/2** **31:3/4**	+ 8 Estimate the product	+ Tables Concept
13:1/2 **13:3/4**	Averages Probability	Concept Chance	**32:1/2** **32:3/4**	Language Estimating chance	ID Card D Chance
14:1/2 **14:3/4**	÷ 2, ÷ 4 24-hour time	÷ Tables Measure	**33:1/2** **33:3/4**	Divisibility Square numbers	Concept Concept
15:1/2 **15:3/4**	÷ 3, ÷ 6 Problem solving	÷ Tables Strategy Time	**34:1/2** **34:3/4**	Factors Problem solving	Concept Strategy Time
16:1/2 **16:3/4**	− 9, − 5 Problem solving	− Tables Strategy Time	**35:1/2** **35:3/4**	Crossnumber puzzle Reflections	Concept Concept
17:1/2 **17:3/4**	+ 7, + 9 Language	+ Tables ID Card B	**36:1/2** **36:3/4**	− 6, − 8 Average speed	− Tables Measure
18:1/2 **18:3/4**	× 6, × 9 Survey	Concept × Tables	**37: 1/2** **37: 3/4**	Language Personal measures	ID Card C Measure
19:1/2 **19:3/4**	× 7, × 8 Length	× Tables Measure	**Answers**	These can be found in the middle of this book on pages A1 to A12.	

 ISBN 978 1 4886 2192 5

Arithmetic Card

	A	B	C	D	E	F	G	H	I	J	K	L	M
1	20	9	110	20	6	11	$100	$\frac{67}{100}$	0·52	97%	$\frac{56}{100}$	20	67
2	16	1	170	50	14	21	$32	$\frac{3}{10}$	0·2	52%	$\frac{8}{100}$	50	62
3	12	6	200	10	2	27	$48	$\frac{75}{100}$	0·75	39%	$\frac{27}{100}$	10	50
4	18	2	130	70	18	25	$90	$\frac{46}{100}$	0·39	74%	$\frac{15}{100}$	70	41
5	13	8	160	100	10	13	$117	$\frac{5}{100}$	0·4	63%	$\frac{88}{100}$	100	33
6	15	5	180	30	16	17	$150	$\frac{9}{10}$	0·98	6%	$\frac{42}{100}$	30	26
7	19	3	150	80	4	29	$76	$\frac{14}{100}$	0·67	18%	$\frac{74}{100}$	80	19
8	14	7	190	60	12	15	$28	$\frac{83}{100}$	0·5	45%	$\frac{66}{100}$	60	14
9	11	4	140	90	20	23	$55	$\frac{6}{10}$	0·13	87%	$\frac{39}{100}$	90	7
10	17	10	120	40	8	19	$85	$\frac{1}{100}$	0·8	21%	$\frac{95}{100}$	40	3

How to Use This Card

If students were told to "subtract B from C", they would write:

❶ 110 – 9 = 101 ❷ 170 – 1 = 169 ❸ 200 – 6 = 194 ❹ 130 – 2 = 128 ❺ 160 – 8 = 152
❻ 180 – 5 = 175 ❼ 150 – 3 = 147 ❽ 190 – 7 = 183 ❾ 140 – 4 = 136 ❿ 120 – 10 = 110

Other instructions might be:

- **What is left from $200 if I spend the amount in column G?**
- **What multiplied by 10 gives column C?**
- **Subtract column I from column L.**
- **Write column J as a decimal.**
- **Multiply column B by 4.**
- **Add columns A and C.**
- **Add columns H and K.**
- **Square column B.**
- **Halve column E.**

The applications of this card are endless.

ID Card A

Do not write on this card.

1 **m** stands for m ______	2 **mm** stands for m ______	3 **cm** stands for c ______	4 **km** stands for k ______	5 **L** stands for l ______
6 **mL** stands for m ______	7 **g** stands for g ______	8 **kg** stands for k ______	9 **s** stands for s ______	10 **min** stands for m ______
11 **h** stands for h ______	12 **cm^2** stands for s ______ c ______	13 **m^2** stands for s ______ m ______	14 **ha** stands for h ______	15 **cm^3** stands for c ______ c ______
16 **m^3** stands for c ______ m ______	17 **°C** stands for d ______ C ______	18 **( )** are called g ______ symbols.	19 **am** means b ______ n ______	20 **pm** means a ______ n ______
21 **1, 2, 3, …** are the c ______ numbers.	22 **2, 4, 6, …** are the e ______ numbers.	23 **1, 3, 5, …** are the o ______ numbers.	24 **1st, 2nd, …** are the o ______ numbers.	25 **208 650** has 6 d ______
26 **1, 4, 9, 16, 25, …** are the s______ numbers.	27 **The factors of 8** are 1, 8, ______ and ______	28 **7, 14, 21, …** are multiples of ______	29 **35, 40 and 45** are all divisible by ______	30 $5\overline{)47}$ = **9 r 2**; "r" means r ______

See page A1 for answers.

 ISBN 978 1 4886 2192 5

ID Card B

Do not write on this card.

ID Card B

1 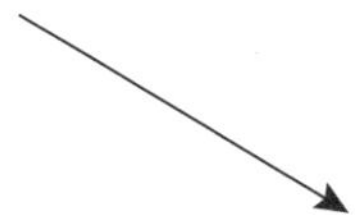
This part of a line is a r ____________

2 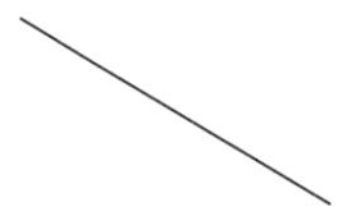
This part of a line is an i ____________

3 
s ____________ line

4 
c ____________ line

5 
w ____________ line

6 
z____________ line

7 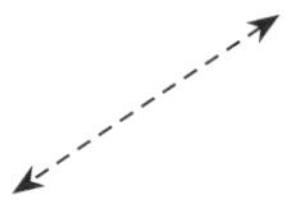
d____________ line

8 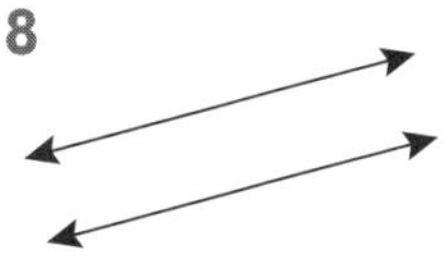
p ____________ lines

9 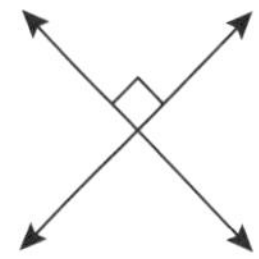
p ____________ lines

10 
h ____________ line

11 
v ____________ line

12 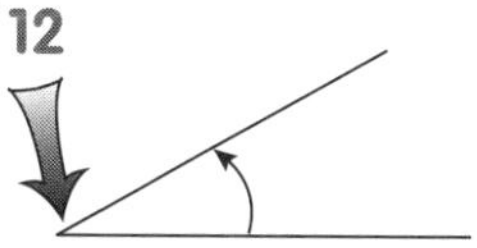
c ____________ (or vertex of an angle)

13 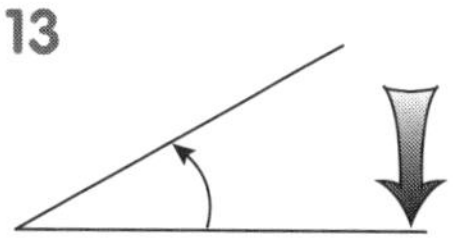
a ____________ of an angle

14 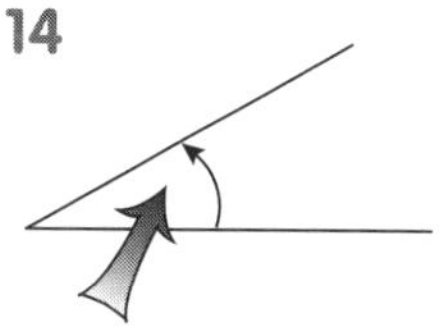
a ____________ angle

15 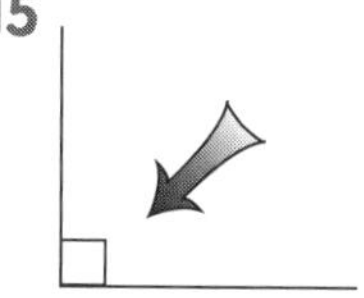
r ____________ angle

16 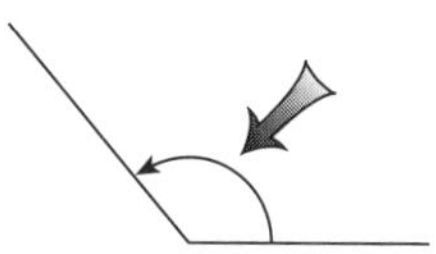
o ____________ angle

17 
s ____________ angle

18 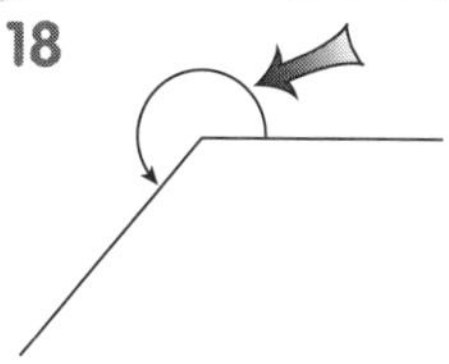
r ____________ angle

19 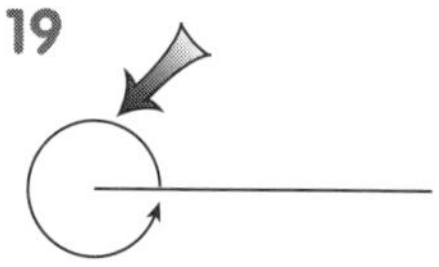
r ____________

20 
t ____________

21 
r ____________

22 
t ____________

23 
r ____________

24 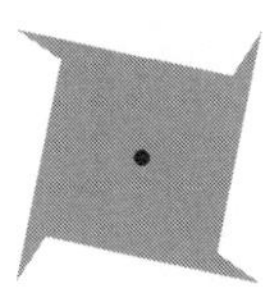
This has r ____________
s ____________

25 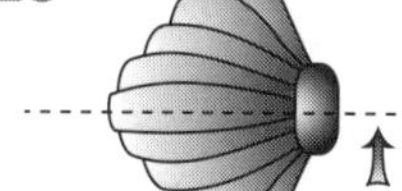
axis of s ____________

26 
a _____ of symmetry

27 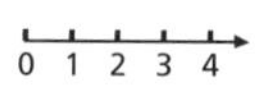

n ____________ line

28 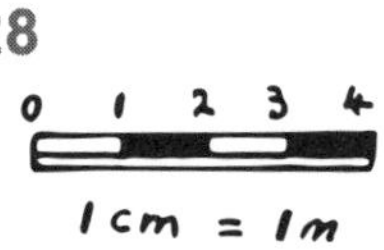

s ____________

29 The scale

1 cm = 1 m

is 1: ____________

30 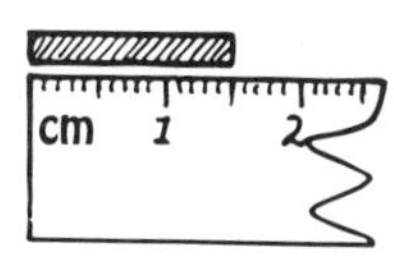

The length is ____ mm.

See page A1 for answers.

AUSTRALIAN SIGNPOST MATHS 6 MENTALS • ISBN 978 1 4886 2192 5

ID Card C

Do not write on this card.

1

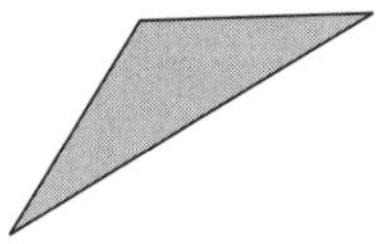

t ____________

2

s ____________

3

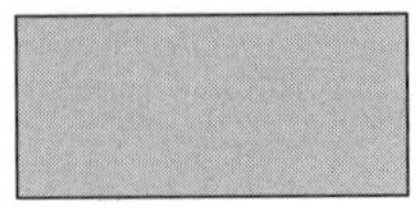

r ____________

4

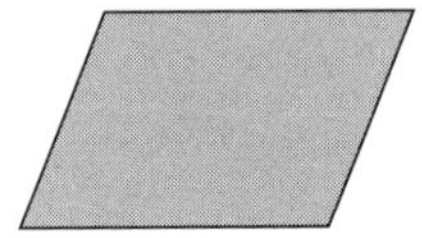

p ____________

5

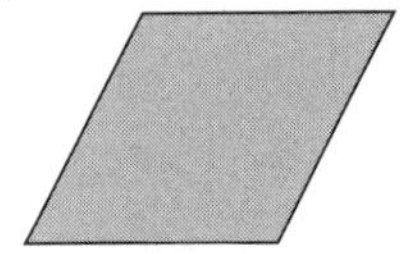

r ____________

6

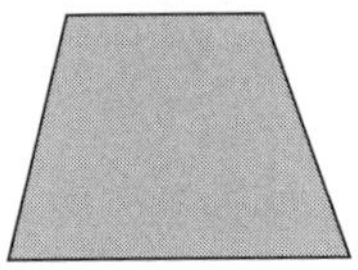

t ____________

7

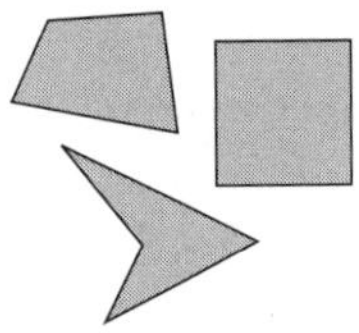

q ____________

8

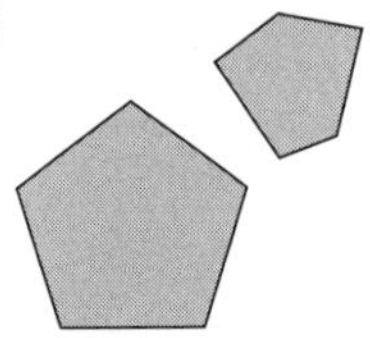

p ____________

9

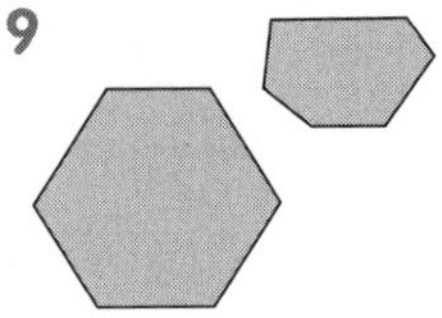

h ____________

10

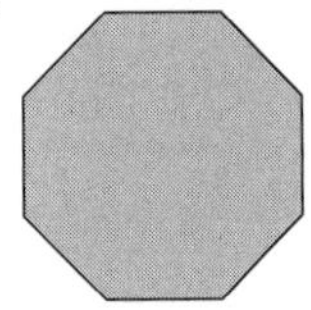

o ____________

11

c ____________

12

o ____________

13

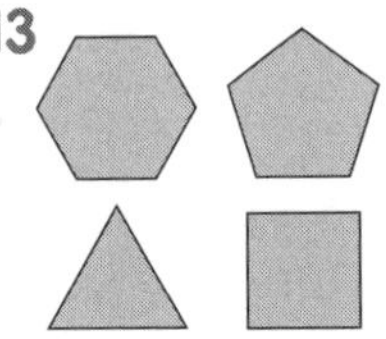

r ____________ shapes

14

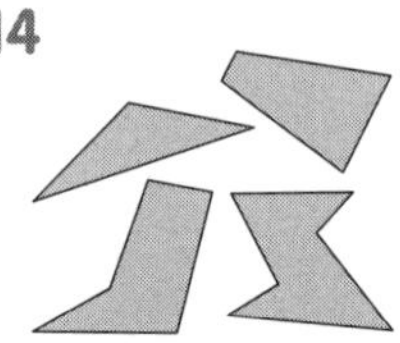

i ____________ shapes

15

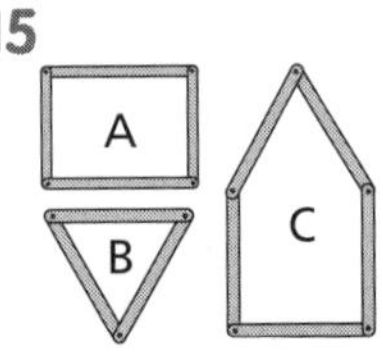

Shape ______ is rigid.

16

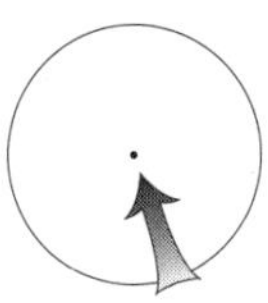

c ____________

17

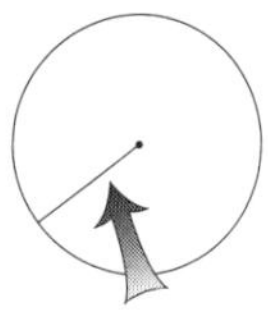

r ____________

18

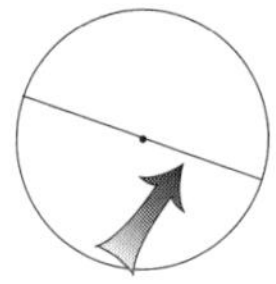

d ____________

19

The distance around a circle is called the

c ____________

20

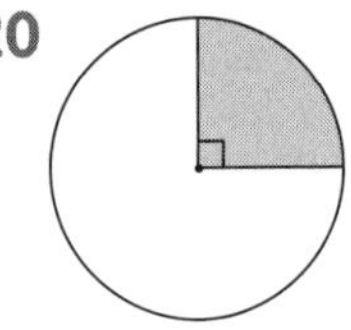

q ____________

21

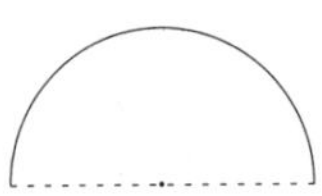

semi- ____________

22

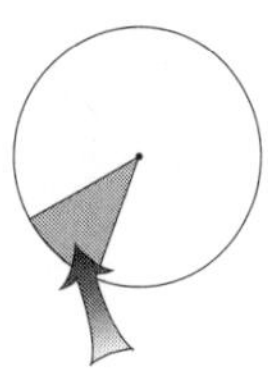

s ____________

23

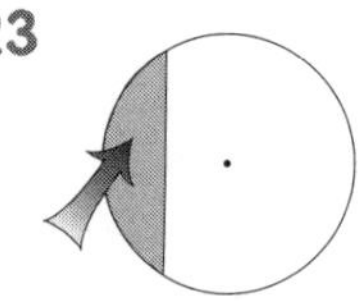

s ____________

24

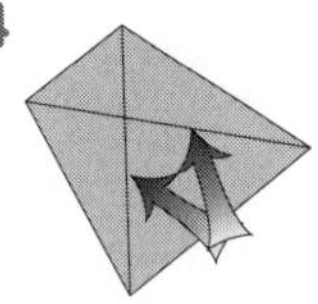

d ____________

25

1 cm^3

has the same volume as

______ mL of liquid.

26

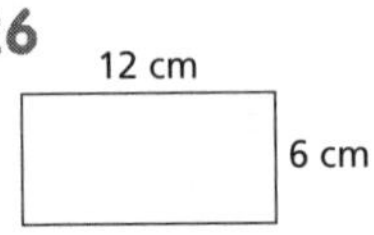

length = ________

breadth = ________

27

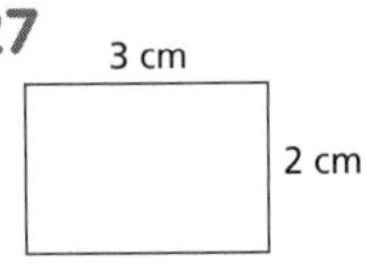

perimeter = ________

28

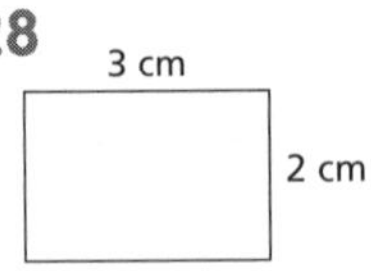

area = ________

29

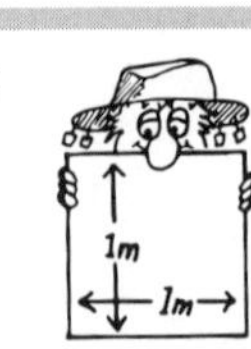

1 square

m ____________

30

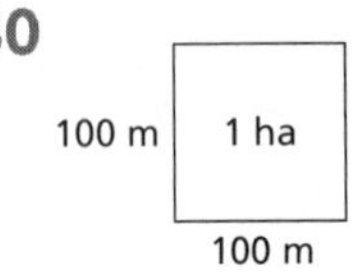

The area is

1 ha ____________

See page A1 for answers.

 ISBN 978 1 4886 2192 5

ID Card D

Do not write on this card.

1

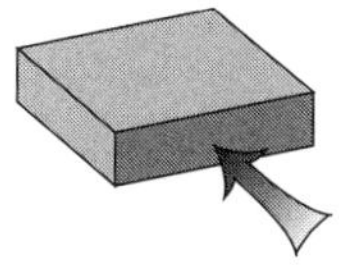

f ____________

2

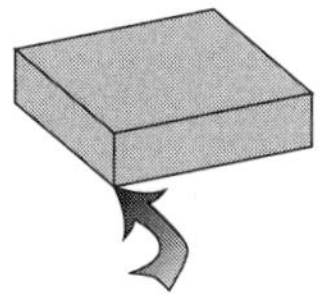

c ____________

or v ____________

3

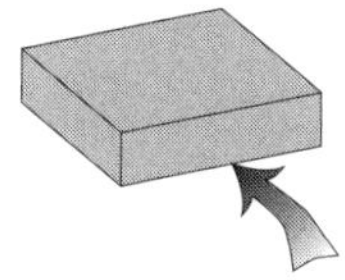

e ____________

4

c ____________

5

r ____________

p ____________

6

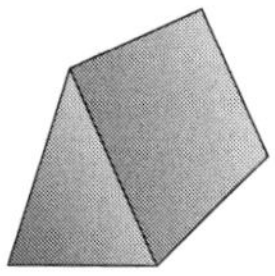

t ____________

p ____________

7

h ____________

p ____________

8

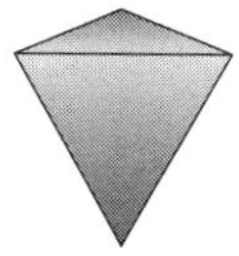

t ____________

p ____________

9

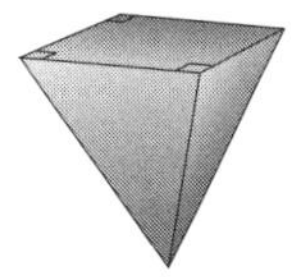

s ____________

p ____________

10

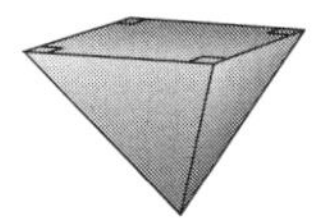

r ____________

p ____________

11

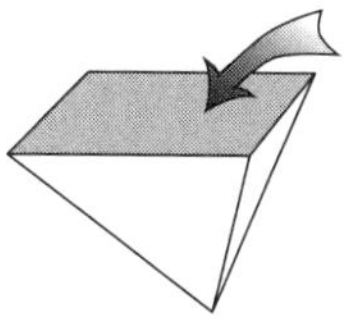

b ____________

12

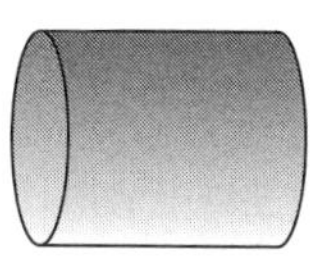

c ____________

13

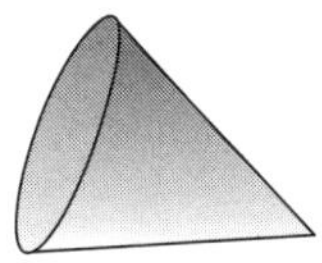

c ____________

14

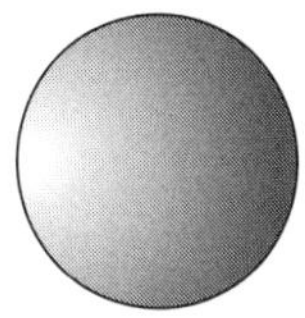

s ____________

15

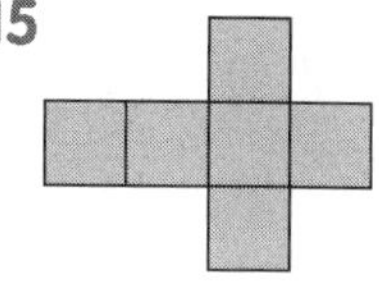

net of a c ____________

16

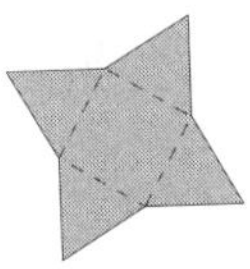

net of a s ____________

p ____________

17

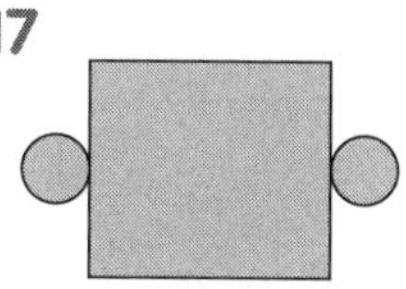

net of a c ____________

18

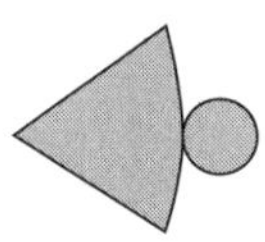

net of a c ____________

19

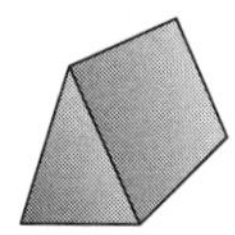

Side view is:

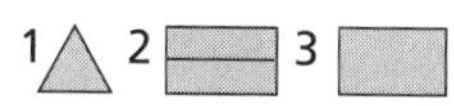

20

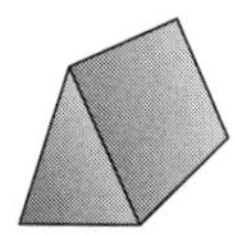

Front view is:

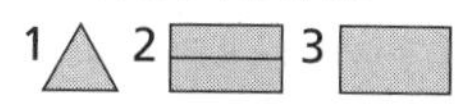

21

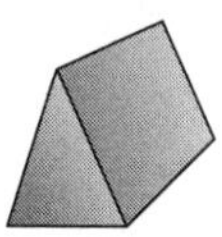

Top view is:

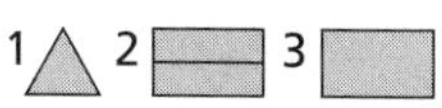

22

7:30 pm

in 24-hour time is

____ : ____

23

05:40

in digital time is

____ : ____ ____

24

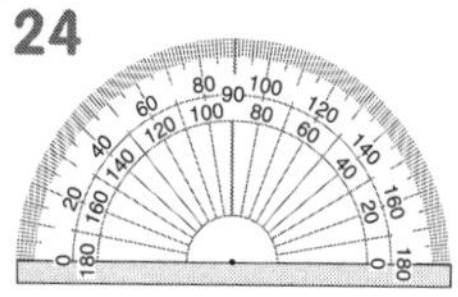

p ____________

25

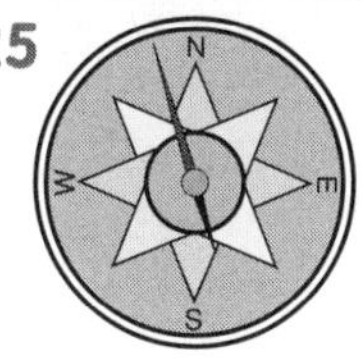

c ____________

26

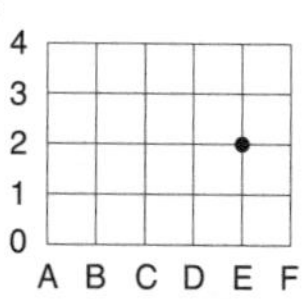

The c ____________ of the dot are E2.

27

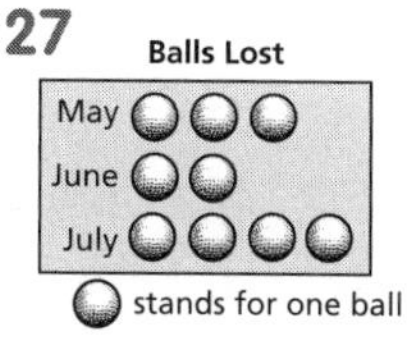

p ____________ graph

28

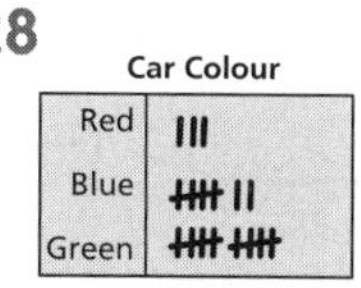

This is a t ____________

29

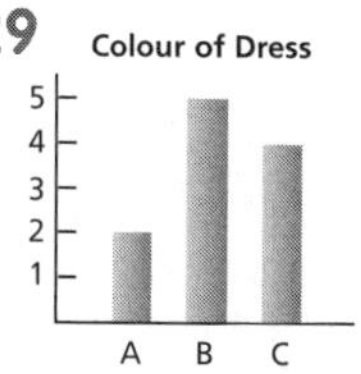

c ____________ graph

30

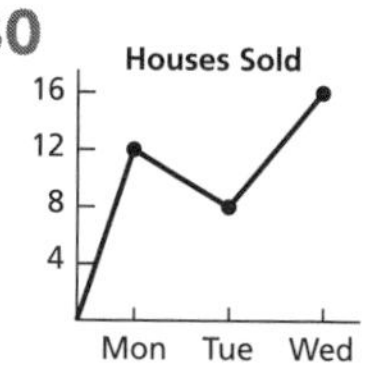

l ________ graph

See page A1 for answers.

1:1 ☐ out of 19

1. 8 + 7 ____
2. 4 × 6 ____
3. 15 − 7 ____
4. 4 × 4 ____
5.
```
   19
 + 21
```
6. 6 × 9 ____
7. 20 ÷ 2 ____
8. Add 9 and 6. ____
9. Take 4 from 9. ____
10.
```
   26
 −  8
```

11. Thousands in 7802? ____
12. Which is smaller, 687 or 587? ____
13. 80 000 + 6000 + 600 + 20 + 4 ____
14. Write 3 out of 10:
    a as a fraction ____
    b as a decimal ____
15. Complete the labels for the shaded section.

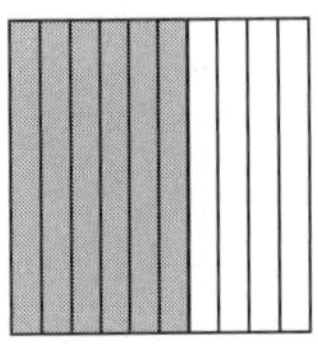

____ tenths or 0· ____

16. 4 baskets with 20 eggs each. ____ eggs
17. List all the factors of 32. ____

____

18. 6 m 80 cm = ____ centimetres
19.

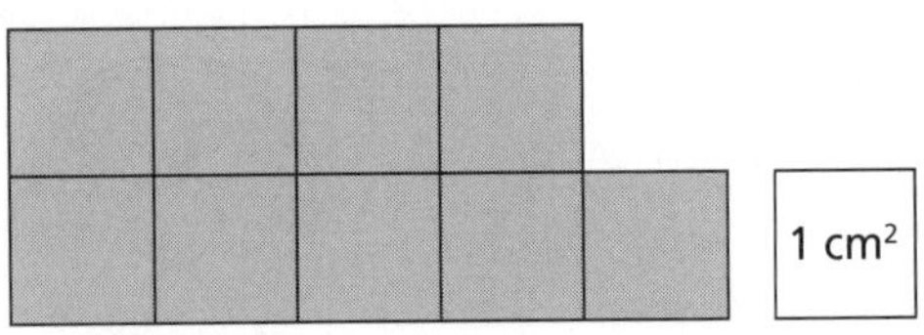

a What is the area? ____
b What is the perimeter? ____

1:2 ☐ out of 15

1. 22 + 72 ____
2. 8 × 8 ____
3. 15 − 5 ____
4. 6 × 30 ____
5.
```
   24
 + 76
```
6. 12 × 5 ____
7. 15 × 3 ____
8. 7 × 7 ____
9. Take 4 from 39. ____
10.
```
   91
 − 12
```

11. Round off the answer to Question 10, correct to the nearest 10. ____
12. Write fifty-one hundredths:
    a as a decimal ____
    b as a percentage ____
13. Shade seven tenths and complete the labels.

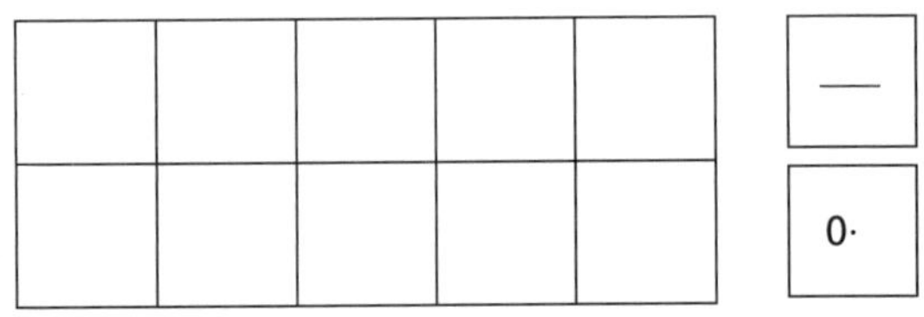

14. List all:
    a vertical lines ____
    b horizontal lines ____
    c sloping lines ____
    d lines parallel to **A** ____

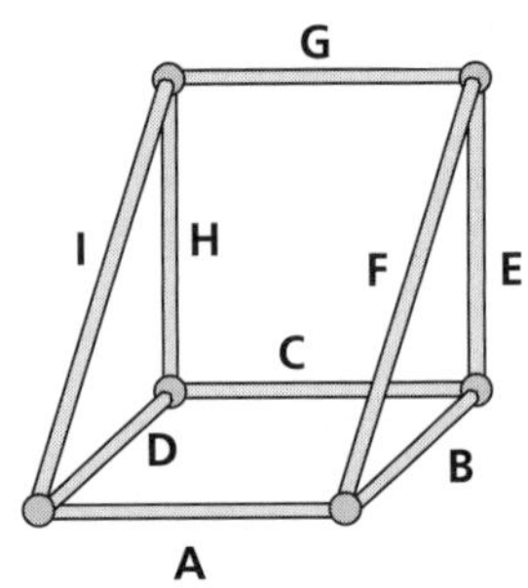

15. How many mugs are needed to hold 14 coffees, 12 teas and 8 hot chocolates? ____

+ Tables

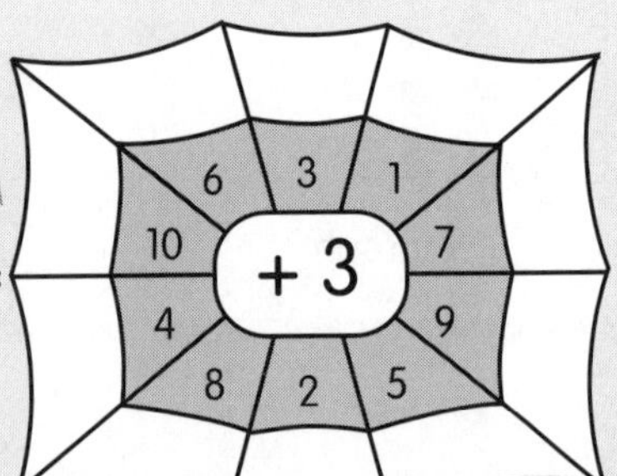

even + odd = ____
odd + odd = ____

 • *AUSTRALIAN SIGNPOST MATHS 6 MENTALS* • ISBN 978 1 4886 2192 5

1:3 — ☐ out of 14

1
$$\begin{array}{r} 592 \\ +\ 348 \\ \hline \end{array}$$

2

T	U
6	2
− 4	8

3 Days in a fortnight. ______

4 Hours in 6 days. ______

5 True or false?
4693 rounds off to 5000. ______

6 How many 50c apples can be bought for $3.70? ______

7 Subtract 8 from 23. ______

8 Years in a decade. ______

9 **a** Colour $\frac{1}{4}$ of this shape red.

b Colour $\frac{1}{3}$ of this shape blue.

c Is $\frac{1}{3}$ smaller than $\frac{1}{4}$? ______

10 How many teams of six can be made using 59 children? ______

11 Fill in this numeral expander for 4902.

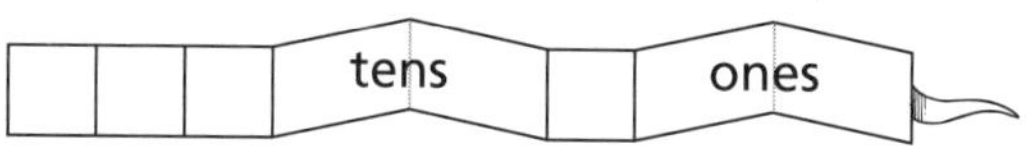

12 How many axes of symmetry does a square have? ______

13 **a** 3 m 2 cm = ______ cm

b 320 cm = ____ m ____ cm

14 The day before Tuesday? ______

1:4 — Extension — ☐ out of 5

1 True or false?

a $3 \times 6 = 6 \times 3$ ______

b $11 - 6 = 6 - 11$ ______

2 For this solid, calculate the number of corners plus the number of faces minus the number of edges. ______

3 Into each of 8 boxes, 4 or 5 books were put. There were 35 books altogether. How many boxes had 4 books? ______

4 Use the jump strategy for 856 + 26. ______

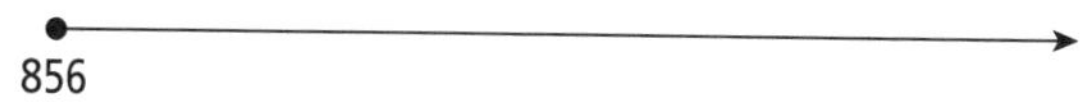

5 I bought at least one of each of these items. The cost was $3.85. How many apples did I buy? ______

Challenge

Write number sentences with the answer 36.

______

______

______

______

______

______

Fill out this table about yourself, a relative or a friend.

Name: ______ **Date:** ______

Age: ______	Mass: ______ kg	Shoe size: ______
Height: ______ cm	Waist: ______ cm	Neck size: ______ cm

2:1 ☐ out of 20

1. $24 \div 4$ ____
2. $0 + 8$ ____
3. 6×6 ____
4. $27 - 14$ ____
5. $\begin{array}{r} 3 \\ \times\ 9 \\ \hline \end{array}$
6. $27 \div 3$ ____
7. Take 12 from 36. ____
8. 5 more than 22. ____
9. Triple 4. ____
10. $\begin{array}{r} 88 \\ -\ 25 \\ \hline \end{array}$
11. The value of the 9 in 298 554? ____
12. Write 7 163 in its expanded form. ____

13. 

 a What fraction is shaded? ____
 b What fraction is not shaded? ____
14. a Is 84 divisible by 7? ____
 b Is 84 a multiple of 7? ____
15. What shape has 4 right angles and has its opposite sides equal? ____
16. a 868 cm = ____ m ____ cm
 b 1·5 m = ____ cm

17. Use the short form to write:
 a four hundred and ten grams ____
 b six hundred and six millilitres ____
18. Reflection, translation or rotation? ____

19. 0·43 = ____ out of ____ = ____%
20. Continue this pattern.
 0·7, 0·8, 0·9, ____, ____, ____

2:2 ☐ out of 18

1. 3×9 ____
2. $13 - 8$ ____
3. $60 + 50$ ____
4. 4×80 ____
5. $\begin{array}{r} 15 \\ +\ \ 9 \\ \hline \end{array}$
6. $81 \div 9$ ____
7. $67 + 42$ ____
8. Reduce 101 by 8. ____
9. 5×5 ____
10. $\begin{array}{r} \$2.87 \\ +\ \$1.61 \\ \hline \end{array}$

11. Round off the answer to Question 10, correct to the nearest 10 cents. ____
12. a 700 000 + 7 000 + 7 ____
 b Use all the odd numbers less than 10 to make as large a number as possible. ____
13. The first 3 multiples of 8. ____
14. How many axes of symmetry has a regular pentagon? ____
15. a The coordinates of **Z**. ____
 The letter found at:
 b **B2** ____
 c **D1** ____
 d **F3** ____
 e **E3** ____

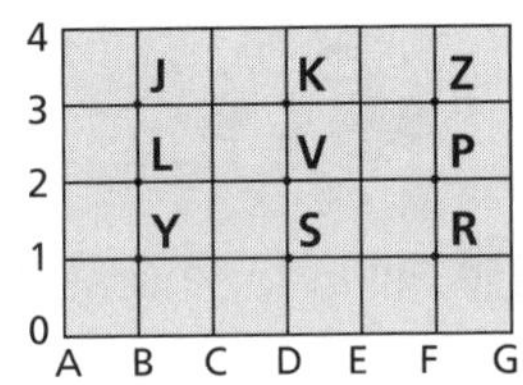

16. Write the numeral for 50 000 + 5 000 + 50 + 5. ____
17. The fraction for:
 a zero point nine nine ____
 b one point eight ____
18. a The difference between 94 and 60. ____
 b The sum of 46 and 53. ____

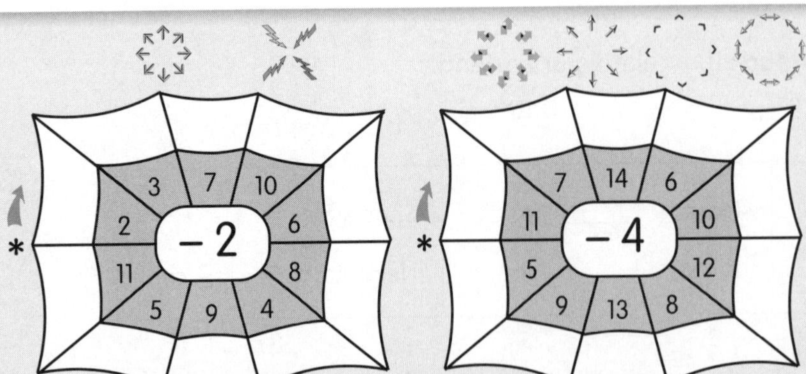

 ISBN 978 1 4886 2192 5

2:3 ☐ out of 11

1

697
+ 136

2

297
+ 324

3

387
+ 165

4 A B

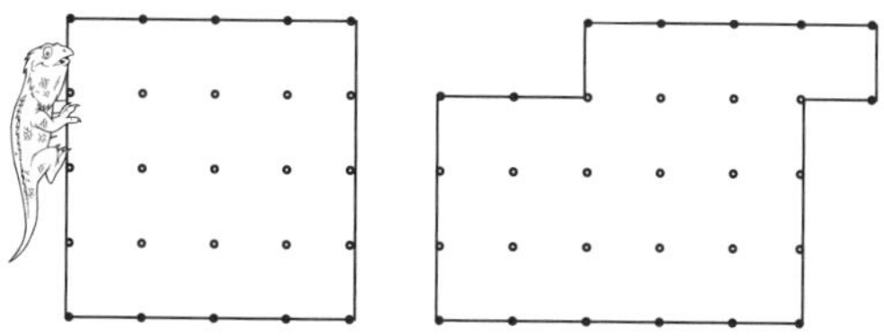

Which shape has the greater:

a area? ______ **b** perimeter? ______

5 In which season is January? ______

6 Write the fraction for zero point nine. ______

7 An eight-sided shape. ______

8 Share 16 mangoes between 8 people. One share = ______

9 These shapes fit together without gaps or overlaps.

They t ______.

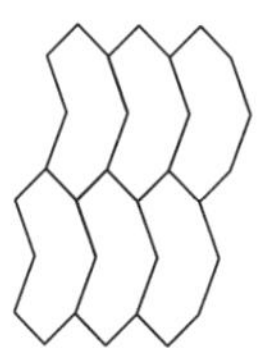

10 Write 37c in decimal form. ______

11 Draw the axes of symmetry on this shape.

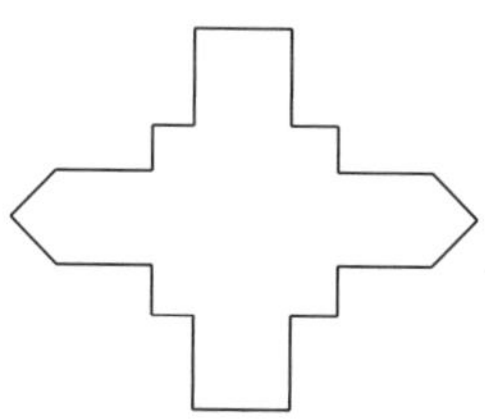

2:4 ☐ out of 4 **Extension**

1 Complete this pattern.

1st number	50	51	52	53
2nd number	65	66	67	

Write a rule for the pattern above. ______

2nd number = ______

2 In one week, Chloe watched 14 h 30 min of TV. Jenna watched 10 h 45 min. How much did they watch altogether? ______

3 Enlarge this shape using a scale factor of 3. Multiply the distance of each point from the centre by 3.

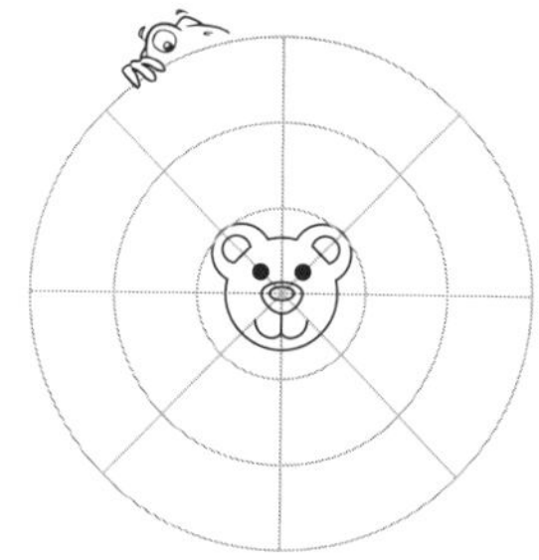

4 **a** 104 more than 5066. ______

b 320 more than 7680. ______

Challenge

Draw a tessellation.

Turn to ID Card D on page 9.

Give the answers for these numbers.

(1) ______ (2) ______

(3) ______ (11) ______

(12) ______ (13) ______

(14) ______ (15) net of a ______

(17) net of a ______ (18) net of a ______

3:1

out of 16

1. 8×4 ____
2. $9 - 6$ ____
3. $14 \div 7$ ____
4. $55 + 6$ ____
5. $\begin{array}{r} 22 \\ -\ 8 \\ \hline \end{array}$
6. Half of 120. ____
7. 70 take away 3. ____
8. 10×7 ____
9. 28 plus 4. ____
10. $\begin{array}{r} 85 \\ -\ 40 \\ \hline \end{array}$

11. Name these 3D shapes.

a

____

b

____

12. 27 exercise books shared between 5 students.

Books each = ____

Remainder= ____

13. 9000 + 700 + 8 ____

14. Join:
1 and 5, 5 and 9, 9 and 1,
2 and 6, 6 and 10, 10 and 2,
3 and 7, 7 and 11, 11 and 3,
4 and 8, 8 and 12, 12 and 4.
What have you drawn?

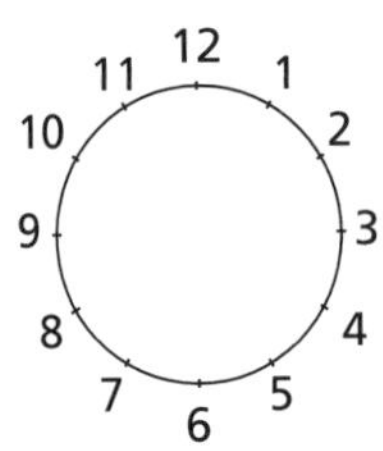

____

15. Write as a numeral "four million four thousand and forty". ____

16. Which of these angles is:

a acute? ____

b obtuse? ____

3:2

out of 16

1. 3×10 ____
2. $16 - 9$ ____
3. $23 + 5$ ____
4. 9×5 ____
5. $\begin{array}{r} 62 \\ +\ 37 \\ \hline \end{array}$
6. $30 \div 3$ ____
7. $99 + 32$ ____
8. $\square \times 8 = 40$, $\square =$ ____
9. $\square \div 5 = 20$, $\square =$ ____
10. $\begin{array}{r} 31 \\ +\ 27 \\ \hline \end{array}$

11. 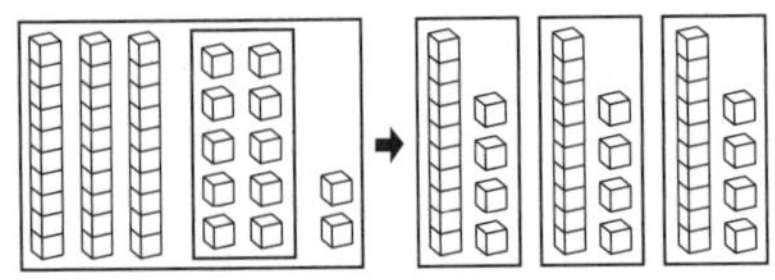

Share 42 among 3. One share = ____

12. Which angle is:

a obtuse? ____

b acute? ____

c straight? ____

d reflex? ____

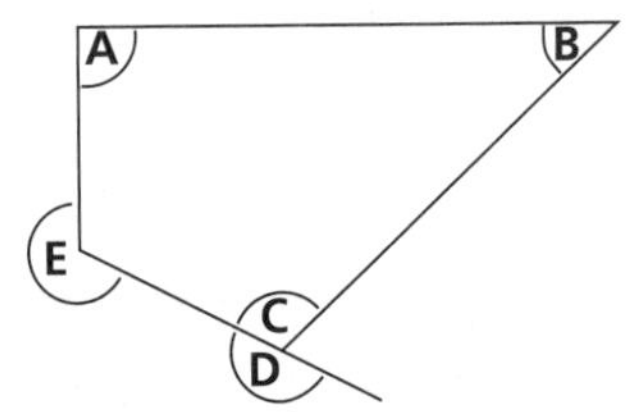

13. Use < or > in:

a 6 073 491 ____ 6 173 492

b 7 340 511 ____ 7 343 611

14. 307 + 71 ____

15. Which of the following would not fold to make a solid shape like this?

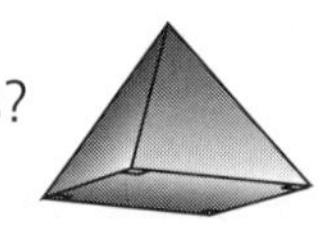

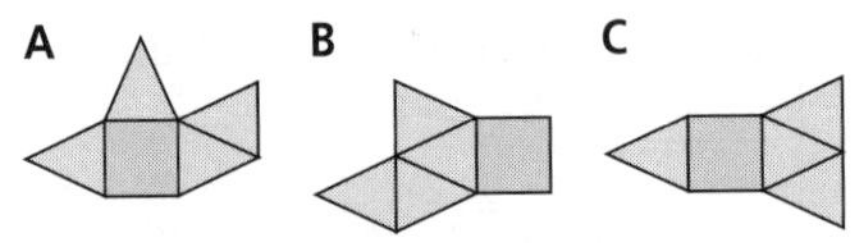

____

16. Reflection, translation or rotation?

____

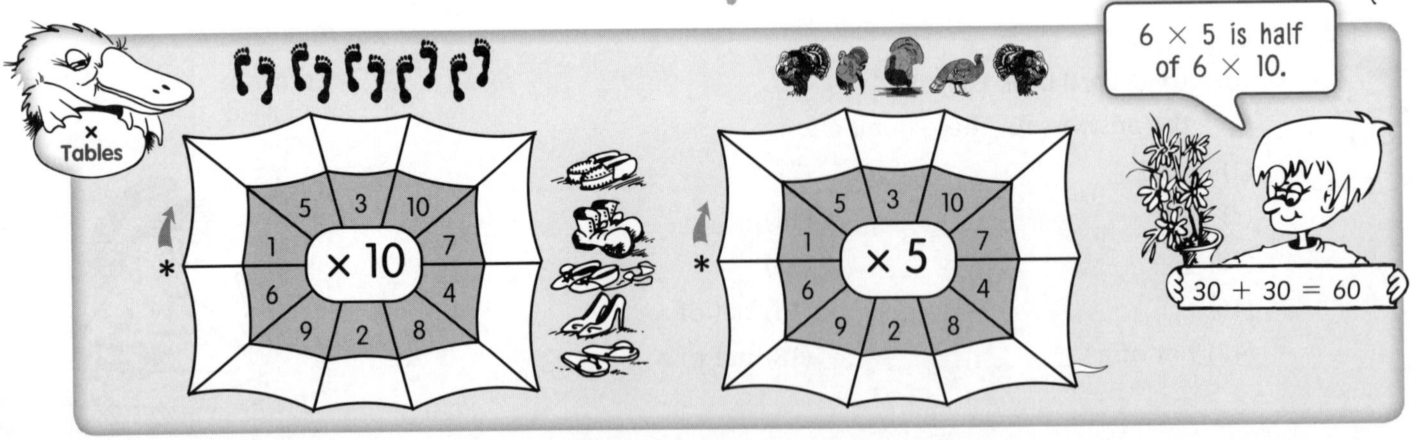

 AUSTRALIAN SIGNPOST MATHS 6 MENTALS • ISBN 978 1 4886 2192 5

3:3  ☐ out of 10

1
$$\begin{array}{r} \$40.23 \\ +\ \$32.85 \\ \hline \end{array}$$

2
$$\begin{array}{r} \$33.56 \\ +\ \$21.29 \\ \hline \end{array}$$

3 True or false?

a 4639 rounds off to 4600. ______

b 3216 rounds off to 3300. ______

4

For these trees, how many groups of:

a 6 trees? ______ groups ______ left

b 5 trees? ______ groups ______ left

5 6 lots of 7 buttons. ______ buttons

6 600 + 80 + 2 + 0·05 ______

7 Write 41 000 004 in words. ______

______

8 Degrees in a straight angle. ______

9 Name the solid for each net below.

a

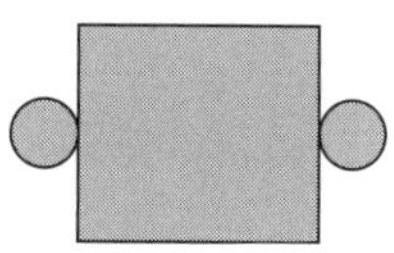

______

b

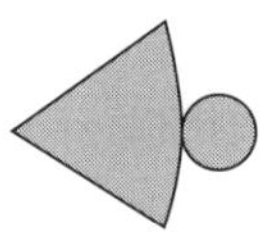

______

10

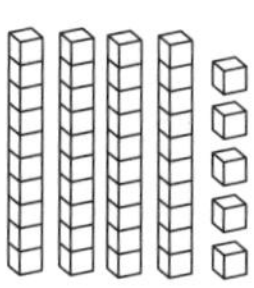

How many people could be given 15?

______

3:4 Extension ☐ out of 6

1 How many groups of 51 in 255? ______

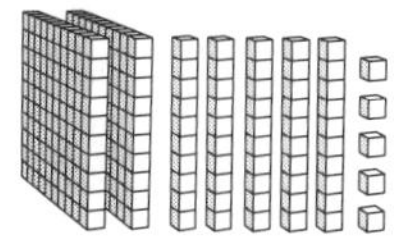

2 After opening a book the sum of the two page numbers I could see was 145. What were the page numbers? ______

3 Which of the shapes below can be joined to shape **S** to make a square? ______

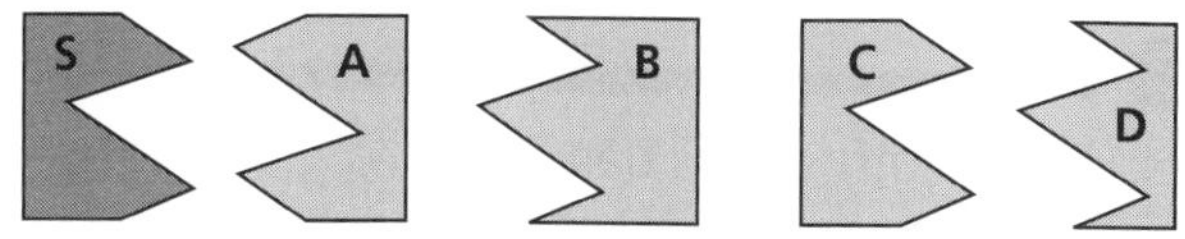

4 In how many different ways can you make 40c using 5c, 10c and 20c coins? ______

5 How many $1 coins (2·5 cm wide) are needed side by side to reach 30 cm? ______

6 345 tens and 7 ones. ______

Challenge

Write facts about the number 13 546 200.

______

______

______

______

______

To round off to the nearest 5 cents, give the closest answer that ends in 5 or 0.

a Is $37.47 closer to $37.45 or $37.50? ______

Round each of these to the nearest 5 cents.

b $43.88 ______ **c** $29.99 ______ **d** $84.63 ______

e $117.12 ______ **f** $265.14 ______ **g** $630.97 ______

4:1 ☐ out of 15

1. 26 + 4 ____
2. 7 × 8 ____
3. 12 − 5 ____
4. 5 ÷ 5 ____
5. $\begin{array}{r} 50 \\ \times\ \ 4 \\ \hline \end{array}$
6. 3 squared. ____
7. 91 subtract 11. ____
8. Divide 33 by 3. ____
9. Add 30 and 17. ____
10. $\begin{array}{r} 72 \\ +\ 18 \\ \hline \end{array}$

11.
The length of this bar. ______ mm

12. Equal numbers of birds are put in four cages. If there are 24 birds, how many are in each cage? ______

13. Complete this picture so that it is symmetrical about the dotted line.

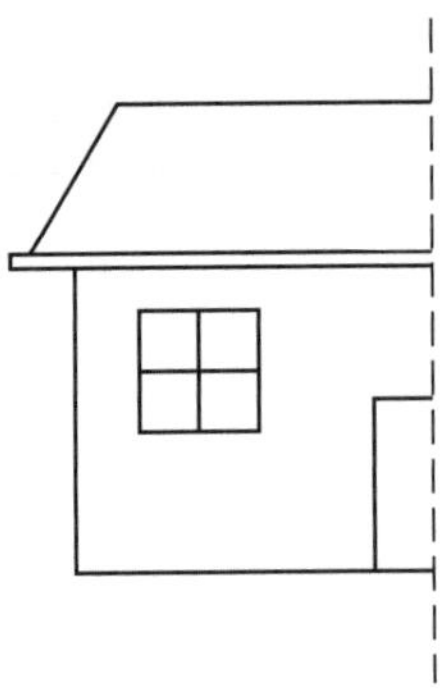

14. Which of these shapes will tessellate?

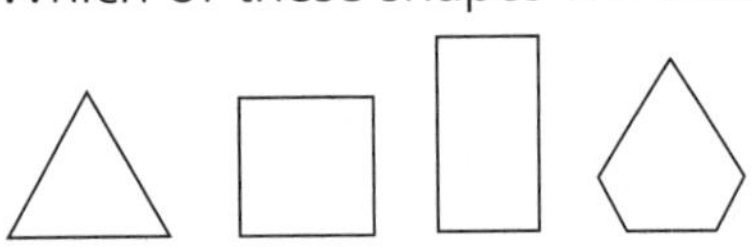

A B C D ______

15. The value of the 2 in 2 001 391? ______

4:2 ☐ out of 17

1. 5 squared. ____
2. 14 − 9 ____
3. 34 + 4 ____
4. 6 × 90 ____
5. $\begin{array}{r} 190 \\ -\ \ 15 \\ \hline \end{array}$
6. 20 ÷ 4 ____
7. 80 − 12 ____
8. □ − 7 = 63, □ = ____
9. □ + 8 = 27, □ = ____
10. $\begin{array}{r} 468 \text{ cents} \\ -\ 311 \text{ cents} \\ \hline \end{array}$

11. Write down all the factors of 36.
______

12. Write as millimetres:
a 4·5 cm ______ **b** 9·6 cm ______

13. Find the perimeter of each shape.

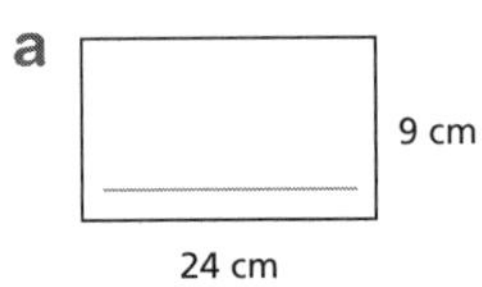

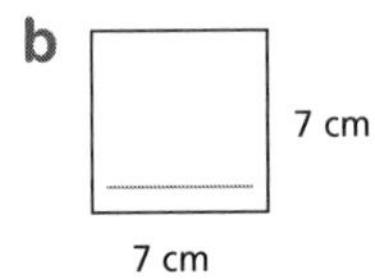

14. 4, 22, 27, 51, 64
Which of these numbers are:
a multiples of 3? ______
b square numbers? ______

15. **a** 7 000 000 + 400 000 ______
b Numeral for $6\frac{1}{2}$ million. ______

16. An angle of size 120° is an ______ angle.

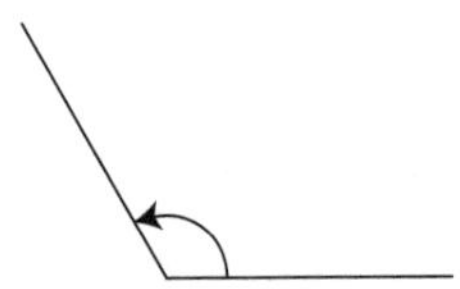

17. How many people could be given 14?
______

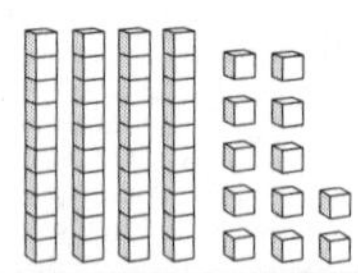

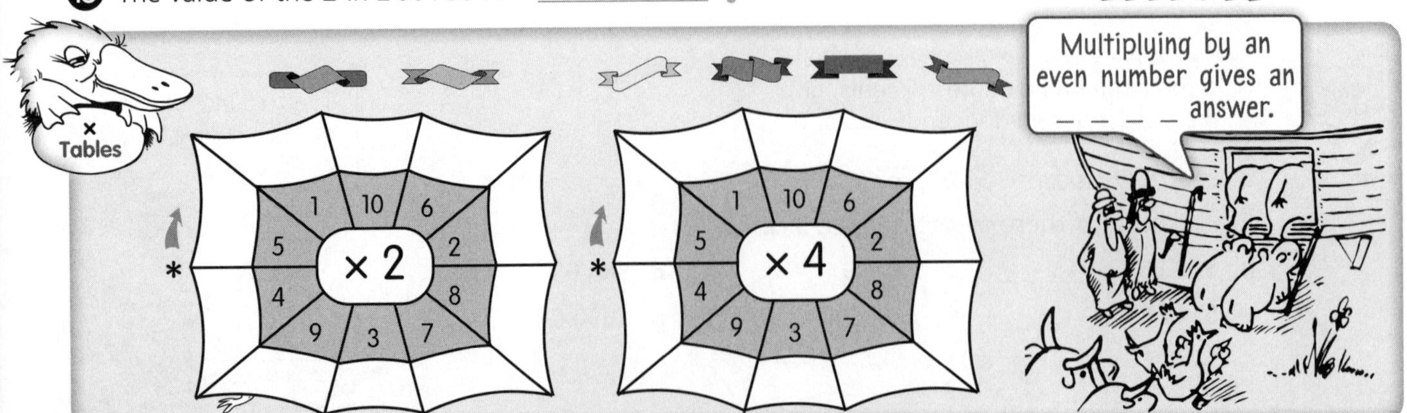

 ISBN 978 1 4886 2192 5

4:3 ☐ out of 11

1.
$$\begin{array}{r} 341 \\ 22 \\ 163 \\ +\ \ 47 \\ \hline \end{array}$$

2.
$$\begin{array}{r} 33 \\ 217 \\ 300 \\ +\ \ 25 \\ \hline \end{array}$$

3.
$$\begin{array}{r} 20 \\ 345 \\ 201 \\ +\ 179 \\ \hline \end{array}$$

4. What is the perimeter of a square if its sides are 8 cm long? ______

5. 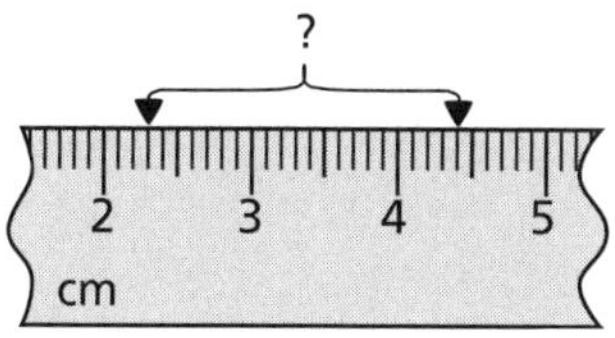

What is the distance between the marks above the ruler? ______

6. The dotted line represents the axis of: ______

7. Millimetres in:
   a 50 cm ______ b 2·5 m ______

8. 6 squared. ______

9. The numeral for nine million nine hundred and ninety-nine thousand. ______

10. How many 30° angles make a right angle? ______

11. How many groups of 6 in 25?
    ______ groups of 6
    ______ left over

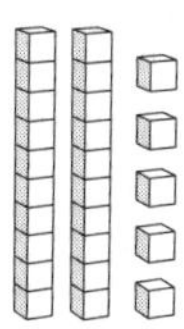

4:4 Extension ☐ out of 5

1. 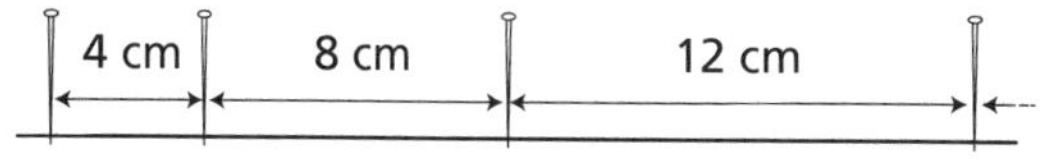

Pins were stuck onto a board using the pattern shown above.
What was the distance between:
   a the 5th and 6th pins? ______
   b the 1st and 6th pins? ______

2. 12 boxes of pens held either 5 or 6 pens. There was a total of 64 pens. How many boxes held 6 pens? ______

3. The smallest even number that is a multiple of 9. ______

4. a $6\frac{1}{2} + 13\frac{1}{2}$ ______

   b $20 - 3\frac{1}{2}$ ______

5. I can run around the large square once or around the small square four times. What is the difference in distance? ______

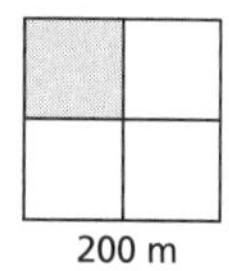

Challenge

List as many square numbers as you can using number sentences, e.g. $2 \times 2 = 4$, 2 squared = 4 or $2^2 = 4$.

______
______
______
______

The Square of a Number

To square a number multiply it by itself.

$6 \times 6 = 6$ squared

$6 \times 6 = 6^2$

Find the value of:

a 5 squared ______	b 3 squared ______	c 10^2 ______
d 4 squared ______	e 8^2 ______	f 1^2 ______
g 9 squared ______	h 2 squared ______	i 6^2 ______

5:1 — out of 14

1. 9 × 4 ____
2. 18 ÷ 3 ____
3. 23 + 9 ____
4. 12 − 6 ____
5. 30 × 10 ____
6. Multiply 7 by 9. ____
7. Half of 18. ____
8. Sum of 12 and 7. ____
9. 2 less than 90. ____
10. 45 − 40 ____
11. Metres in one kilometre. ____
12. **Tally of Chores Done**

Setting table	𝍸 𝍸
Clearing table	𝍸 𝍷
Sweeping floor	𝍸
Wiping benches	𝍸 𝍸 𝍷𝍷𝍷𝍷

Isabella kept a tally of the jobs she did during the week.

a Which job did she do 14 times? ____

b How many jobs were recorded altogether? ____

13. The length of this black line. ____

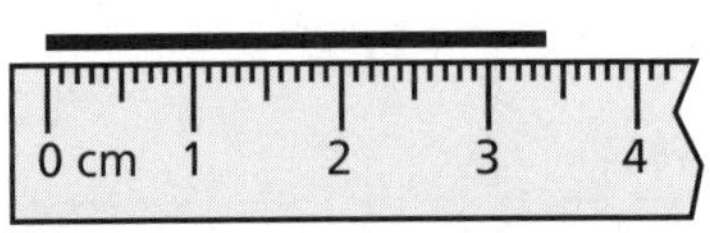

14. Arrange in ascending order.
7 157 743, 1 795 178, 1 204 155, 7 050 705

____

____

5:2 — out of 16

1. 44 + 3 ____
2. 6 squared. ____
3. 13 − 6 ____
4. 4 × 7 ____
5. 52 − 4 ____
6. 24 ÷ 4 ____
7. 40 × 2 ____
8. 756 − 200 ____
9. 8756 − 2000 ____
10. \$1.70 + \$0.34 ____
11. Round off 7 814 200 correct to the nearest million. ____
12. What is the value of the 4 in 3 425 601? ____
13. **People at the Pool**

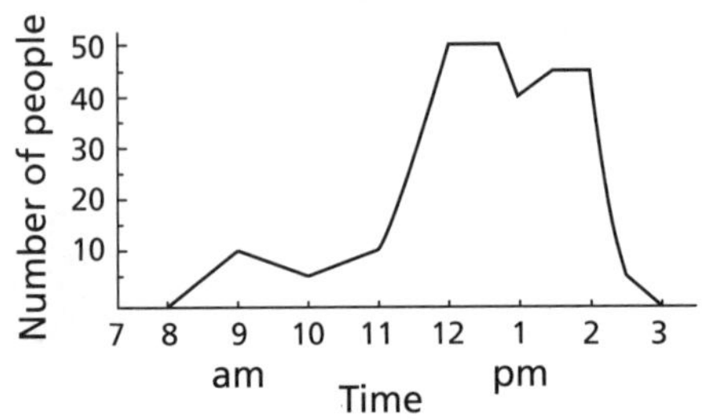

a How many people at 9 am? ____

b What was the maximum number of people at the pool? ____

During which hour did the number:

c increase the most? ____

d decrease the most? ____

14. Which unit of measure (km, m or cm) would be used to measure the height:
a of a building? ____ b of a salt shaker? ____
15. 63 mm = ____ cm ____ mm
16. 5 squared. ____

even + even = ____
odd + even = ____

5:3 ☐ out of 10

❶
```
   531
   243
   604
+   17
```

❷
```
   430
   281
   123
+  347
```

❸
```
   165
   256
   323
+  157
```

❹ The length of this pencil.

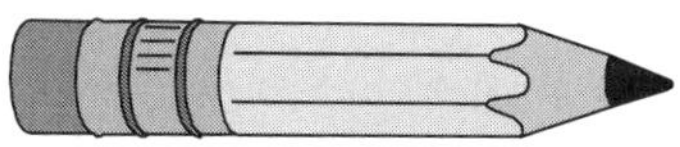

Estimate = _______ mm

Measure = _______ mm

❺ How many different lines of 3 circles can be found on this picture? ____________

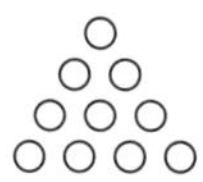

❻ **Money Raised for Charity**

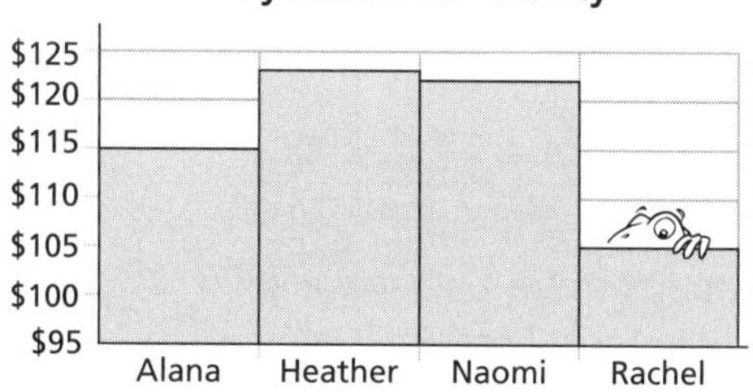

a How much did Rachel raise? ____________

b How much did these girls raise together? ____________

❼ Haley cut 15 cm from a 1 m ruler. How much of the ruler remained? ____________

❽ What is the perimeter of this rectangle? ________

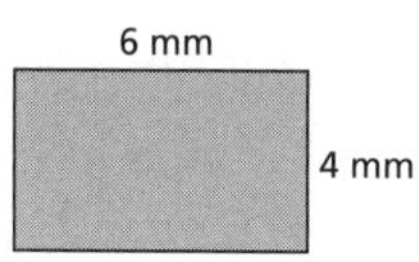

❾ Five squared. ________

❿ Is a population of 2 706 000 closer to 2 000 000 or 3 000 000? ____________

5:4 Extension ☐ out of 5

❶ a The sum of the first four square numbers. ____________

b The product of the first three square numbers. ____________

❷

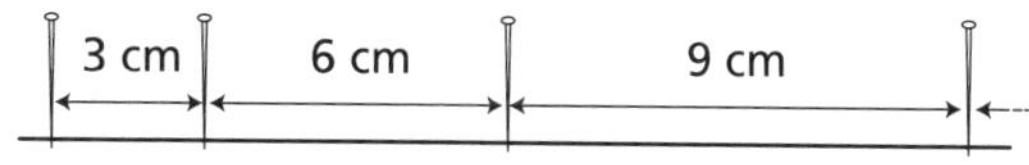

Pins were stuck onto a board using the pattern shown above. What was the distance between:

a the 7th and 8th pins? ____________

b the 1st and 8th pins? ____________

❸ Halve the number that is 53 bigger than 177. ____________

❹ If 4 small squares make a quado and 2 quados make an octo, could 68 small squares make:

a 7 quados and 5 octos? ____________

b 4 quados and 7 octos? ____________

❺ The smallest square number that is also a multiple of 8. ____________

Challenge

Complete this algorithm, then create a number story for the problem.

```
  56839
– 32963
```

____

____

____

____

____

Travel Graph

a At how many *floors* did the lift stop? ________

b How long does the lift stop for at the 2nd floor? ________

c How many floors are in the building? ________

d How long did it take for the lift to return to the ground floor? ________

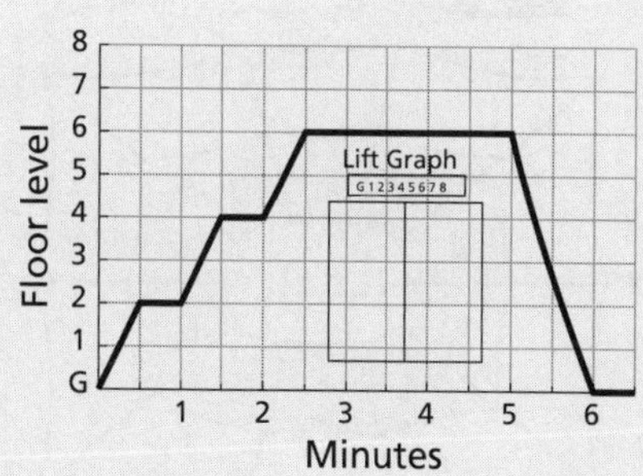

 • *AUSTRALIAN SIGNPOST MATHS 6 MENTALS* • ISBN 978 1 4886 2192 5

6:1 out of 18

1. 20 − 8 ____
2. 4 × 7 ____
3. 16 ÷ 4 ____
4. 16 + 16 ____
5. $\begin{array}{r} 12 \\ +\ \ 9 \\ \hline \end{array}$
6. Double 9. ____
7. 80 minus 2. ____
8. 96 plus 4. ____
9. Half of 54. ____
10. $\begin{array}{r} 12 \\ \times\ \ 4 \\ \hline \end{array}$
11. 100 000 + 7 000 + 300 + 8 ____
12. Which Australian coins are silver?

____

13. Complete the labels.

a

after

b

to

14. Four places before 53rd. ____
15. What is the value of the 6 in 2 160? ____
16. **a** What size is angle **A**?

____

b What size is angle **B**?

____

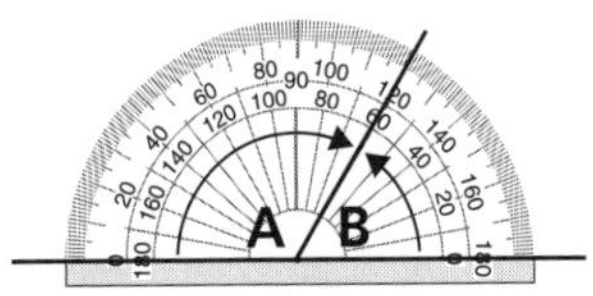

17. The number for each tally.

a 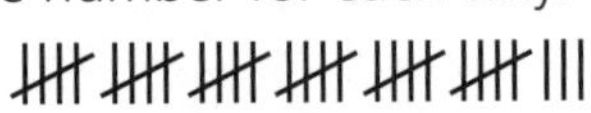 ____

b  ____

18. To square a number, multiply it by i______.

6:2 out of 17

1. 4 × 8 ____
2. 32 − 8 ____
3. 7 × 7 ____
4. 50 + 40 ____
5. $\begin{array}{r} 38 \\ +\ 81 \\ \hline \end{array}$
6. 18 + 6 × 10 ____
7. 50 × 6 ____
8. 4 × □ = 28, □ = ____
9. 28 ÷ 7 = □, □ = ____
10. $\begin{array}{r} \$6.72 \\ +\ \$9.16 \\ \hline \end{array}$

11. 20 − 2 × 5 ____
12. Write as kilometres:

a 6 500 metres ____ **b** 900 metres ____

13.

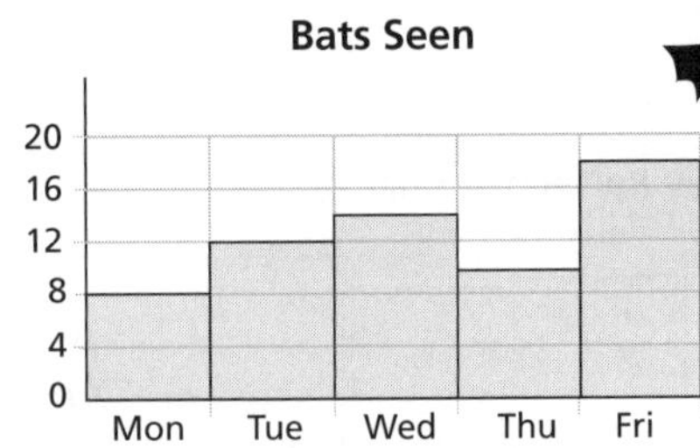

a How many more bats were seen on Friday than Monday? ____

b On which two days were the least number of bats seen? ____

14. Millimetres in 14 cm 6 mm. ____
15.

What is the length of this line to the nearest millimetre? ____

16. Two more than 7 squared. ____
17. Arrange in descending order: 31 673 316, 37 631 713, 33 761 301, 31 763 116.

____

____

6:3 ☐ out of 11

1

Tens	Ones
4	0
− 3	7

2

Tens	Ones
5	6
− 1	9

3 Write the value of 8 in:

a 7 380 213 ______

b 9 041 805 ______

4 Write 7th in words. ______

5 Is this a reflection, translation or rotation? ______

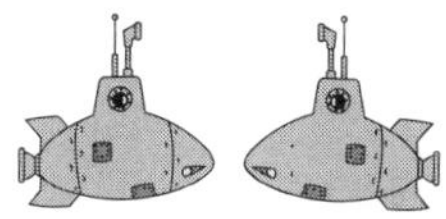

6 18 shoes are in the shop window. How many pairs are there? ______

7 **a** Complete the parallelograms.

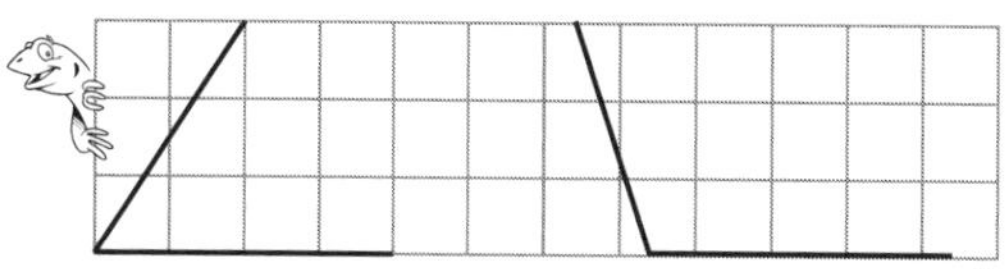

b Are opposite sides of a parallelogram equal? ______

8 Find the difference between 14 and 76. ______

9 Estimate the size of these angles.

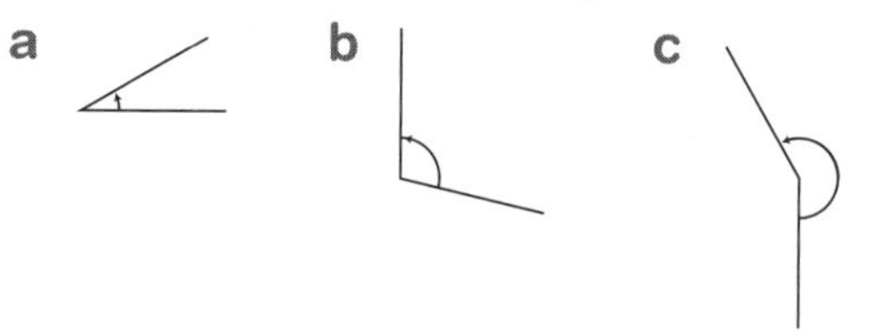

______ ______ ______

10 How many kilometres in 5 000 m? ______

11 The next two square numbers after 30. ______

6:4 Extension ☐ out of 6

1 The shortest distance by road from:

a **A** to **F** ______ **b** **C** to **D** ______

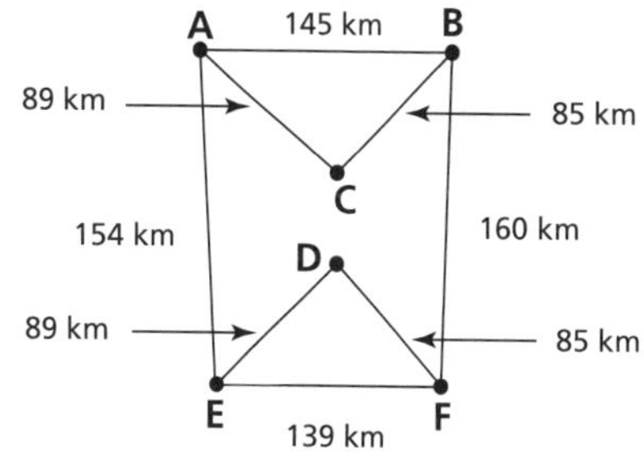

2 I am paid between \$12 and \$14 an hour. Which could be my pay for 6 hours work: \$70.50, \$72.00, \$83.10 or \$84.00? ______

3 Minutes in 9 hours. ______

4 ☐ ÷ 2 = 55, ☐ = ______

5 The shaded part has value 30. What is the value of the whole? ______

6 If 3 small squares make a *trio* and 3 *trios* make a *nino*, could 57 small square make:

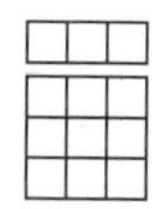

a one *trio* and 6 *ninos*? ______

b 7 *trios* and 4 *ninos*? ______

Challenge

Write number sentences with the answer 14, e.g. 4 + 5 × 2 − (4 × 0) = 14

______

______

______

Concept

Order of Operations

Example

28 − (7 − 3) ÷ 2

Remove the ( ).

= 28 − 4 ÷ 2

Do × and ÷.

= 28 − 2

= 26

Order
1 ( )
2 × and ÷
3 + and −
(going from left to right)

a 6 + 3 × 5 ______ **b** 10 − 2 × 4 ______

c 7 − (10 − 3) ______ **d** 28 − (20 − 10) ______

e 10 − 3 + 4 ______ **f** 10 − (3 + 4) ______

g 20 − 4 + 9 ______ **h** 25 − 19 + 1 ______

i 20 ÷ 5 × 12 ______ **j** 20 ÷ (5 × 2) ______

k 10 + (6 ÷ 2) × 3 + 15 ÷ 3 ______

7:1 ☐ out of 18

1. 6 − 6 ____
2. 64 + 8 ____
3. 21 ÷ 3 ____
4. 9 × 100 ____
5. $\begin{array}{r} 38 \\ +\ \ 4 \\ \hline \end{array}$
6. 1 squared. ____
7. 8 groups of 4. ____
8. 5 more than 33. ____
9. 71 take away 4. ____
10. $\begin{array}{r} 42 \\ -\ \ 3 \\ \hline \end{array}$
11. Which angle is:
    a reflex? ____
    b straight? ____
    c acute? ____
    d obtuse? ____

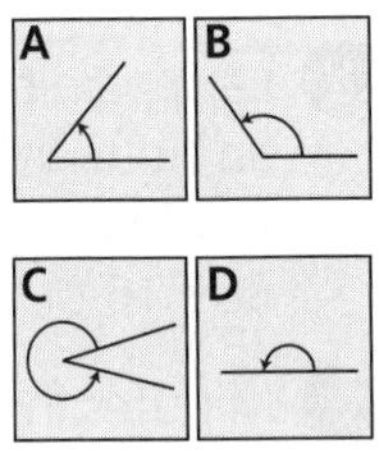

12. Subtract 8 from 12. ____
13. 6000 + 400 + 7 ____
14. Use < or > in:
    a 82 095 ____ 82 210 **b** 30 979 ____ 30 997
15. Round off 6389 correct to the nearest hundred. ____
16. 62, 64, 66, ____, ____, ____
17. In this space draw a shape that will tessellate.
18. 6 squared. ____

7:2 ☐ out of 18

1. 61 + 8 ____
2. 4 × 9 ____
3. 15 + 6 ____
4. 5 × 60 ____
5. $\begin{array}{r} 21 \\ \times\ 10 \\ \hline \end{array}$
6. 90 ÷ 10 ____
7. 20 × 4 ____
8. 4 × ☐ = 36, ☐ = ____
9. 80 ÷ ☐ = 8, ☐ = ____
10. $\begin{array}{r} 378 \\ +\ \ 46 \\ \hline \end{array}$
11. Round off the answer to Question 10, correct to the nearest 100. ____
12. (6 × 5) + 7 = ____
13. Name this solid.

____

14. **a** Are opposite sides of a rectangle equal? ____
    b Do the diagonals cut each other in half? ____

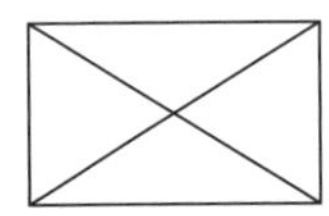

15. Round off 1742 to the nearest hundred. ____
16. 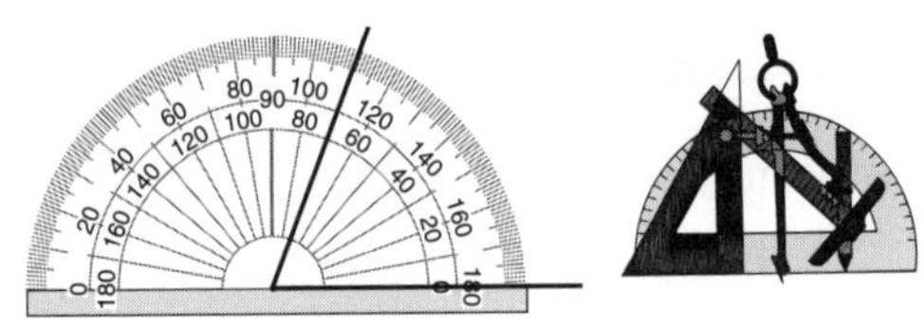
    a The size of the angle shown? ____
    b Is this angle acute or obtuse? ____
17. 4 squared. ____
18. **a** $\begin{array}{r} 134 \\ \times\ \ \ 5 \\ \hline \end{array}$ **b** $\begin{array}{r} 218 \\ \times\ \ \ 4 \\ \hline \end{array}$

Order of Operations

❶ ( ) ❷ × and ÷ ❸ + and −

Example

4 × (11 − 9) + 20 ÷ 2

Remove the ( ).

= 4 × 2 + 20 ÷ 2

Do × and ÷, (left to right).

= 8 + 10

= 18

a 11 − (8 − 3) ____
b 14 − (20 − 10) ____
c 8 + 2 × 4 ____
d 16 − 2 × 6 ____
e 20 − 12 ÷ 4 ____
f 15 + 6 ÷ 3 ____
g 6 ÷ 3 × 2 ____
h 20 ÷ 5 × 4 ____
i 11 − 4 + 5 ____
j 21 − 11 + 6 ____
k 63 + 12 ÷ 6 − (8 + 12) ÷ (9 − 4 + 5) ____

 ISBN 978 1 4886 2192 5

7:3  ☐ out of 12

1.
```
  2793
−  242
```

2.
```
  8790
−  357
```

3.
```
  300
−  52
```

4.
```
  20
×  4
```

5.
```
  700
×   3
```

6.
```
  9000
×    4
```

7. How many are left over if 22 toys are shared by:

   a 3 girls? ________ **b** 4 girls? ________

8. How many minutes in 8 hours? ________

9. Two darts are thrown into this dartboard. Which totals (below 16) are impossible to obtain? ________

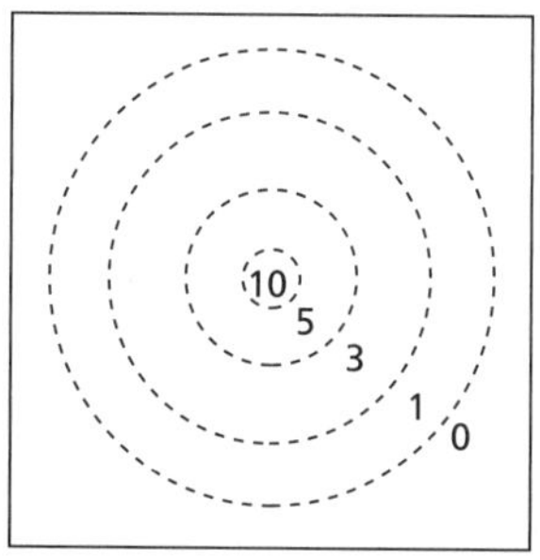

10. A book has 82 pages. How many times was the digit 8 used in numbering its pages? ________

11. Use your ruler and protractor to find:

    a the number of equal sides ________

    b the number of equal angles ________

12. 1, 15, 23, 49, 60
    Which of these numbers are:

    a multiples of 5? ________

    b square numbers? ________

7:4 Extension ☐ out of 7

1. $(5 \times 37) + (5 \times 37) =$ ________

2. Which number below is a multiple of 5, 6 and 7? ________

   1764 1470 1120 1560

3. How many octagons of any shape are present? ________

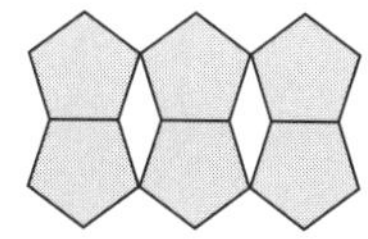

4. **a** A whale weighs 140 000 kg. How many tonnes is this? ________

   b A car had a mass of 1·8 t. How many kg is this? ________

5. 374 + 279 ________

6. Which is larger,
   $2^2 + 3^2 + 4^2$ or $1^2 + 5^2$? ________

7. Circle the square below that completes the pattern.

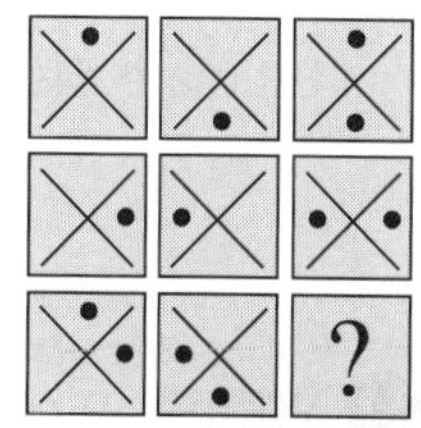

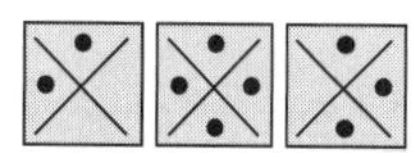

Challenge

Describe this angle. List places you might see an angle this size.

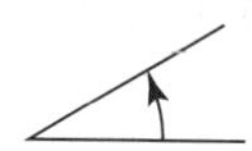

____

____

____

____

____

Turn to ID Card B on page 7.
Give the answers for these numbers.

(7)	________	line	(8)	________	lines
(10)	________	line	(11)	________	line
(14)	________	angle	(15)	________	angle
(16)	________	angle	(17)	________	angle
(18)	________	angle	(19)	________	

 • *AUSTRALIAN SIGNPOST MATHS 6 MENTALS* • ISBN 978 1 4886 2192 5

8:1 ☐ out of 17

1. 8 × 9 ____
2. 6 + 15 ____
3. 12 ÷ 4 ____
4. 11 + 7 ____
5. $\begin{array}{r} 6 \\ \times\ 0 \\ \hline \end{array}$
6. Divide 16 by 4. ____
7. The square of 9. ____
8. Multiply 8 by 7. ____
9. Total 19 and 4. ____
10. $\begin{array}{r} 64 \\ -\ 52 \\ \hline \end{array}$

11. Draw lines to join equivalent numbers.

0·61	80%
0·49	61%
0·80	25%
0·10	49%
0·25	10%

12. 100 m + 70 m + 9 m ____
13. Estimate then measure this length.

Estimate = ________ cm

Measurement = ________ cm

14. Write 149 cm in metres and centimetres. ____
15. Chen saved $6 per week for four weeks. How much has he saved? ____
16. "km" stands for ________.
17. Colour the car that is correctly parked.

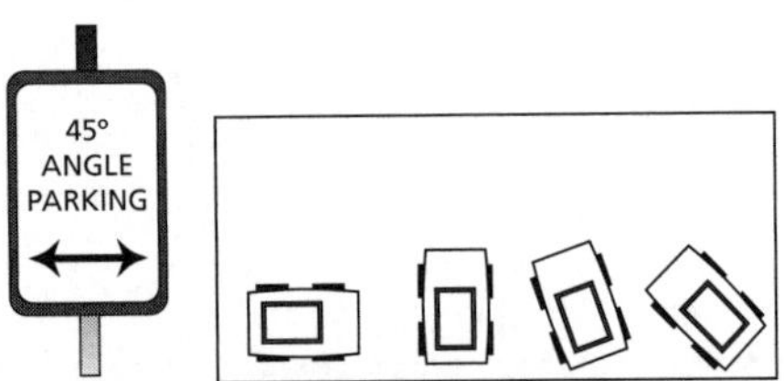

8:2 ☐ out of 22

1. 5 × 90 ____
2. 10 × 10 ____
3. 12 − 5 ____
4. 8 × 60 ____
5. $\begin{array}{r} 34 \\ \times\ 10 \\ \hline \end{array}$
6. 30 + 80 ____
7. 36 ÷ 4 ____
8. ☐ × 5 = 45, ☐ = ____
9. 23 − ☐ = 15, ☐ = ____
10. $\begin{array}{r} \$1.11 \\ +\ \$2.09 \\ \hline \end{array}$
11. 10 − 10 + 17 − 9 ____
12. How many degrees are in a straight angle? ____
13. a Millimetres in 8 cm. ____
    b Centimetres in 90 mm. ____
14. I had 48 fish but lost half of them. How many do I have left? ____

15. I need new sets of horse shoes for thirteen of my horses. How many shoes do I need? ____

16. Write 18th in words. ____
17. What is the value of the 4 in 17 462? ____
18. How many days in March? ____
19. Which is larger, 0·09 or 0·12? ____
20. 1m   40 cm   200 m   0·8 m
    Which of these is closest to the diameter of a car's steering wheel? ____
21. 0·98 as a percentage. ____%
22. (9 × 6) − (4 × 6) ____

a Colour 34% red.
Colour 27% blue.
Colour 19% yellow.
What percentage is left uncoloured?

____

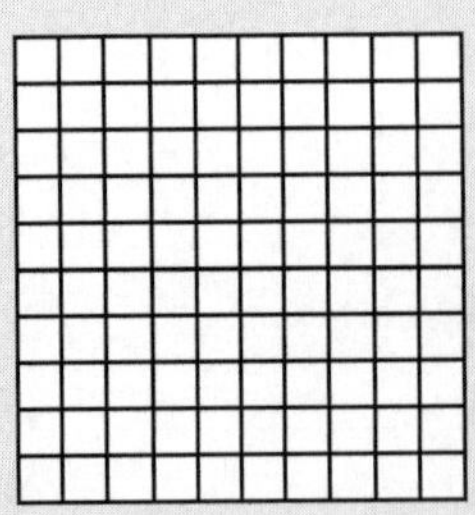

b Colour 9% orange.
Colour 41% green.
Colour 38% purple.
What percentage is left uncoloured?

____

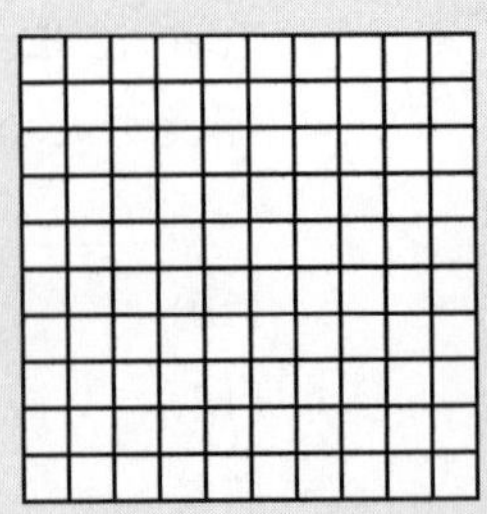

 • *AUSTRALIAN SIGNPOST MATHS 6 MENTALS* • ISBN 978 1 4886 2192 5

8:3 ☐ out of 12

1
```
  1 9 4
×     5
```

2
```
  2 1 9
×     4
```

3 Is the height if an adult giraffe closer to 5 metres or 3 metres? ____________

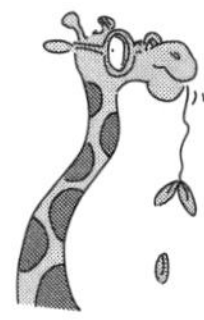

4 Write as metres:
a 310 cm ______ **b** 1 104 cm ______

5 Use the decimal form to write 2 m 63 cm in metres. ______

6 If one cake will serve 7 people, how many are needed to serve 100? ______

7

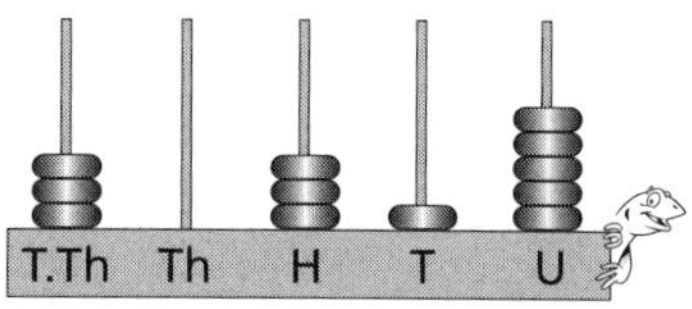

The number shown above. ______

8 Write 8·421 km as metres. ______

9 Use the decimal form to write 6 metres 39 centimetres. ______ m

10 Colour 66% of this square.

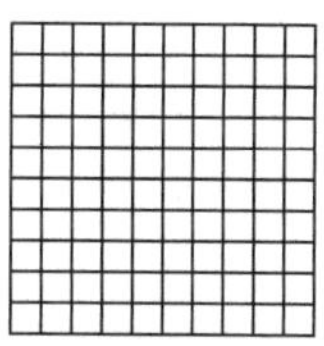

11 The size of a reflex angle is "between 180° and 360°". The size of an obtuse angle is: ____________

12 5 + (9 ÷ 3) × 2 ______

8:4 ☐ out of 6

Extension

1 (13 × 9) + (13 × 1) ______

2 The angle size between the hands of a clock at 20 past 6. ______

3 What percentage of a metre is 1 cm? ______

4 A truck loaded with sand begins a trip with a gross mass of 27 t and finishes with 26·7 t. How much sand was lost? ______

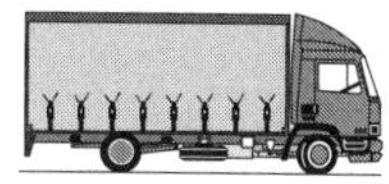

5 In how many ways can we draw 3 crosses in a row, on this grid? ______

×			×	×	×
	×				
		×			

6 Adam cuts the bread like this to make four sandwiches. A loaf of bread usually contains 24 slices. How many sandwiches can Adam make from one loaf of bread? ______

Challenge

Draw and label 3D objects, showing their features.

Complete this table for the shaded part.

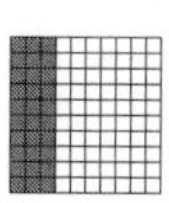	$\frac{}{10}$	$\frac{}{100}$	0·__	__%
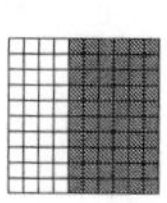	$\frac{}{10}$	$\frac{}{100}$	0·__	__%

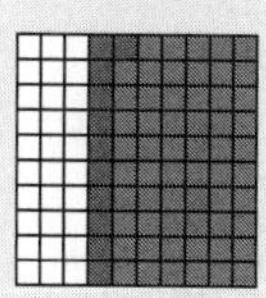

9:1 ☐ out of 19

1. 7×4 ____
2. 8×10 ____
3. $20 - 10$ ____
4. $20 \div 10$ ____
5. $\begin{array}{r} 32 \\ +\ 61 \\ \hline \end{array}$
6. Triple 7. ____
7. 7 groups of 5. ____
8. Take 3 from 48. ____
9. Increase 47 by 4. ____
10. $\begin{array}{r} 61 \\ \times\ \ 3 \\ \hline \end{array}$
11. Complete the labels for the shaded part.

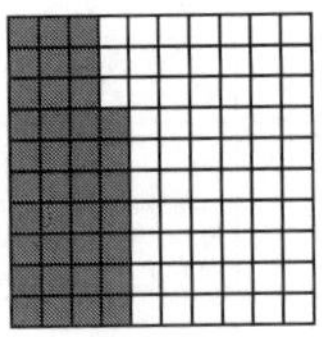

·	$\frac{}{100}$	%

12. Use the decimal form to write 29 mm as cm. ____
13. 81% means ______ out of ______.
14. Thomas drew 4 red monsters. He gave each one 8 legs. How many legs altogether? ____
15. Write 243 in words. ____
16. 675 cents in decimal form. ____
17. What is the value of the 5 in 2567? ____
18. 100 cm, 2 m, 4000 mm, 2000 cm

    Which of these is the best estimate for the length of a bed? ____
19. Metres in 5 km. ____

9:2 ☐ out of 18

1. 8×90 ____
2. $13 - 5$ ____
3. $31 + 7$ ____
4. 5×7 ____
5. $\begin{array}{r} 60 \\ \times\ \ 3 \\ \hline \end{array}$
6. $28 \div 4$ ____
7. 30×3 ____
8. $9 + 8 + 2 + 4$ ____
9. $7 + 9 + 8 + 1$ ____
10. $\begin{array}{r} 70 \\ \times\ \ 6 \\ \hline \end{array}$
11. $56 \div (11 - 9)$ ____
12. 76 out of 100 $= \frac{76}{100}$ = ____·____

    = ____ %
13. 3·85 m = ____ m ____ cm
14. Write as a percentage:

    a 0·35 ____ **b** $\frac{1}{4}$ ____
15. Write 50%:

    a as a decimal ____

    b as a fraction ____
16. Write 6·508 km as metres. ____
17. 

    What is the average amount in each mug? ____
18. 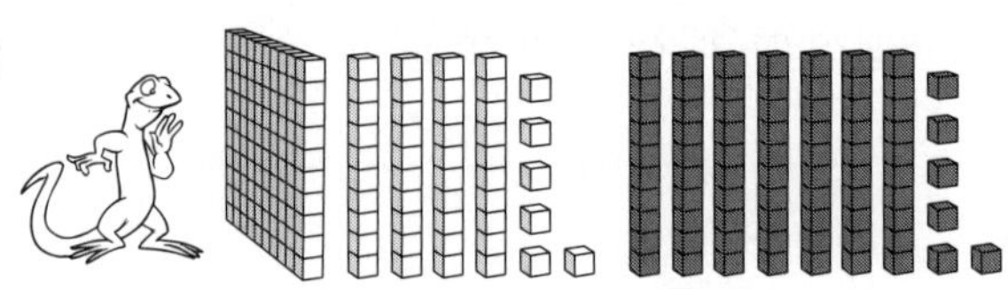

    a 146 + 76 ____ **b** 146 − 76 ____

Multiplying Numbers Ending in Zeros

× Tables

Write down the end zeros, and multiply the other numbers.

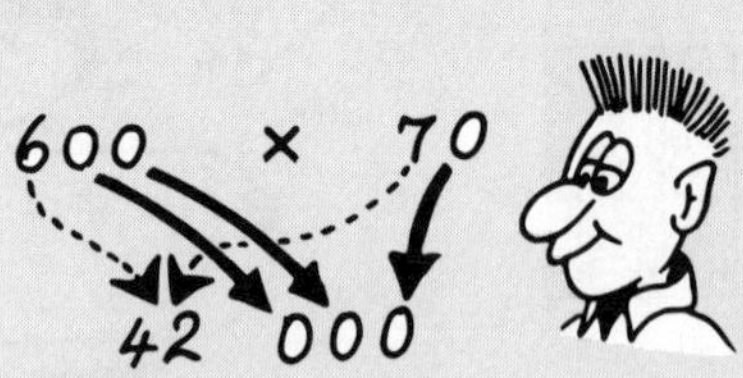

a 50×30 ____ **b** 70×80 ____

c 40×60 ____ **d** 50×50 ____

e 90×50 ____ **f** 100×50 ____

g 80×50 ____ **h** 300×40 ____

i 50^2 ____ **j** 800^2 ____

9:3 out of 11

1. 200×5

2. $\$67.51 + \$32.12$

3. $9000 - 2135$

4. Round off each number to the nearest hundred, then use these to estimate:
   a 873 − 204 ______ b 1907 − 743 ______

5. a Write 3 m and 56 cm in metres as a decimal. ______
   b Write 406 cm as metres and centimetres. ______

6. a Fraction shaded ______
   b Decimal shaded ______
   c Percentage shaded ______
   d Percentage not shaded ______

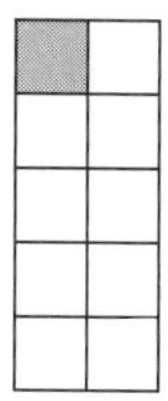

7. Write as a percentage:
   a 0·72 ______
   b 0·09 ______

8. Write the numeral for seven thousand, four hundred and thirty-one. ______

9. Use the graph to convert to pounds:
   a 1 kg ______
   b 0·8 kg ______

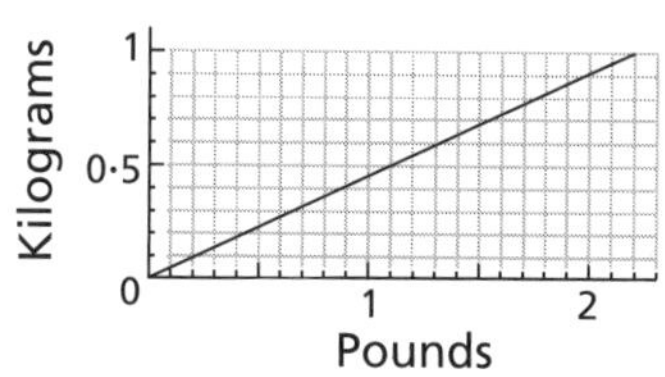

10. Carlos has a part-time job. He is paid $148 per week. From this amount $16 is deducted as tax. How much does he receive for 3 weeks work? ______

11. $74 - 6 \times 4$ ______

9:4 Extension out of 4

1. I am able to save $9 each week. How many weeks will it take me to save $684? ______

2. The top 5 countries in gold medals per ten million people in the 1996 Atlanta Olympics are shown.

Country	Gold Medals ptmp*
Australia	5
Cuba	6·36
Denmark	8
New Zealand	8·57
Switzerland	5·71

*ptmp = per ten million people

   a Which country did the best? ______
   b Australia's population was 18 million. How many gold medals did we win? ______

   By how much did New Zealand beat:
   c Denmark? ______ gold medals ptmp
   d Australia? ______ gold medals ptmp

3. Does $2{\cdot}5^2 = 1{\cdot}5^2 + 2^2$? ______

4. Which is closest to 4000, 4396, 3514 or 3606? ______

Challenge

Represent 0·20 in as many ways as you can.

Complete this grid to write the distances in three ways.

8·375 km	8 km 375 m	8375 m
		2914 m
5·446 km		
	9 km 125 m	

10:1 out of 19

1. 13 − 5 ______
2. 7 + 6 ______
3. 22 ÷ 2 ______
4. 8 × 5 ______
5. $\begin{array}{r} 50 \\ \times\ 3 \\ \hline \end{array}$
6. 10 times 6. ______
7. Take 9 from 41. ______
8. Total of 5 and 38. ______
9. 5 rows of 8. ______
10. $\begin{array}{r} 144 \\ -\ 144 \\ \hline \end{array}$

11. Write 9 m 35 cm in decimal form. ______
12. Circle the numbers that round off to 4000.

    3650 4732 3364 4092
13. **a** The analogue time. ______

    b How many minutes past 11? ______

14. The month before May. ______
15. How many groups of 5 fish in 27?

    ______ groups. ______ left over.

16. Threes in 30. ______
17. How many socks in 4 pairs? ______
18. **a** 12 + 5 + 10 + 4 ______

    b Write 126 in words. ______

    ______
19. **a** The sum of 8 and 7. ______

    b Subtract 67 from 70. ______

10:2 out of 16

1. 81 − 6 ______
2. 7 × 6 ______
3. 66 + 5 ______
4. 63 − 58 ______
5. $\begin{array}{r} 600 \\ \times\ 3 \\ \hline \end{array}$
6. 24 ÷ 3 ______
7. 9 × 8 ______
8. 8 × □ = 64, □ = ______
9. □ − 15 = 13, □ = ______
10. $\begin{array}{r} 9529 \\ -\ 3817 \\ \hline \end{array}$
11. Write 0·45 as a percentage. ______
12.

	Miss Breakfast			Arrive Late		
	Primary (%)	High (%)	Total (%)	Primary (%)	High (%)	Total (%)
Always	16	24	20	9	3	6
Often	37	31	34	24	18	21
Occasionally	27	25	26	23	21	22
Rarely	14	2	8	35	39	37
Never	6	18	12	9	19	14

    a What fraction of students always miss breakfast? ______

    b What percentage said they always or often arrive late? ______

    c If 1000 students were surveyed, how many *never* miss breakfast? ______
13. Draw lines to connect equal numbers.

0·6	$\frac{1}{2}$	0·06	$\frac{5}{100}$

50%	6%	60%	5%

14. Write 607 cm as metres and centimetres.

    ______
15. **a** 8 lots of 20. ______

    b Share 21 biscuits among 7 children. ______ each

16. 100 − 20 × (5 − 3) ______

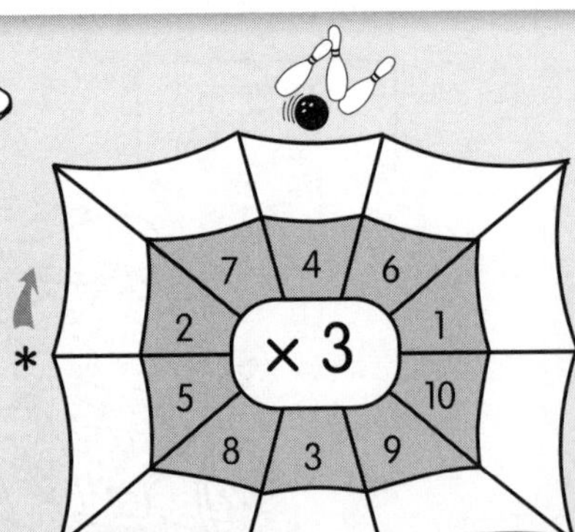

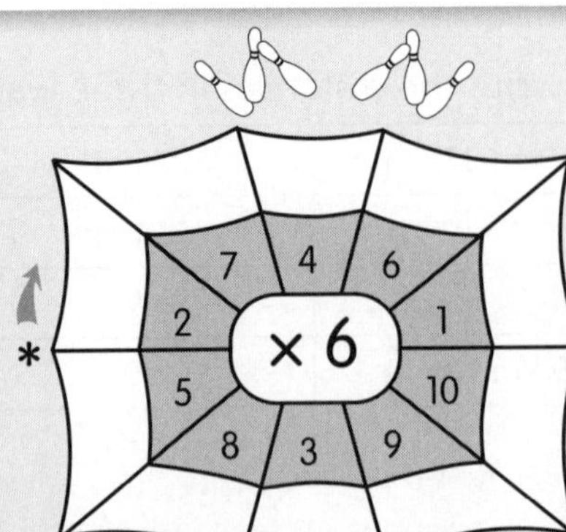

 ISBN 978 1 4886 2192 5

10:3 out of 12

1. 800 − 43 =

2. \$49.97 + \$37.03 =

3. 3000 × 7 =

4. A bunch of bananas costs \$1.50. How many bunches can be bought with \$5? ________

5. Write the percentage equivalent for:
   a $\frac{60}{100}$ ________ **b** 0·3 ________

6. How do you change 5 209 into:
   a 5 249 ________
   b 5 009 ________

7. (60 × 5) + (60 × 5) = ________

8. Complete these numbers facts.
   If 13 × 5 = 65, then:
   a 5 × 13 = ____ **b** ____ ÷ 5 = 13

9. 6 bags of 10 rolls. ______ rolls

10. Write in metres as a decimal:
    a 3 m 56 cm ________
    b 15 m 9 cm ________

11. Convert to yen:
    a 25c ____
    b 60c ____
    Convert to cents:
    c 40 yen ____
    d 60 yen ____

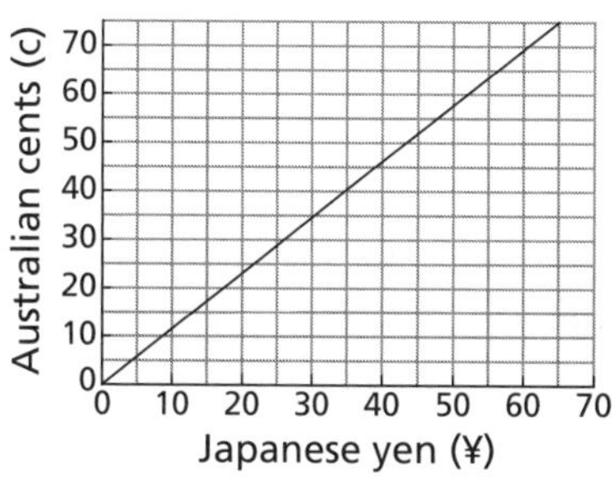

12. Write as centimetres:
    a 0·71 m ________ **b** 2·4 m ________

10:4 Extension out of 6

1. One pizza is enough for 4 people. How many do I need to satisfy 33 people? ________

2. True or false?
   a 0·60 ≠ 0·06 ________
   b 0·70 = $\frac{7}{10}$ ________

   ≠ means "is not equal to".

3. This clock face was seen in a mirror. What time was it? ________

4. True or false?
   0·25 = 25% = $\frac{1}{4}$ ________

5. **a**

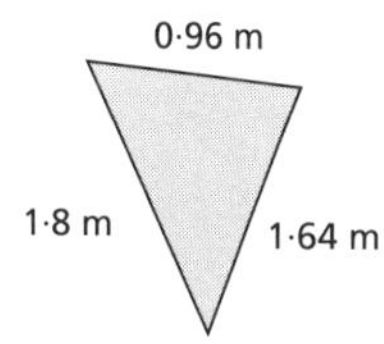

   Perimeter = ______

   b

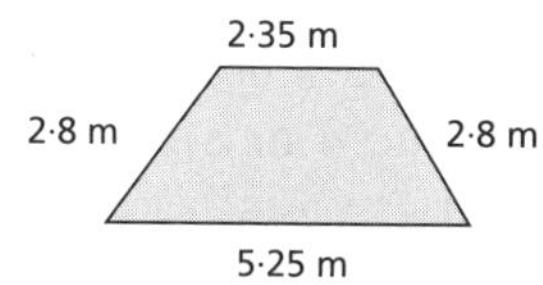

   Perimeter = ______

6. I have 6 shirts and 4 ties. In how many ways can I choose one of each? ________

Challenge

Four people measured the length of a field and all recorded different measurements. How is this possible?

____
____
____

Arkos wanted to find the thickness of a sheet of paper. He found that a 200-page book was 1 cm thick.

a How many sheets of paper make 200 pages? ________

b Complete this table.

Thickness	10 mm	1 mm	0·1 mm
Number of sheets	100		

c How thick would a book of 160 pages be? ________

11:1 out of 20

1. 9 + 5 ____
2. 6 × 4 ____
3. 15 − 6 ____
4. 36 ÷ 4 ____
5. $\begin{array}{r} 60 \\ \times\ 8 \\ \hline \end{array}$
6. 4 squared. ____
7. Double 63. ____
8. Add 8 and 56. ____
9. 14 minus 7. ____
10. $\begin{array}{r} 490 \\ +\ 10 \\ \hline \end{array}$
11. **a** Write the fraction 7 out of 10. ____
    b Write the fraction $\frac{1}{6}$ in words. ____
12. The product of 12 and 3. ____
13. 48 grapes are shared fairly among 4 girls. How many grapes were given to each girl? ____
14. Write in words the number ten less than one thousand. ____
15. 900 + 400 ____
16. Circle the larger number:
    3 243 703 3 301 792
17. List all the factors of 40.
    1, 40, 2, ___, ___, ___, ___, ___
18. Write the numeral for 10^2 ____
19. Write 860 mm as cm. ____
20. The value of the 7 in 4790. ____

11:2 out of 19

1. 5 × 80 ____
2. 13 − 9 ____
3. 83 + 6 ____
4. 4 × 6 ____
5. $\begin{array}{r} 700 \\ \times\ 10 \\ \hline \end{array}$
6. 32 ÷ 4 + 4 ____
7. 20 − 2 × 9 ____
8. □ × 8 = 72, □ = ____
9. 7 × □ = 35, □ = ____
10. $\begin{array}{r} 800 \\ \times\ \ 6 \\ \hline \end{array}$

11. Round off the answer to Question 10, correct to the nearest 1 000. ____
12. The size of the missing angle.
    a ____ **b** ____

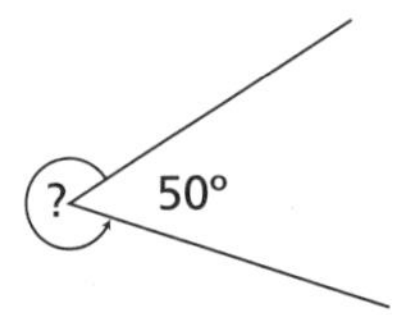

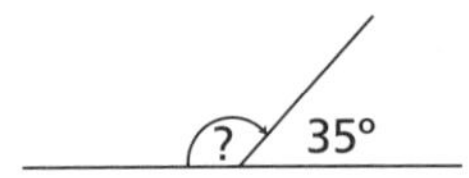

13. True or false? odd × odd = odd ____
14. Underline those numbers that are *not* multiples of 12?
    3 24 4 36 6
15. Write 5 605 in words. ____
16. **a** $4\overline{)49}$ r **b** $7\overline{)62}$ r
17. $10^3 + 10^2 + 10 + 1$ ____
18. 8 m 6 cm as centimetres. ____
19. Write $\frac{83}{100}$ as:
    a a percentage ____ **b** a decimal ____

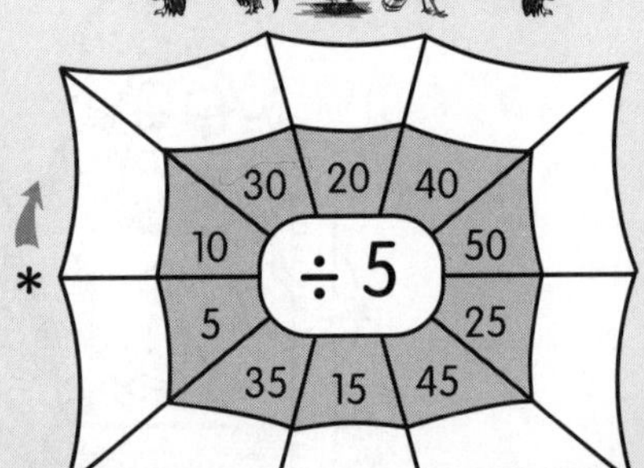

 • *AUSTRALIAN SIGNPOST MATHS 6 MENTALS* • ISBN 978 1 4886 2192 5

11:3 — out of 12

1

Tens	Ones
7	1
− 3	4

2

Tens	Ones
8	2
− 6	9

3 $2\overline{)42}$

4 $3\overline{)186}$

5 $5\overline{)7550}$

6 **a** 0·7 = ______ % **b** 0·1 = ______ %

c 0·07 = ______ % **d** 0·01 = ______ %

7 **a**

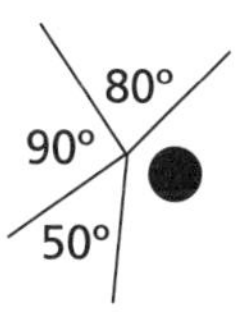

b

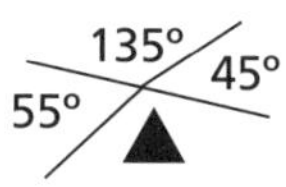

● = ______ ▲ = ______

8 Write the numeral for ninety-eight million and twenty. ______

9 A man's step is 80 cm long. How far does he walk in 4 steps? ______

10 Gabriela has 4000 stamps. Beau has 8 times as many. How many stamps does Beau have?

______

11 $(7 \times 10^3) + (2 \times 10^2) + (7 \times 10^1) + 7$ ______

12 Write in metres as a decimal.

a 3 m 56 cm ______

b 15 m 9 cm ______

Extension 11:4 — out of 7

1 How long would it take me to pay for a stove that costs \$490 if I pay \$99 each week?

______

2 Write 73% as a decimal. ______

3 What two numbers have a difference of 3 and a product of 130? ______

4 If $10^3 = 1000$ and $10^2 = 100$ and $10^1 = 10$, what is the value of 10^0? ______

5 Write the numeral for:

a LXXXI ______ **b** CLXII ______

c CCXVI ______ **d** CXCIV ______

6 Two tins of fish are sold for \$5.50. Find:

a the cost of 1 tin ______

b the cost of 8 tins ______

7 Which of the numbers 9, 14 and 17 have exactly 2 factors? This is called a "prime number". ______

Challenge

Write numerals then record them as powers of ten, e.g.

$8724 = (8 \times 10^3) + (7 \times 10^2) + (2 \times 10^1) + 4$

______

______

______

______

Using a Model

Alan, Rhonda, Rachel and Heather will sit on the four seats shown.
Rhonda will sit between Rachel and Alan.
Who will sit in seat number:

a 1? ______ **b** 2? ______

c 4? ______

12:1 out of 18

1. 14 − 4 ____
2. 4 × 6 ____
3. 30 ÷ 10 ____
4. 27 + 7 ____
5. $\begin{array}{r} 137 \\ +\ \ \ 3 \\ \hline \end{array}$
6. 8 lots of 3. ____
7. 6 times 8. ____
8. 2 less than 70. ____
9. 8 more than 33. ____
10. $\begin{array}{r} \$1.22 \\ \times\ \ \ \ \ 3 \\ \hline \end{array}$

11. What is the size of angle **A**? ____

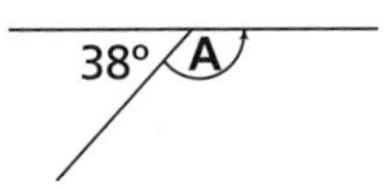

12. Write the numeral fifty-one million four hundred and twenty-eight thousand two hundred and eleven.

____

13. Priscilla has 54 shells. How many more does she need to have 91? ____

14. A straight angle measures: ____°.
15. Make the largest number you can with the digits 2, 5, 6 and 8. ____
16. **a**

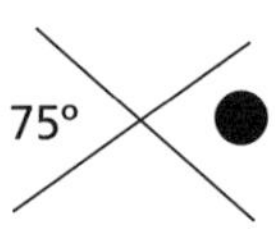

b

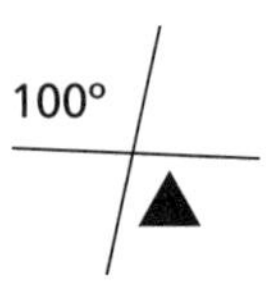

● = ____ ▲ = ____

17. Write the numeral for 10^3. ____
18. Write 0·85 as a percentage. ____

12:2 out of 20

1. 61 − 5 ____
2. 92 + 6 ____
3. 8 × 7 ____
4. 7 squared. ____
5. $\begin{array}{r} 300 \\ -\ \ \ \ 9 \\ \hline \end{array}$
6. 80 ÷ 10 ____
7. (6 + 8) × 2 ____
8. □ ÷ 3 = 8, □ = ____
9. 42 ÷ □ = 7, □ = ____
10. $\begin{array}{r} 9000 \\ \times\ \ \ \ \ \ 6 \\ \hline \end{array}$
11. Write 20 ha in words. ____
12. The value of the 4 in 6·724? ____
13. What part is shaded?

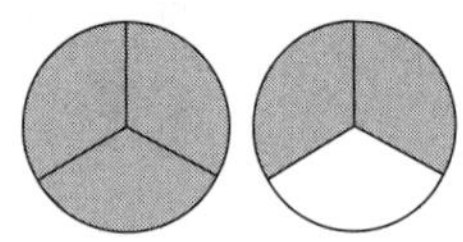

____

14. Use numerals to write:
    a eighteen point zero eight ____
    b six tens and six hundreths ____
15. Which is closest to 6: 5·84, 6·6, 5·09 or 6·23? ____
16. The numeral for two million two hundred thousand and six. ____
17. The perimeter of this rectangle. ____

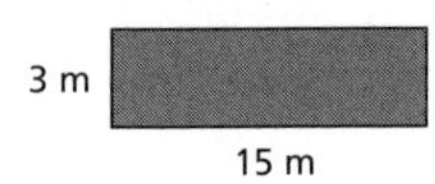

18. What size is the missing angle? ____

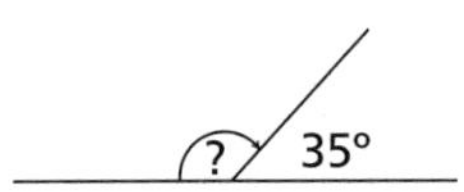

19. 800 000 + 50 000 + 300 + 6 ____
20. My car can travel 12 km on one litre of petrol. How far can I go with four litres? ____

Turn to ID Card A on page 6.

Give the answers for these numbers.

(11) ____ (12) ____

(13) ____ (14) ____

(15) ____ (26) ____ numbers

(27) ____ (28) ____

(29) ____ (30) ____

Multiples of 5 end with 5 or 0.

12:3 ☐ out of 16

1 $3\overline{)27}$

2 $5\overline{)20}$

3 $7\overline{)49}$

4 Complete this pattern,
0·88, 0·89, 0·9, ______, ______, ______

5 Colour one third of these birds.

6 Use < or > in:

a 4·392 ____ 4·282

b 6·021 ____ 6·103

7 Write the numeral for two hundred and forty-seven thousand three hundred and sixty-eight. ______

8 On a cube, what is the number of:

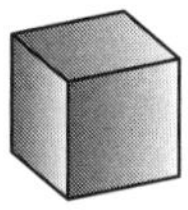

a faces? ______

b corners? ______

9 220 − ☐ = 80, ☐ = ______

10 95 cents minus 15 cents. ______

11 The number 6 more than 77. ______

12 How many thousand in 1 million? ______

13 Find the perimeter of a square with a side length of 6 m. ______

14 How big is the acute angle? ______

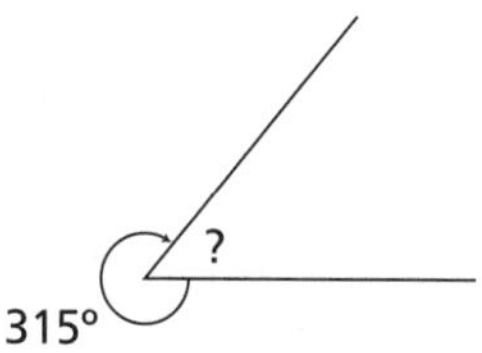

15 $(9 \times 10^4) + (6 \times 10^3) + (4 \times 10^2) + 8$ ______

16 Write 0·9 as a percentage. ______

12:4 ☐ out of 7

Extension

1 Find the perimeter of a square of side length:

a 2·25 m ____ **b** 9·05 m ____

2 The Roman numeral for 36. ______

3 6 rolls of cloth each contain 24 m of cloth, while 2 other rolls each contain 86 m. What is the total length of cloth? ______

4 If this net is folded to make a cube, which side would be opposite **A**? ______

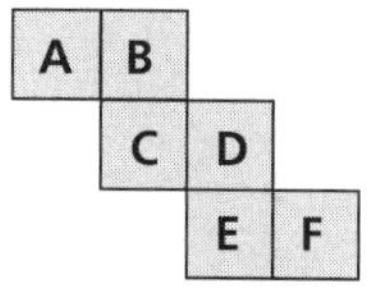

5 These are finishing times for a race. Who came 2nd? ______

Ty	21:54·69
Kim	21:53·45
Ron	22:01·56
Sue	21:54·71

6 $\frac{1}{10}$ of one kilogram = ____ g

7 The smallest two-digit square number that is also odd. ______

Challenge

List groups of numbers and record the average of each group.

______

______

______

______

Average

$$= \frac{\text{sum of the items}}{\text{number of items}}$$

Find the average of 8, 7, 11, 27 and 12.
= (8 + 7 + 11 + 27 + 12) ÷ 5
= 13

Find the average of:

a 6 m, 15 m, 8 m and 7 m ______

b 71 g, 132 g and 88 g ______

c 463, 684 and 671 ______

d 7, 9, 1, 4 and 9 ______

e 81, 43, 70 and 58 ______

13:1 ☐ out of 17

1. 4 + 7 ____
2. 8 × 4 ____
3. 16 − 8 ____
4. 0 ÷ 2 ____
5. $\begin{array}{r} 100 \\ \times \quad 6 \\ \hline \end{array}$
6. 13 take away 6. ____
7. Half of 0. ____
8. 6 plus 9. ____
9. 7 lots of 6. ____
10. $\begin{array}{r} 68 \\ -\ 25 \\ \hline \end{array}$
11. Write the numeral for 10^4. ____
12. The size of angle **B**. ____

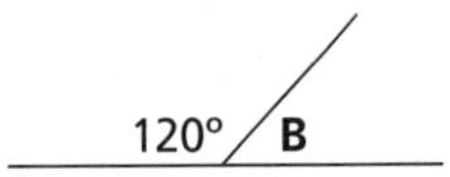

13. What is unlikely to happen today?

____

14. Rewrite these numbers from smallest to largest:
    a 6, 37, 43, 22, 39

    ____

    b 3651, 3472, 3960, 3399

    ____
15. The ordinal number after 600th? ____
16. 

    What number would be at:
    a **A**? ____ **b** **B**? ____ **c** **C**? ____
17. A rectangle measures 7 cm by 8 cm. What is its:
    a perimeter? ____
    b area? ____

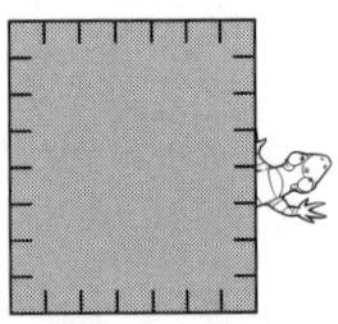

13:2 ☐ out of 15

1. 7 × 9 ____
2. 18 − 9 ____
3. 77 + 0 ____
4. 8 × 8 ____
5. $\begin{array}{r} 60 \\ \times\ 6 \\ \hline \end{array}$
6. 150 ÷ 10 ____
7. 14 − (20 − 9) ____
8. ☐ ÷ 6 = 7, ☐ = ____
9. 25 + ☐ = 39, ☐ = ____
10. $\begin{array}{r} 99 \\ +\ 99 \\ \hline \end{array}$
11. Round off the answer to Question 10, correct to the nearest ten. ____
12. **a**

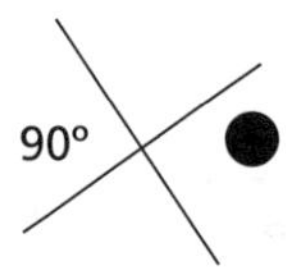

    b

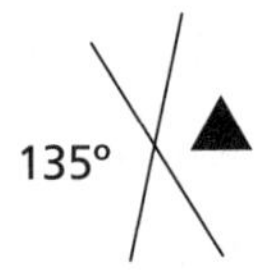

    ● = ____ ▲ = ____
13. 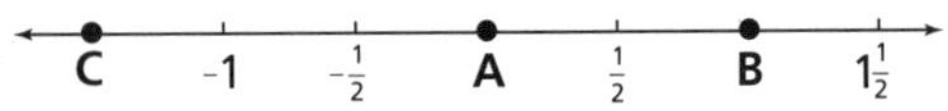

    What number would be at:
    a **A**? ____ **b** **B**? ____ **c** **C**? ____
14. **a** Which letter has a 50% chance that the spinner will land on it?

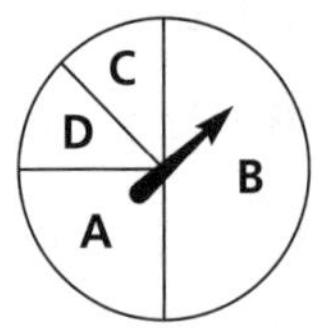

    ____

    What is the chance, as a decimal, that the spinner will land on:
    b **B**? ____ **c** **A**? ____
15. The size of each missing angle.
    a

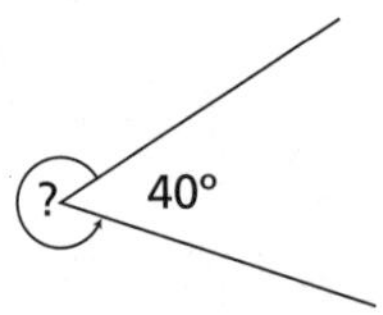

    b

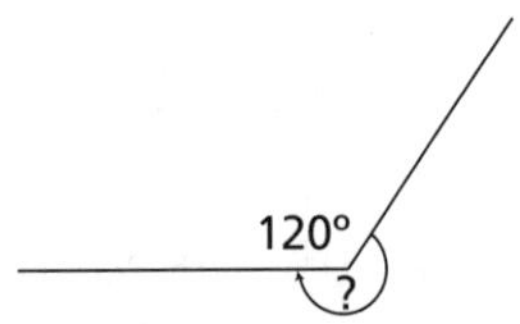

    ____ ____

Averages

Measure the pictures in mm to obtain your answers.

a

Average length = ____
Average height = ____

b

Average mass = ____
Average width = ____

c

Average capacity = ____
Average height = ____

 ISBN 978 1 4886 2192 5

13:3 ☐ out of 13

Write each answer for Questions 1 to 3 as a mixed numeral.

1 $6\overline{)41}$ **2** $7\overline{)75}$ **3** $9\overline{)5}$

4

$$\begin{array}{r} 36705 \\ 14054 \\ +\ 23109 \\ \hline \end{array}$$

5

$$\begin{array}{r} 73000 \\ 14000 \\ 3100 \\ +\ 1053 \\ \hline \end{array}$$

6 An angle of 360° is a ____________.

7

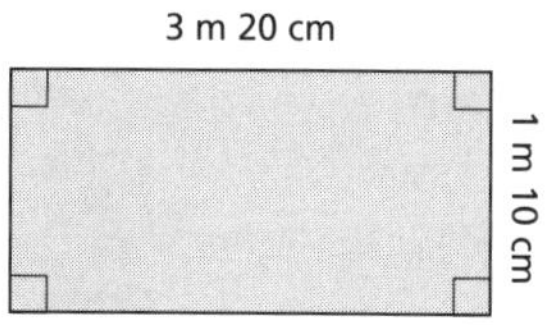

Perimeter = ________

8 Arrange in descending order:
67 541 234, 67 647 324, 67 747 324

____

9 0·7 − 0·3 ________

10 Write 72·69 in words. ________

____

11 Which letter has a 25% chance that the spinner will land on it? ________

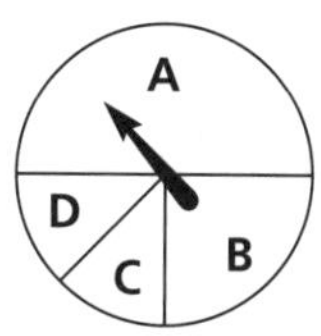

12 Find the size of the reflex angle. ________

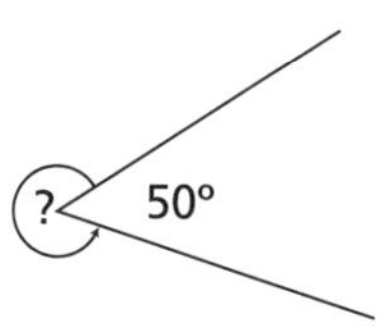

13 $(5 \times 10^4) + (3 \times 10^3) + (8 \times 10^2) + 3$ ________

13:4 Extension ☐ out of 7

1 Find the perimeter of each rectangle.

a

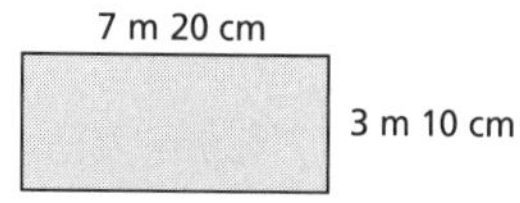

b

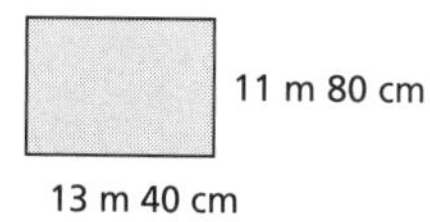

________ ________

2 "Common" means "belongs to all". What is the lowest common multiple of:

a 4 and 6? ____ **b** 3 and 5? ____

3 The sum of the first 6 consecutive even counting numbers. ________

4 Write 80 in Roman numerals. ________

5 Which of the numbers below are square numbers? ________

49, $2^2 + 3^2$, 16, 9 + 4

6 Write the numeral for:

a 36 tens and 7 ones ________

b 46 tens and 8 tenths ________

7 LII − XI ________

Challenge

Write your own number sentences that have an answer that is a negative number, e.g. 14 ÷ 2 − 10 = −3.

____

____

____

____

What is the Probability of Success?

Estimate the place for each letter and write it above the scale.

A The next baby born in Melbourne will be a girl.

B Australia will be a powerful nation in the year 2030.

C I will go to the movies next month.

D I will get a 6 if I throw a dice once.

E Our teacher will become prime minister tomorrow.

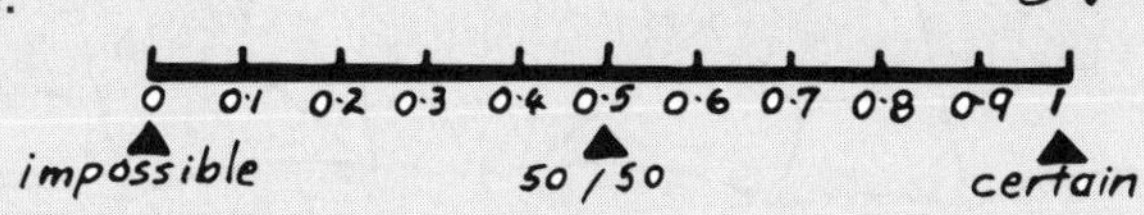

14:1 ☐ out of 16

1. 0×4 ____
2. $12 - 4$ ____
3. $8 + 5$ ____
4. $35 \div 5$ ____
5. $\begin{array}{r} 18 \\ +\ 22 \\ \hline \end{array}$
6. Double 34. ____
7. Multiply 9 by 8. ____
8. Take 7 from 20. ____
9. Sum of 9 and 8. ____
10. $\begin{array}{r} 100 \\ \times\ \ \ 7 \\ \hline \end{array}$
11. 

What number would be at:
a A? ____ **b** B? ____ **c** C? ____
12. Arrange in descending order:
1 227 436, 1 049 415, 1 248 976
____
13. **a** Round 46 496 507 correct to the nearest ten million. ____
b Write 0·631 in words. ____
14. Years in 2 centuries. ____
15. Which month is two months after September? ____
16. For this spinner, which result:
a is least likely? ____
b has an even chance of occuring? ____

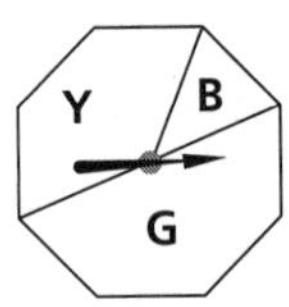

Y = yellow
B = blue
G = green

14:2 ☐ out of 17

1. $50 + 44$ ____
2. 9×7 ____
3. $36 - 4$ ____
4. 6×8 ____
5. $\begin{array}{r} 41 \\ +\ \ 8 \\ \hline \end{array}$
6. $45 \div 5$ ____
7. $\square \times 6 = 36,\ \square =$ ____
8. $36 \times \square = 360,\ \square =$ ____
9. $8 + 4 \times 7$ ____
10. $\begin{array}{r} \$2.62 \\ -\ \$0.70 \\ \hline \end{array}$
11. Round off the answer to Question 10, correct to the nearest 5c. ____
12. What is the value of 5 in 7 354 130? ____
13. If a train leaves at 11:38 am and arrives at 12:12 pm, how long does the journey take?

____
14. What is the perimeter of this shape?
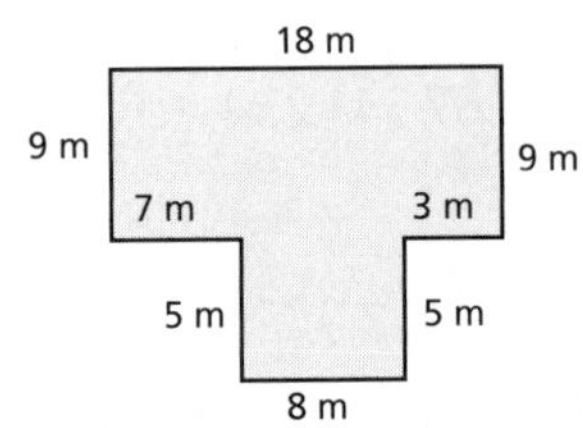

____
15. Hours from 10 am to:
a 3 pm ____ **b** midnight ____
16. The size of:
a angle **A** ____
b angle **B** ____
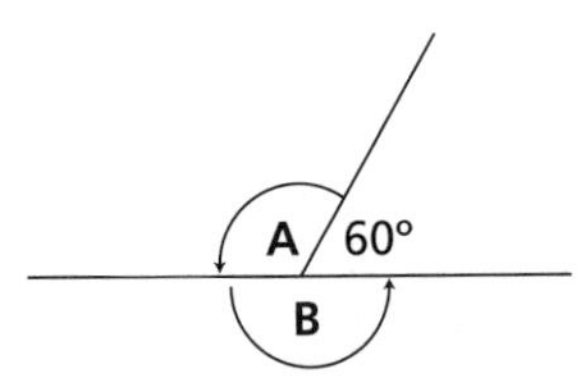

17. Two heads, two tails, or a head and a tail could result from tossing two coins.
What is the most likely result? ____

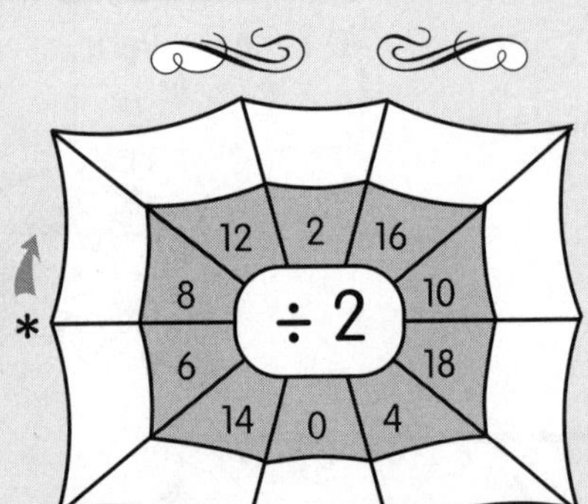

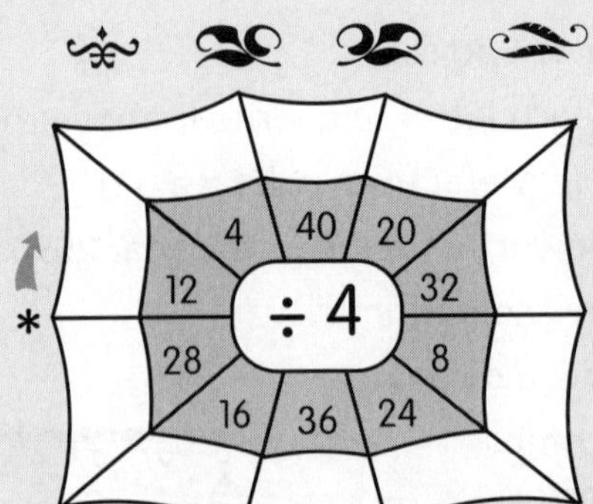

$\square \times 4 = 28,\ \square =$ ____

© PEARSON AUSTRALIA 2018 • *AUSTRALIAN SIGNPOST MATHS 6 MENTALS* • ISBN 978 1 4886 2192 5

14:3 ☐ out of 12

1
```
  23724
  51514
+  1689
```

2
```
  29580
  15547
+ 21342
```

3
```
  82105
− 24053
```

4
```
  4125
+ 5329
```

5 

What number would be at:

a A? ______ **b** B? ______ **c** C? ______

6 Write 4:28 pm in 24-hour time. ______

7 Kim's bus came at 7:50 am. She arrived at the station at 8:20 am. How long did the journey take? ______

8 There are 3600 seconds in 1 hour. How many seconds are there in a 6-hour school day? ______

9 How many school days in 7 weeks? ______

10 Weeks in half a year. ______

11 If this spinner is spun, which result, **Y**, **B** or **G**,

a is most likely? ______

b has a 25% chance of occurring? ______

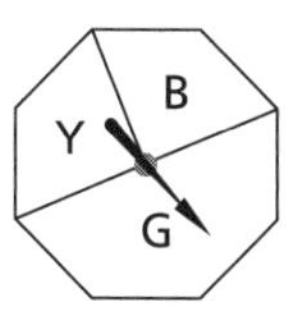

12 **a** $5\overline{)27}$ r ______ **b** $4\overline{)27}$ r ______

14:4 Extension ☐ out of 3

1 We wish to build a border around this garden. It is to be three paving stones wide. How many paving stones will be used altogether?

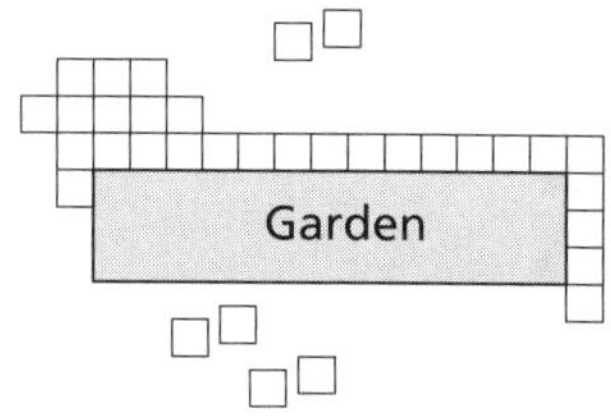

______

2 3 days from now it will be Saturday. What day was it 30 days ago? ______

3

Bus timetable	
May St	08:54
Joy Ave	09:12
Red St	09:37
Fig St	09:48
Rae St	10:04

How long does it take to travel from:

a May St to Joy Ave? ______

b Red St to Rae St? ______

c May St to Rae St? ______

Challenge

Make a list of events and estimate the probability of each event, as a percentage.

______

______

______

______

24-hour Time

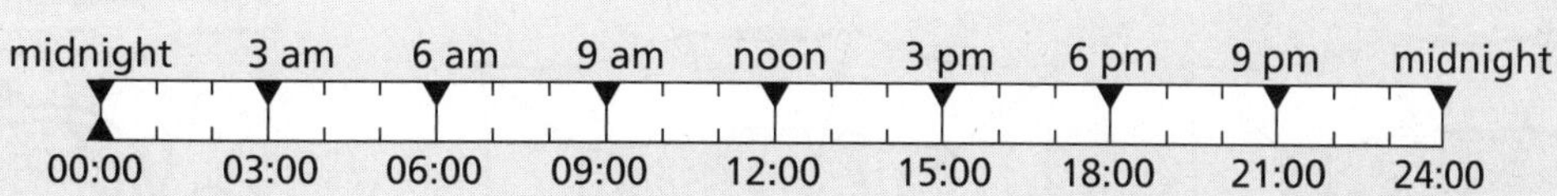

Write the 24-hour time for each of these digital times.

a 6 pm ______ **b** 9:30 am ______

c 7 am ______ **d** 10:30 pm ______

e noon ______ **f** midnight ______ or ______

15:1 ☐ out of 15

1. 9 × 9 ____
2. 13 − 8 ____
3. 40 ÷ 5 ____
4. Ten fives. ____
5. $\begin{array}{r} 15 \\ +\ \ 7 \\ \hline \end{array}$
6. 5 rows of 4. ____
7. 81 subtract 7. ____
8. Increase 55 by 7. ____
9. Half of 88. ____
10. $\begin{array}{r} 60 \\ -\ 18 \\ \hline \end{array}$

11. 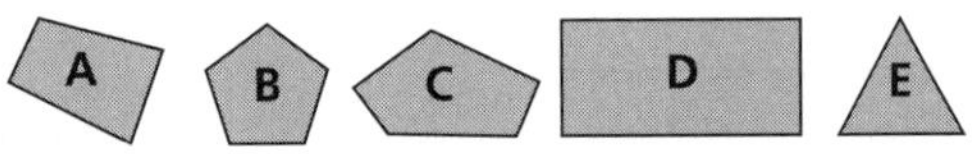

   a Which shapes are regular? ____
   b Which shapes have all angles obtuse? ____

12. Round off 3 421 030 to the nearest million. ____
13. These are ____________ lines.

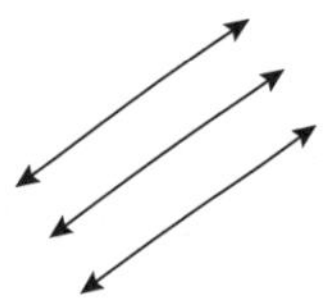

14. Find the area of this shape.

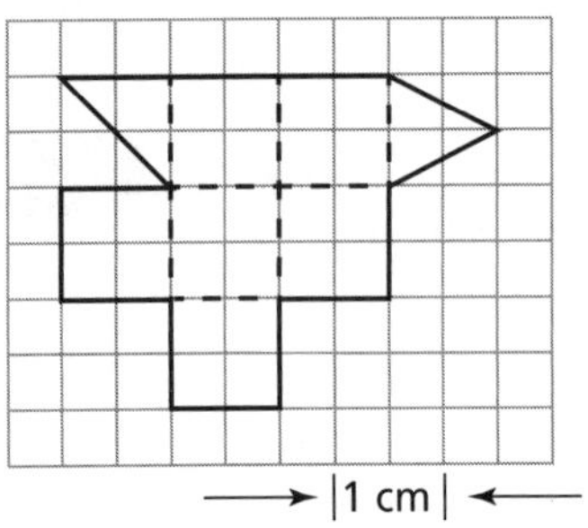

____

15. Show the time 20 minutes after noon.

a 

b 

15:2 ☐ out of 18

1. 112 − 4 ____
2. 9 × 6 ____
3. 70 + 60 ____
4. 7 × 8 ____
5. $\begin{array}{r} 30 \\ \times\ \ 8 \\ \hline \end{array}$
6. 25 ÷ 5 ____
7. Tens in 470. ____
8. 470 ÷ 10 ____
9. 7 × 5 + 3 × 5 ____
10. $\begin{array}{r} 60 \\ \times\ \ 7 \\ \hline \end{array}$

11. How many minutes in:
   a $1\frac{1}{2}$ hours? ____
   b $2\frac{1}{4}$ hours? ____

12. How much further must this car travel before the odometer shows 1 000 km?

____

13. How many sides on a hexagon? ____
14. Find the area of a rectangle measuring 16 m by 5 m. ____
15. Use 24-hour time to write 3:30 pm. ____
16. The 3rd month of the year. ____
17. 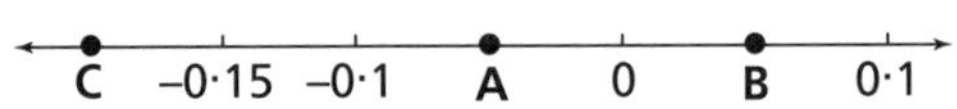

   What number would be at:
   a A? ____ b B? ____ c C? ____

18. Find the change from $50 if the total is rounded off to the nearest 5 cents.

$ 4.34
$ 1.96
$ 2.44
$ 1.88

____

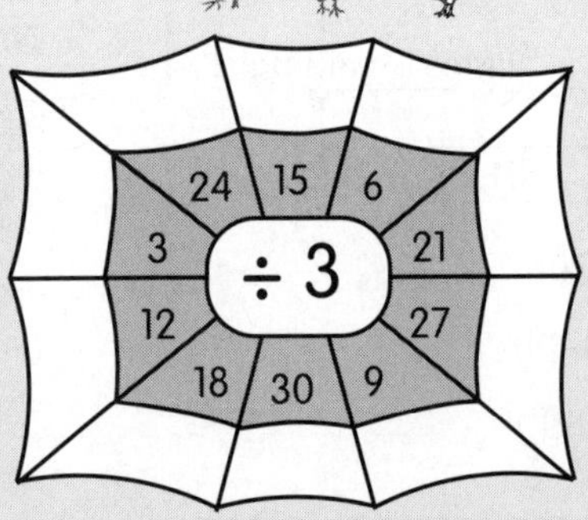

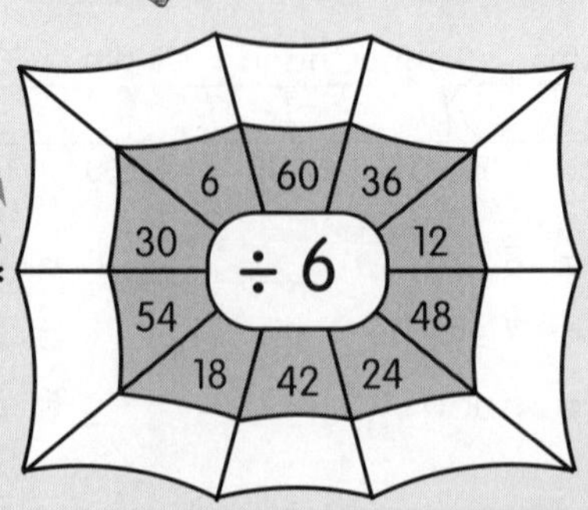

☐ × 3 = 24, ☐ = ____
☐ × 6 = 48, ☐ = ____

 ISBN 978 1 4886 2192 5

15:3 out of 7

1.
```
  $4 3 7 2 1
+ $1 5 5 8 4
```

2.
```
  9 0 0 0 0
−   8 2 0 0
```

3. A photographer allows 10 minutes to take one family portrait. How many families can be photographed from 9 am to 12:30 pm? ______

4. 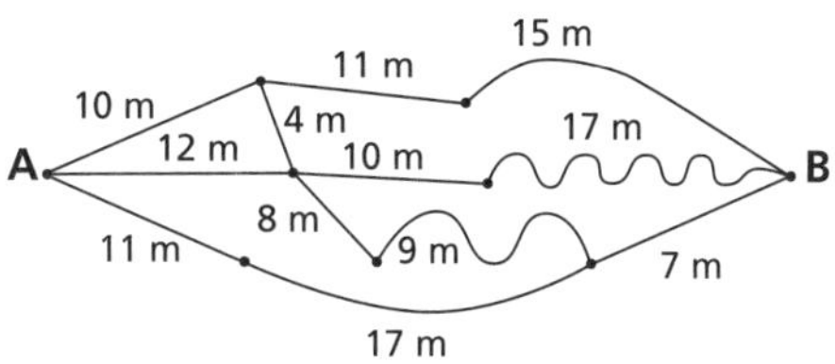

The shortest distance from **A** to **B**. ______

5. If a car travelled 50 km per hour for 4 hours, how far would it travel? ______

6. Write as 24-hour time:
a 8:50 am ______ **b** 8:50 pm ______

7.

Income	Gabby	Priscilla	Ilya
Mowing lawns	$30	0	$10
Babysitting	0	$28	$12
Washing cars	$18	$8	$12
Odd jobs	$16	$23	$25
TOTAL	$ ______	$ ______	$ ______

How much was earned by:
a Gabby? ______ **b** Ilya? ______
c Gabby, Priscilla and Ilya altogether? ______

15:4 out of 5

Extension

1. Which group of shapes below can be rearranged to make the flag on the right? ______

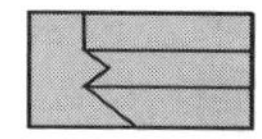

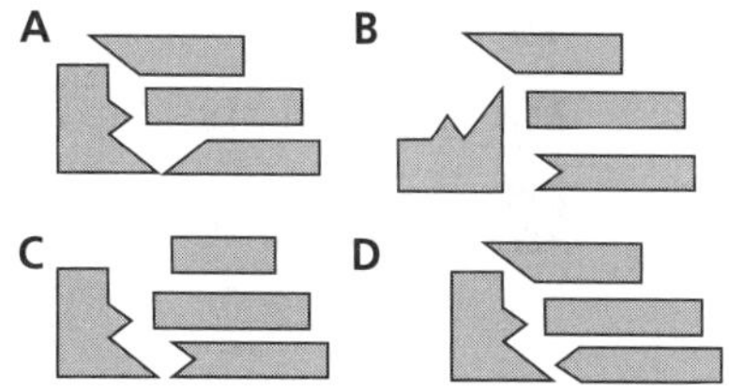

2. Aaron mowed the lawn from 3:39 pm till 5:06 pm. How long did he take? ______

3. The Roman numeral for 299. ______

4. Use the digits 1, 4, 5, 6 and 8 to make the number closest to:
a 60 000 ______ **b** 30 000 ______

5. November 8th 2012 is a Thursday. What day is it on November 8th 2013? ______

Challenge

Draw and describe the features of a parallelogram.

______

______

______

______

______

Eliminating Possibilities

How old is Alan if:

- reversing the digits of Naomi's age gives Alan's age,
- the total of their ages is 66,
- Naomi is under 20 years of age.

Alan's age = ______

 • *AUSTRALIAN SIGNPOST MATHS 6 MENTALS* • ISBN 978 1 4886 2192 5

16:1 ☐ out of 16

1. 5 × 7 ____
2. 16 − 7 ____
3. 2 ÷ 2 ____
4. 24 ÷ 6 ____
5. $\begin{array}{r} 25 \\ +\ \ 4 \\ \hline \end{array}$
6. Take 10 from 17. ____
7. Multiply 3 by 9. ____
8. Double 80. ____
9. Total 16 and 8. ____
10. $\begin{array}{r} \$5.00 \\ -\ \$0.87 \\ \hline \end{array}$
11. The sides of a square are ____________.
12. **a** In which direction does a compass needle always point? ____________

    b The angle between the compass directions, South and East? ____________

13. One million twelve thousand and twelve as a numeral. ____________
14. In this trapezium name two lines that are:

    a parallel ____________

    b at right angles to one another ______

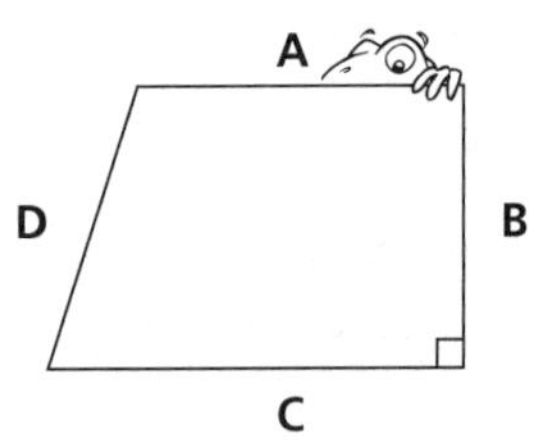

15. **a** Days in May. ____________

    b Days in autumn. ____________
16. What is the area of the shaded shape? ____________

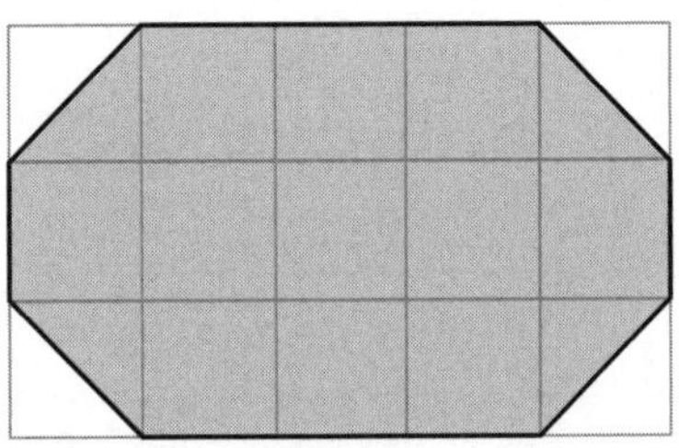

16:2 ☐ out of 16

1. 41 − 8 ____
2. 6 × 7 ____
3. 25 + 2 ____
4. 3 + 4 × 8 ____
5. $\begin{array}{r} 400 \\ \times\ \ \ 5 \\ \hline \end{array}$
6. 36 ÷ 4 ____
7. 760 ÷ 10 ____
8. □ + 81 = 99, □ = ____
9. 90 − □ = 35, □ = ____
10. $\begin{array}{r} \$1.17 \\ \times\ \ \ \ 4 \\ \hline \end{array}$
11. 62 − 6 − 6 − (6 − 5) ____________
12. Write this as 24-hour time. ____________

13. Find the area of each rectangle.

a

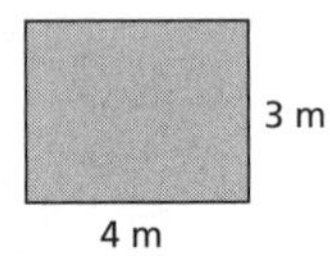

____

b

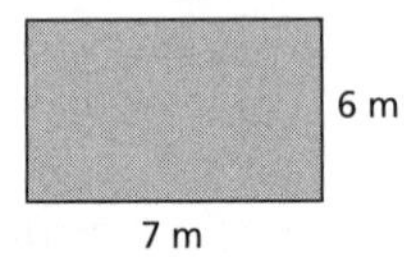

____

14. If a car travelled at 60 km per hour for $3\frac{1}{2}$ hours, how far would it travel? ______
15. Write the digital time for:

    a 15:36 ____________ **b** 07:05 ____________
16. Gillian began with this amount. She bought these items.

$15 $35.40 $1.80

Total amount spent: ______ Amount left: ______

 ISBN 978 1 4886 2192 5

16:3 — out of 8

1

$$\begin{array}{r} \$35.25 \\ \$16.35 \\ \$4.20 \\ +\ \$6.30 \\ \hline \end{array}$$

2

$$\begin{array}{r} 33 \\ 421 \\ 173 \\ +\ 256 \\ \hline \end{array}$$

3 3 × (4 + 6) ________

4 Is a square a quadrilateral? ________

5 How many sides on a hexagon? ________

6 If **E** has 10% of market share, what percentage has:

a **D**? ________

b **C**? ________

Market Share

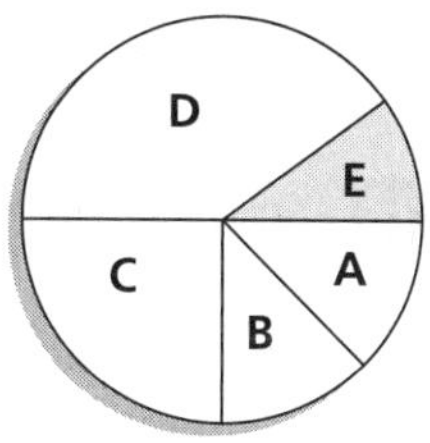

7

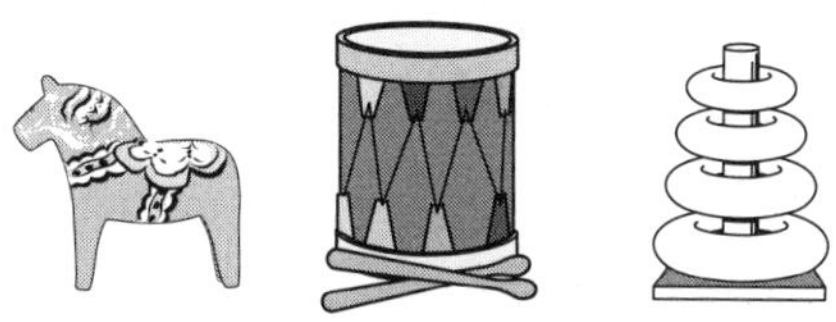

$4.20 $7.60 $1.90

a Circle the best estimate for the cost of 3 ring toys.

$3 $6 $8 $11

b If each item were reduced by fifty cents, what is the total cost of a drum and a toy horse?

____

c Circle the best estimate for the cost of 2 drums.

$10 $13 $15 $18

8 11, 22, 33, ____, ____, ____, ____

16:4 — out of 5

Extension

1 Insert grouping symbols to make this number sentence true.

18 − 5 × 3 = 39

2 How many days from 2nd August to 14th September? ________

3 What is the greatest number of shape **A** that could be cut out from shape **B**?

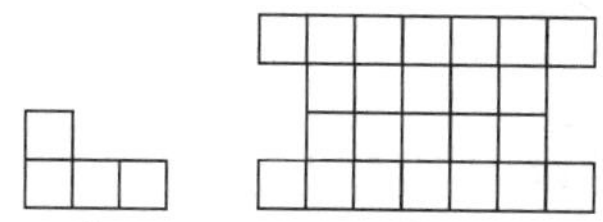

A **B**

____

4 $\frac{30}{100}$ of the townspeople were men, $\frac{27}{100}$ women and $\frac{51}{100}$ male.

men
women
boys
girls

What percentage of the people are:

a female? ________ **b** boys? ________

c girls? ________ **d** not men? ________

5 The angle between the compass directions:

a North and North-east? ________

b South-west and North? ________

N

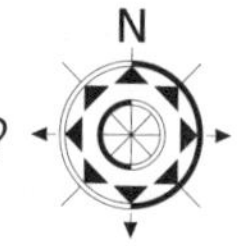

Challenge

Describe the position of items on this grid, e.g. the pentagon is north-east of the triangle.

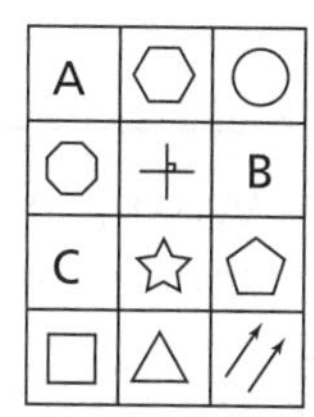

____

____

____

Consecutive numbers follow one another.

4, **5** and **6** are three **consecutive** numbers. Their sum is 15.

a On the list to the right, cross out those numbers that are the sum of 2 consecutive numbers, 3 consecutive numbers etc, up to the sum of 7 consecutive numbers.

b Which numbers are left? ________

What kind are they? ________

1			
2	3	4	5
6	7	8	9
10	11	12	13
14	15	16	17
18	19	20	21
22	23	24	25
26	27	28	29
30	31	32	33

17:1 ___ out of 16

1. 5×6 ___
2. $10 - 4$ ___
3. 9×6 ___
4. $70 + 18$ ___
5. $3\overline{)12}$
6. 2 squared. ___
7. Add 6 and 17. ___
8. 4 rows of 9. ___
9. Take 40 from 95. ___
10. $10\overline{)70}$
11. $0{\cdot}5 + 0{\cdot}5$ ___
12. Name a shape with 6 sides. ___
13. 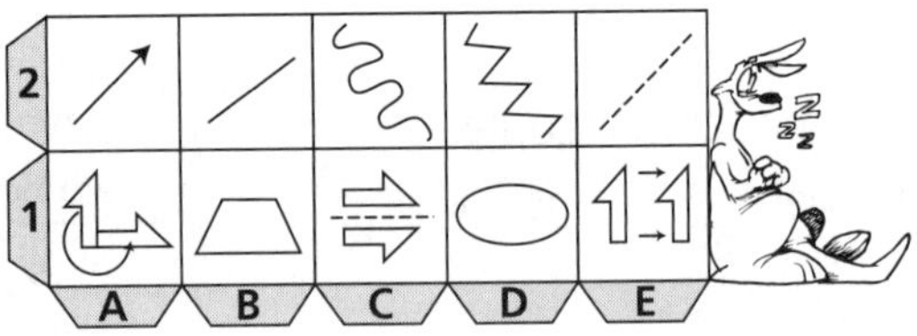

Give the name of the figure at:

a **E2** ___ **b** **B1** ___
c **C1** ___ **d** **D1** ___
e **E1** ___ **f** **A1** ___
g **D2** ___ **h** **B2** ___

14. A shape with five straight sides is called a ___.
15. 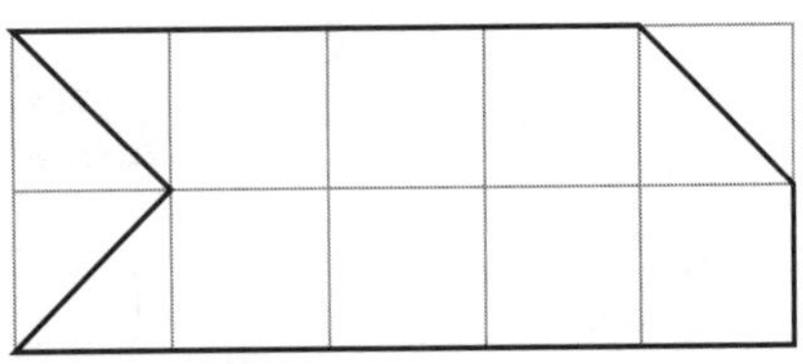

What is the area of this shape in square centimetres? ___ cm^2

16. The difference between 14:30 and:

a 08:30 on the same day. ___
b 08:30 on the next day. ___

17:2 ___ out of 17

1. 9×3 ___
2. $32 - 3$ ___
3. 6×7 ___
4. $8 + 41$ ___
5. $4\overline{)36}$
6. $0{\cdot}7 + 0{\cdot}3$ ___
7. $\square \times 10 = 100$, $\square =$ ___
8. $0{\cdot}1 + 0{\cdot}9$ ___
9. $180 - 2 \times 70$ ___
10. $5\overline{)36}$ r

11. **a** $4 \times 8 + 10$ ___

b $16 \div 4 + 20 \div 5$ ___

12. At a speed of 60 km/h, how far would I travel in 2 hours? ___
13. What is the area of a rectangular dance floor that has a length of 12 m and a width of 6 m? ___

14. How many sides does an octagon have? ___
15. $0{\cdot}8$, $1{\cdot}0$, $1{\cdot}2$, ___, ___
16. Minutes in $4\frac{1}{2}$ hours. ___
17. Heidi began with $30 and bought these items.

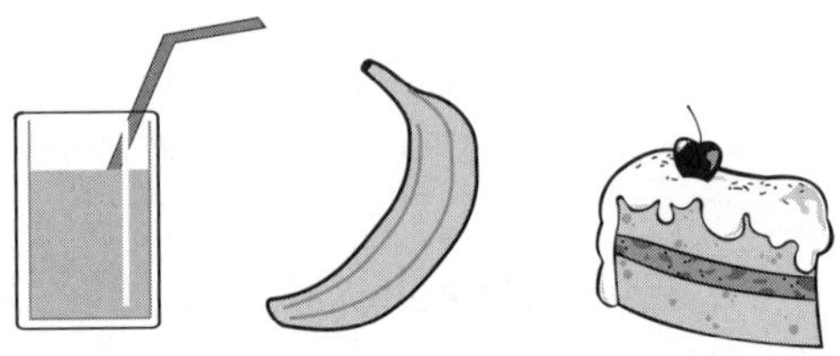

$2.80 **$1.70** **$1.40**

Total spent = ___

Amount left = ___

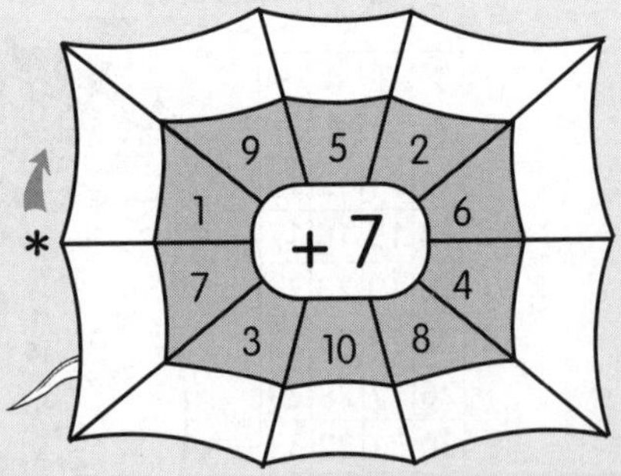

Answers

ID Card Answers

ID Card A

1 metres 2 millimetres 3 centimetres 4 kilometres 5 litres
6 millilitres 7 grams 8 kilograms 9 seconds 10 minutes 11 hours
12 square centimetres 13 square metres 14 hectares
15 cubic centimetres 16 cubic metres 17 degrees Celsius
18 grouping symbols 19 before noon (or ante meridiem)
20 after noon (or post meridiem) 21 counting numbers
22 even numbers 23 odd numbers 24 ordinal numbers 25 digits
26 square numbers 27 2, 4 28 7 29 5 30 remainder

ID Card B

1 ray 2 interval 3 straight line 4 curved line 5 wavy line
6 zigzag line 7 dotted line 8 parallel lines 9 perpendicular lines
10 horizontal line 11 vertical line 12 corner (or vertex) of an angle
13 arm of an angle 14 acute angle 15 right angle 16 obtuse angle
17 straight angle 18 reflex angle 19 revolution 20 tessellation
21 reflection (flip) 22 translation (slide) 23 rotation (turn)
24 rotational symmetry 25 axis of symmetry 26 axes of symmetry
27 number line 28 scale 29 1 : 100 30 15 mm

ID Card C

1 triangle 2 square 3 rectangle 4 parallelogram 5 rhombus
6 trapezium 7 quadrilaterals 8 pentagons 9 hexagons
10 octagon 11 circle 12 oval 13 regular shapes 14 irregular shapes
15 Shape B is rigid. 16 centre 17 radius 18 diameter 19 circumference
20 quadrant 21 semi-circle 22 sector 23 segment 24 diagonals
25 1 mL 26 length = 12 cm, breadth = 6 cm 27 perimeter = 10 cm
28 area = 6 cm^2 29 1 square metre 30 hectare

ID Card D

1 face 2 corner or vertex 3 edge 4 cube 5 rectangular prism
6 triangular prism 7 hexagonal prism 8 triangular pyramid
9 square pyramid 10 rectangular pyramid 11 base 12 cylinder
13 cone 14 sphere 15 net of a cube 16 net of a square pyramid
17 net of a cylinder 18 net of a cone 19 Side view is 3.
20 Front view is 1. 21 Top view is 2. 22 19:30 (or 1930)
23 5:40 am 24 protractor 25 compass 26 coordinates
27 picture graph 28 tally 29 column graph 30 line graph

1:1

1 15 2 24 3 8 4 16 5 40 6 54 7 10 8 15 9 5
10 18 11 7 (thousands) 12 587 13 86 624 14 a $\frac{3}{10}$ b 0·3
15 6 (tenths) or 0·6 16 80 (eggs) 17 1, 32, 2, 16, 4, 8
18 680 (centimetres) 19 a 9 cm^2 b 14 cm

1:2

1 94 2 64 3 10 4 180 5 100 6 60 7 45 8 49 9 35
10 79 11 80 12 a 0·51 b 51% 13 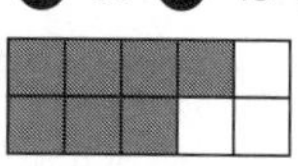 $\frac{7}{10}$, 0·7
14 a E, H b A, B, C, D, G c F, I d C, G 15 34 (mugs)

Activity

13, 9, 6, 4, 10, 12, 8, 5, 11, 7
15, 11, 8, 6, 12, 14, 10, 7, 13, 9
even + odd = *odd*, odd + odd = *even*

1:3

1 940 2 14 3 14 (days) 4 144 5 true 6 7 (apples)
7 15 8 10
9 a and b 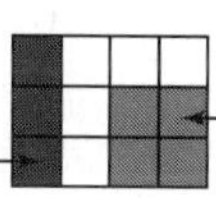

c no 10 9 (teams)

11 | 4 | 9 | 0 | tens | 2 | ones |
12 4 13 a 302 cm b 3 m 20 cm 14 Monday

1:4

1 a true b false 2 8 + 6 − 12 = 2 3 5 4 882 5 5

Challenge

Answers will vary. One answer is 4 × 9 = 36

Activity

Answers will vary.

2:1

1 6 2 8 3 36 4 13 5 27 6 9 7 24 8 27 9 12
10 63 11 90 thousands 12 7000 + 100 + 60 + 3 13 a $\frac{6}{8}$ (or $\frac{3}{4}$)
b $\frac{2}{8}$ (or $\frac{1}{4}$) 14 a yes b yes 15 rectangle (and square)
16 a 8 m 68 cm b 150 cm 17 a 410 g b 606 mL 18 reflection
19 43 out of 100 = 43% 20 1·0 (or 1), 1·1, 1·2

2:2

1 27 2 5 3 110 4 320 5 24 6 9 7 109 8 93 9 25
10 $4.48 11 $4.50 12 a 707 007 b 97 531 13 8, 16, 24 14 5
15 a F3 b L c S d Z e J 16 55 055
17 a $\frac{99}{100}$ b $1\frac{8}{10}$ (or $\frac{18}{10}$ or $1\frac{4}{5}$) 18 a 34 b 99

Activity

0, 1, 5, 8, 4, 6, 2, 7, 3, 9
7, 3, 10, 2, 6, 8, 4, 9, 5, 1
even − even = *even*, odd − even = *odd*

2:3

1 833 2 621 3 552 4 a B b B 5 summer 6 $\frac{9}{10}$
7 octagon 8 2 (mangoes) 9 tessellate 10 $0.37 11 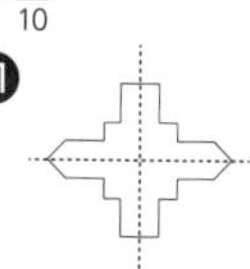

2:4

1

1st number	50	51	52	53
2nd number	65	66	67	68

2nd number = 1st number + 15

2 25 h 15 min 3  4 a 5170 b 8000

Challenge

Answers will vary. A tessellation will be drawn.

Activity

(1) *face* (2) *corner* or *vertex* (3) *edge* (11) *base* (12) *cylinder*
(13) *cone* (14) *sphere* (15) net of a *cube* (17) net of a *cylinder*
(18) net of a *cone*

3:1

1 32 2 3 3 2 4 61 5 14 6 60 7 67 8 70 9 32
10 45 11 a cylinder b sphere 12 Books each = 5, remainder = 2

 • *AUSTRALIAN SIGNPOST MATHS 6 MENTALS* • ISBN 978 1 4886 2192 5

13 9708 **14**

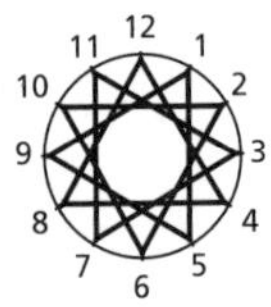

a 12-point star **15** 4004040

16 **a** B **b** A

3:2

1 30 **2** 7 **3** 28 **4** 45 **5** 99 **6** 10 **7** 131 **8** 5 **9** 100
10 58 **11** 14 **12** **a** C **b** B **c** D **d** E **13** **a** $<$ **b** $<$ **14** 378
15 A **16** rotation

Activity

10, 50, 30, 100, 70, 40, 80, 20, 90, 60
5, 25, 15, 50, 35, 20, 40, 10, 45, 30

3:3

1 \$73.08 **2** \$54.85 **3** **a** true **b** false
4 **a** 4 groups 2 left **b** 5 groups 1 left **5** 42 (buttons) **6** 682·05
7 forty-one million and four **8** 180 (degrees)
9 **a** cylinder **b** cone **10** 3 (people)

3:4

1 5 **2** 72 and 73 **3** D **4** 9 **5** 12 **6** 3457

Challenge

Answers will vary. One answer could include: 13546200 is an even number. It has 8 digits and rounds to 14000000, when rounding to the nearest million. It has 2 hundreds.

Activity

a \$37.45 **b** \$43.90 **c** \$30.00 **d** \$84.65 **e** \$117.10
f \$265.15 **g** \$630.95

4:1

1 30 **2** 56 **3** 7 **4** 1 **5** 200 **6** 9 **7** 80 **8** 11 **9** 47
10 90 **11** 57 mm **12** 6 (birds) **13**

14 A, B, C
15 2000000 (or 2 million)

4:2

1 25 **2** 5 **3** 38 **4** 540 **5** 175 **6** 5 **7** 68 **8** 70
9 19 **10** 157 cents **11** 1, 36, 2, 18, 3, 12, 4, 9, 6
12 **a** 45 mm **b** 96 mm **13** **a** 66 cm **b** 28 cm **14** **a** 27, 51 **b** 4, 64
15 **a** 7400000 **b** 6500000 **16** obtuse **17** 3 (people)

Activity

10, 2, 20, 12, 4, 16, 14, 6, 18, 8
20, 4, 40, 24, 8, 32, 28, 12, 36, 16
Multiplying by an even number gives an even answer.

4:3

1 573 **2** 575 **3** 745 **4** 32 cm **5** 21 mm (or 2·1 cm)
6 symmetry **7** **a** 500 (mm) **b** 2500 (mm) **8** 36 **9** 9999000
10 3 **11** 4 groups of 6, 1 left over

4:4

1 **a** 20 cm **b** 60 cm **2** 4 **3** 18 **4** **a** 20 **b** $16\frac{1}{2}$ **5** 600 m

Challenge

Answers will vary.

Activity

a 25 **b** 9 **c** 100 **d** 16 **e** 64 **f** 1 **g** 81 **h** 4 **i** 36

5:1

1 36 **2** 6 **3** 32 **4** 6 **5** 300 **6** 63 **7** 9 **8** 19
9 88 **10** 5 **11** 1000 (m) **12** **a** wiping benches **b** 35 (jobs)
13 34 mm (or 3·4 cm) **14** 1204155, 1795178, 7050705, 7157743

5:2

1 47 **2** 36 **3** 7 **4** 28 **5** 48 **6** 6 **7** 80 **8** 556
9 6756 **10** \$2.04 **11** 8000000 **12** 400000
13 **a** 10 (people) **b** 50 (people) **c** 11 am till noon **d** 2 pm till 3 pm
14 **a** m **b** cm **15** **a** 6 cm 3 mm **16** 25

Activity

5, 13, 9, 6, 10, 8, 12, 7, 11, 14
7, 15, 11, 8, 12, 10, 14, 9, 13, 16
even + even = *even*, odd + even = *odd*

5:3

1 1395 **2** 1 181 **3** 901
4 Estimates will vary. Measure = 44 or 45 mm **5** 9
6 **a** \$105 **b** \$465 **7** 85 cm **8** 20 mm **9** 25 **10** 3000000

5:4

1 **a** 30 **b** 36 **2** **a** 21 cm **b** 84 cm **3** 115
4 **a** yes **b** no **5** 16

Challenge

Answer = 23876; Number stories will vary.

Activity

a 4 **b** 30 seconds **c** 9 (including the ground floor) **d** 6 minutes
(It takes 1 minute to get from level 6 to level G.)

6:1

1 12 **2** 28 **3** 4 **4** 32 **5** 21 **6** 18 **7** 78 **8** 100
9 27 **10** 48 **11** 107308 **12** 5c, 10c, 20c, 50c
13 **a** 6 after 4 **b** 28 to 10 **14** 49th **15** 60 **16** **a** 120° **b** 60°
17 **a** 33 **b** 36 **18** itself

6:2

1 32 **2** 24 **3** 49 **4** 90 **5** 119 **6** 78 **7** 300 **8** 7
9 4 **10** \$15.88 **11** 10 **12** **a** 6·5 km **b** 0·9 km **13** **a** 10 (bats)
b Monday and Thursday **14** 146 (mm) **15** 51 or 52 mm **16** 51
17 37631713, 33761301, 31763116, 31673316

Activity

1, 9, 5, 4, 0, 8, 2, 6, 3, 7
5, 1, 7, 6, 2, 10, 4, 8, 3, 9

6:3

1 3 **2** 37 **3** **a** 80 000 **b** 800 **4** seventh **5** reflection

6 9 (pairs) **7** **a** 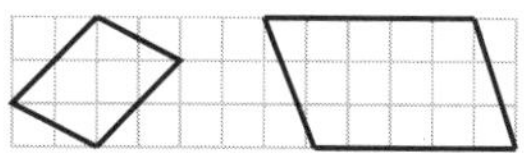 **b** yes **8** 62

9 Answers will vary slightly. **a** 30° **b** 95° **c** 190°

10 5 (km) **11** 36, 49

6:4

1 **a** 293 km **b** 330 km **2** $83.10 **3** 540 min **4** 110 **5** 40

6 **a** yes **b** yes

Challenge

Answers will vary.

Activity

a 21 **b** 2 **c** 0 **d** 18 **e** 11 **f** 3 **g** 25 **h** 7 **i** 48 **j** 2 **k** 24

7:1

1 0 **2** 72 **3** 7 **4** 900 **5** 42 **6** 1 **7** 32 **8** 38

9 67 **10** 39 **11** **a** C **b** D **c** A **d** B **12** 4 **13** 6407 **14** **a** < **b** <

15 6400 **16** 68, 70, 72 **17** Answers will vary. **18** 36

7:2

1 69 **2** 36 **3** 21 **4** 300 **5** 210 **6** 9 **7** 80 **8** 9 **9** 10

10 424 **11** 400 **12** 37 **13** rectangular pyramid **14** **a** yes **b** yes

15 1700 **16** **a** 70° **b** acute **17** 16 **18** **a** 670 **b** 872

Activity

a 6 **b** 4 **c** 16 **d** 4 **e** 17 **f** 17 **g** 4 **h** 16 **i** 12 **j** 16 **k** 63

7:3

1 2551 **2** 8433 **3** 248 **4** 80 **5** 2100 **6** 36 000

7 **a** 1 (toy) **b** 2 (toys) **8** 480 (min) **9** 7, 9, 12, 14 **10** 11

11 **a** 7 **b** 3 **12** **a** 15, 60 **b** 1, 49

7:4

1 370 **2** 1470 **3** 8 **4** **a** 140 (t) **b** 1800 (kg)

5 653 **6** $2^2 + 3^2 + 4^2$ **7** 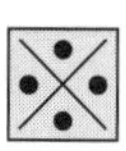

Challenge

Answers will vary. It is less than 90° in size. Places this angle could be seen are: between your fingers in a hand span, at the tip of a pencil or when scissors are open.

Activity

(7) *dotted* line (8) *parallel* lines (10) *horizontal* line
(11) *vertical* line (14) *acute* angle (15) *right* angle (16) *obtuse* angle
(17) *straight* angle (18) *reflex* angle (19) *revolution*

8:1

1 72 **2** 21 **3** 3 **4** 18 **5** 0 **6** 4 **7** 81 **8** 56 **9** 23

10 12 **11** 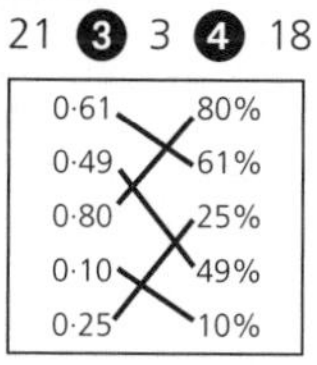

12 179 m **13** your estimate, 6 cm

14 1 m 49 cm **15** $24 **16** kilometres **17** 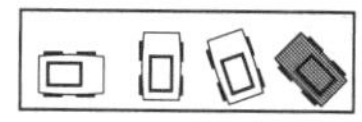

8:2

1 450 **2** 100 **3** 7 **4** 480 **5** 340

6 110 **7** 9 **8** 9 **9** 8 **10** $3.20 **11** 8 **12** 180°

13 **a** 80 (mm) **b** 9 (cm) **14** 24 (fish) **15** 52 **16** eighteenth **17** 400

18 31 days **19** 0·12 **20** 40 cm **21** 98% **22** 30

Activity

a 34 small squares will be red, 27 will be blue and 19 will be yellow. 20% will be left uncoloured.

b 9 small squares will be orange, 41 will be green and 38 will be purple. 12% will be left uncoloured.

8:3

1 970 **2** 876 **3** 5 metres **4** **a** 3·1 m **b** 11·04 cm **5** 2·63 m

6 15 (cakes) **7** 30 315 **8** 8421 m **9** 6·39 m **10** 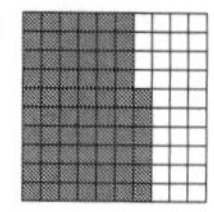

11 between 90° and 180° **12** 11

8:4

1 130 **2** 70° **3** 1% **4** 0·3 t (or 300 kg) **5** 26 **6** 48 (sandwiches)

Challenge

Answers will vary. One answer could be:

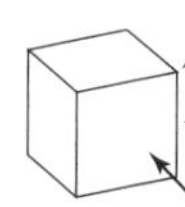

Activity

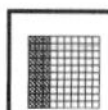	$\frac{3}{10}$	$\frac{30}{100}$	0·3	30%
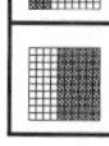	$\frac{6}{10}$	$\frac{60}{100}$	0·6	60%

(The part shaded is $\frac{7}{10}$ or $\frac{70}{100}$ or 0·7 or 0·70 or 70%.)

9:1

1 28 **2** 80 **3** 10 **4** 2 **5** 93 **6** 21 **7** 35 **8** 45

9 51 **10** 183 **11** 0·37, $\frac{37}{100}$, 37% **12** 2·9 cm **13** 81 out of 100

14 32 (legs) **15** two hundred and forty-three **16** $6.75

17 500 **18** 2 m **19** 5000 (m)

9:2

1 720 **2** 8 **3** 38 **4** 35 **5** 180 **6** 7 **7** 90 **8** 23

9 25 **10** 420 **11** 28 **12** 0·76, 76% **13** 3 m 85 cm

14 **a** 35% **b** 25% **15** **a** 0·5 **b** $\frac{50}{100}$ (or $\frac{25}{50}$ or $\frac{1}{2}$)

16 6508 m **17** 94 mL **18** **a** 222 **b** 70

Activity

a 1500 **b** 5600 **c** 2400 **d** 2500 **e** 4500 **f** 5000 **g** 4000
h 12 000 **i** 2500 **j** 640 000

9:3

1 1000 **2** $99.63 **3** 6865 **4** **a** E = 700 **b** E = 1200

5 **a** 3·56 m **b** 4 m 6 cm **6** **a** $\frac{1}{10}$ **b** 0·1 **c** 10% **d** 90%

7 **a** 72% **b** 9% **8** 7431 **9** **a** 2·2 pounds **b** 1·7 (or 1·8) pounds

10 $396 **11** 50

9:4

1 76 (weeks) **2** **a** New Zealand **b** 9 (gold) **c** 0·57 **d** 3·57

3 yes **4** 3606

Challenge

Answers will vary. 0·20 can be represented as: 0·2, $\frac{2}{10}$, $\frac{20}{100}$, 20%, 20 out of 100 or 2 out of 10.

Activity

8·375 km	8 km 375 m	8375 m
2·914 km	2 km 914 m	2914 m
5·446 km	5 km 446 m	5446 m
9·125 km	9 km 125 m	9125 m

10:1

1 8 **2** 13 **3** 11 **4** 40 **5** 150 **6** 60 **7** 32 **8** 43 **9** 40 **10** 0 **11** 9·35 m **12** 3650 and 4092 will be circled. **13** **a** 20 to 12 **b** 40 (minutes) **14** April **15** 5 groups, 2 left over **16** 10 **17** 8 (socks) **18** **a** 31 **b** one hundred and twenty-six **19** **a** 15 **b** 3

10:2

1 75 **2** 42 **3** 71 **4** 5 **5** 1800 **6** 8 **7** 72 **8** 8 **9** 28 **10** 5712 **11** 45% **12** **a** $\frac{1}{5}$ **b** 27% **c** 120

13

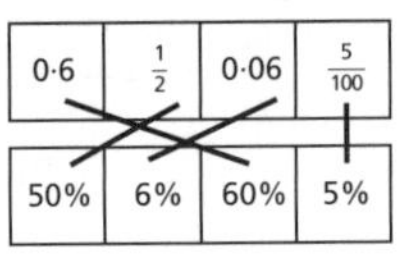

14 6 m 7 cm **15** **a** 160 **b** 3 (each) **16** 60

Activity

6, 21, 12, 18, 3, 30, 27, 9, 24, 15
12, 42, 24, 36, 6, 60, 54, 18, 48, 30

10:3

1 757 **2** $87.00 **3** 21 000 **4** 3 (bunches) **5** **a** 60% **b** 30% **6** **a** Add 40. **b** Subtract 200. **7** 600 **8** **a** 65 **b** 65 **9** 60 (rolls) **10** **a** 3·56 m **b** 15·09 m **11** **a** 22 yen **b** about 52 yen **c** about 47c (or $0.47) **d** about 69c ($0.69) **12** **a** 71 cm **b** 240 cm

10:4

1 9 (pizzas) **2** **a** true **b** true **3** 20 to 4 (or 3:40) **4** true

5 **a** 4·4 m **b** 13·2 m **6** 24 ways

Challenge

It is difficult to be accurate while measuring. The measuring instruments need to be used accurately and carefully and we should always check our measurements, making sure we have used the correct unit.

Activity

a 100 (sheets of paper) **b**

Thickness	10 mm	1 mm	0·1 mm
Number of sheets	100	10	1

c 8 mm (80 sheets)

11:1

1 14 **2** 24 **3** 9 **4** 9 **5** 480 **6** 16 **7** 126 **8** 64 **9** 7 **10** 500 **11** **a** $\frac{7}{10}$ **b** one sixth **12** 36 **13** 12 (grapes) **14** nine hundred and ninety **15** 1300 **16** 3 301 792 **17** 20, 4, 10, 5, 8 **18** 100 **19** 86 cm **20** 700

11:2

1 400 **2** 4 **3** 89 **4** 24 **5** 7000 **6** 12 **7** 2 **8** 9 **9** 5 **10** 4800 **11** 5000 **12** **a** 310° **b** 145° **13** true **14** 3, 4 and 6 will be underlined. **15** five thousand six hundred and five **16** **a** 12 r 1 **b** 8 r 6 **17** 1111 **18** 806 cm **19** **a** 83% **b** 0·83

Activity

2, 6, 4, 8, 10, 5, 9, 3, 7, 1
3, 8, 5, 2, 7, 4, 1, 9, 6, 10

11:3

1 37 **2** 13 **3** 21 **4** 62 **5** 1510 **6** **a** 70% **b** 10% **c** 7% **d** 1% **7** **a** 140° **b** 125° **8** 98 000 020 **9** 320 cm (or 3·2 m) **10** 32 000 (stamps) **11** 7277 **12** **a** 3·56 m **b** 15·09 m

11:4

1 5 weeks **2** 0·73 **3** 10 and 13 **4** 1

5 **a** 81 **b** 162 **c** 216 **d** 194 **6** **a** $2.75 **b** $22 **7** 17

Challenge

Answers will vary.

Activity

a Rachel **b** Rhonda **c** Heather

12:1

1 10 **2** 24 **3** 3 **4** 34 **5** 140 **6** 24 **7** 48 **8** 68 **9** 41 **10** $3.66 **11** 142° **12** 51 428 211 **13** 37 **14** 180° **15** 8652 **16** **a** 75° **b** 100° **17** 1000 **18** 85%

12:2

1 56 **2** 98 **3** 56 **4** 49 **5** 291 **6** 8 **7** 28 **8** 24 **9** 6 **10** 54 000 **11** twenty hectares **12** 4 thousandths **13** $1\frac{2}{3}$ (or $\frac{5}{3}$) **14** **a** 18·08 **b** 60·06 **15** 5·84 **16** 2 200 006 **17** 36 cm **18** 145° **19** 850 306 **20** 48 km

Activity

(11) *hours* (12) *square centimetres* (13) *square metres*
(14) *hectares* (15) *cubic centimetres* (26) *square* numbers (27) *2, 4*
(28) *7* (29) *5* (30) *remainder*

12:3

1 9 **2** 4 **3** 7 **4** 0·91, 0·92, 0·93 **5** 4 birds will be coloured. **6** **a** > **b** < **7** 247 368 **8** **a** 6 **b** 8 **9** 140 **10** 80c **11** 83 **12** 1000 **13** 24 m **14** 45° **15** 96 408 **16** 90%

12:4

1 **a** 9 m **b** 36·2 m **2** XXXVI **3** 316 m **4** D

5 Ty **6** 100 g **7** 25

Challenge

Answers will vary.

Activity

a 9 m **b** 97 g **c** 606 **d** 6 **e** 63

13:1

1 11 **2** 32 **3** 8 **4** 0 **5** 600 **6** 7 **7** 0 **8** 15
9 42 **10** 43 **11** 10 000 **12** 60° **13** Answers will vary.
14 **a** 6, 22, 37, 39, 43 **b** 3399, 3472, 3651, 3960 **15** 601st
16 **a** −2 **b** 1 **c** −5 **17** **a** 30 cm **b** 56 cm^2

13:2

1 63 **2** 9 **3** 77 **4** 64 **5** 360 **6** 15 **7** 3 **8** 42 **9** 14
10 198 **11** 200 **12** **a** 90° **b** 135° **13** **a** 0 **b** 1 **c** $-1\frac{1}{2}$
14 **a** B **b** 0·5 **c** 0·25 **15** **a** 320° **b** 240°

Activity

a length = about 19 mm, height = about 5 mm
b mass = 12 kg, width = about 13 mm
c capacity = 950 mL, height = about 14 mm

13:3

1 $6\frac{5}{6}$ **2** $10\frac{5}{7}$ **3** $\frac{5}{9}$ **4** 73 868 **5** 91 153 **6** revolution
7 8 m 60 cm **8** 67 747 324, 67 647 324, 67 541 234 **9** 0·4
10 seventy-two point six nine **11** B **12** 310° **13** 53 803

13:4

1 **a** 20 m 60 cm **b** 50 m 40 cm **2** **a** 12 **b** 15 **3** 42 **4** LXXX
5 49, 16 **6** **a** 367 **b** 460·8 **7** 41 (or XLI)

Challenge

Answers will vary.

Activity

Answers will vary.
C could be different for each person.

14:1

1 0 **2** 8 **3** 13 **4** 7 **5** 40 **6** 68 **7** 72 **8** 13 **9** 17
10 700 **11** **a** −7 **b** −4 **c** −10 **12** 1 248 976, 1 227 436, 1 049 415
13 **a** 50 000 000 **b** zero point six three one **14** 200 (years)
15 November **16** **a** B (blue) **b** G (green)

14:2

1 94 **2** 63 **3** 32 **4** 48 **5** 49 **6** 9 **7** 6 **8** 10
9 36 **10** $1.92 **11** $1.90 **12** 50 000 **13** 34 min **14** 64 m
15 **a** 5 (h) **b** 14 (h) **16** **a** 120° **b** 180° **17** a head and a tail

Activity

4, 6, 1, 8, 5, 9, 2, 0, 7, 3
3, 1, 10, 5, 8, 2, 6, 9, 4, 7; □ = 7

14:3

1 76 927 **2** 66 469 **3** 58 052 **4** 9454
5 **a** −40% **b** 0 (or 0%) **c** −100% **6** 16:28 (or 1628)
7 30 min **8** 21 600 s **9** 35 (school days) **10** 26 (weeks)
11 **a** G **b** Y and B **12** **a** 5 r 2 **b** 6 r 3

14:4

1 192 **2** Monday **3** **a** 18 min **b** 27 min **c** 1 h 10 min

Challenge

Answers will vary.

Activity

a 18:00 **b** 09:30 **c** 07:00 **d** 22:30 **e** 12:00 **f** 24:00 (or 00:00)

15:1

1 81 **2** 5 **3** 8 **4** 50 **5** 22 **6** 20 **7** 74 **8** 62
9 44 **10** 42 **11** **a** B and E **b** B **12** 3 000 000 **13** parallel (lines)
14 7 cm^2 **15** **a**

b

15:2

1 108 **2** 54 **3** 130 **4** 56 **5** 240 **6** 5 **7** 47 (tens) **8** 47
9 50 **10** 420 **11** **a** 90 (min) **b** 135 (min) **12** 175 km **13** 6 (sides)
14 80 m^2 **15** 15:30 (or 1530) **16** March
17 **a** −0·05 **b** 0·05 **c** −0·2 **18** $39.40

Activity

1, 8, 5, 2, 7, 9, 3, 10, 6, 4
5, 1, 10, 6, 2, 8, 4, 7, 3, 9; □ = 8, □ = 8

15:3

1 $59 305 **2** 81 800 **3** 21 (families) **4** 35 m **5** 200 km
6 **a** 08:50 **b** 20:50 **7** **a** $64 **b** $59 **c** $182

15:4

1 B **2** 1 h 27 min **3** CCXCIX **4** **a** 58 641 **b** 18 654 **5** Friday

Challenge

A parallelogram will be drawn. Answers will vary. One answer could include: It has 4 straight sides and 4 angles. The two opposite sides are parallel and have equal length. The opposite angles are equal. Diagonals bisect each other.

Activity

Alan's age = 51

16:1

1 35 **2** 9 **3** 1 **4** 4 **5** 29 **6** 7 **7** 27 **8** 160 **9** 24
10 $4.13 **11** equal **12** **a** north **b** 90°
13 1 012 012 **14** **a** A and C **b** B and C (or A and B)
15 **a** 31 (days) **b** 92 (days) **16** 13 cm^2

16:2

1 33 **2** 42 **3** 27 **4** 35 **5** 2000 **6** 9 **7** 76 **8** 18 **9** 55
10 $4.68 **11** 49 **12** 14:30 **13** **a** 12 m^2 **b** 42 m^2 **14** 210 km
15 **a** 3:36 pm **b** 7:05 am
16 Total amount spent = $52.20, Amount left = $17.80

Activity

4, 7, 0, 10, 5, 2, 9, 6, 3, 8
0, 8, 2, 7, 10, 3, 6, 9, 4, 5

 • *AUSTRALIAN SIGNPOST MATHS 6 MENTALS* • ISBN 978 1 4886 2192 5

16:3

1 \$62.10 **2** 883 **3** 30 **4** yes **5** 6 (sides) **6** **a** 40% **b** 25%

7 **a** \$6 will be circled. **b** \$10.80 **c** \$15 will be circled.

8 44, 55, 66, 77

16:4

1 $(18 - 5) \times 3 = 39$ **2** 43 (days) **3** 6

4 **a** 49% **b** 21% **c** 22% **d** 70% **5** **a** 45° **b** 135°

Challenge

Answers will vary.

Activity

a Most numbers on the grid will be crossed out.

b 1, 2, 4, 8, 16, 32. These are the powers of 2.

That is, $2^0, 2^1, 2^2, 2^3, 2^4, 2^5$.

17:1

1 30 **2** 6 **3** 54 **4** 88 **5** 4 **6** 4 **7** 23 **8** 36 **9** 55

10 7 **11** 1 **12** hexagon **13** **a** dotted line **b** trapezium

c reflection (or axis of symmetry) **d** oval **e** translation (or slide)

f rotation (or turn) **g** zigzag line **h** interval (or part of a line)

14 pentagon **15** 8·5 cm^2 **16** **a** 6 h **b** 18 h

17:2

1 27 **2** 29 **3** 42 **4** 49 **5** 9 **6** 1 **7** 10 **8** 1 **9** 40

10 7 r 1 **11** **a** 42 **b** 8 **12** 120 km **13** 72 m^2 **14** 8 (sides)

15 1·4, 1·6 **16** 270 min **17** **a** \$5.90 **b** \$24.10

Activity

8, 16, 12, 9, 13, 11, 15, 17, 10, 14
10, 18, 14, 11, 15, 13, 17, 19, 12, 16

17:3

1 121 068 **2** 895·94 **3** **a** 01:30 (or 0130) **b** 13:30 (or 1300)

4 **a** eggs **b** $\frac{1}{4}$ (or $\frac{25}{100}$) **c** 2 (eggs) **d** bacon **e** pastry

5 5 (sides) **6** $\frac{19}{5}$ **7** equal and parallel **8** 10 h **9** **a** 12 **b** 180

17:4

1 **a** \$61.70 **b** \$33.80 **2** **a** 30% **b** 20% **3** **a** $4\frac{3}{10}$ **b** 4·3

Challenge

Answers will vary.

Activity

(9) *perpendicular* lines (13) *arm* of an angle (20) *tessellation*
(21) *reflection* (flip) (22) *translation* (slide) (23) *rotation* (turn)
(24) *rotational symmetry* (26) *axes* (of symmetry) (28) *scale* (29) *1 : 100*

18:1

1 30 **2** 16 **3** 6 **4** 2 **5** 200 **6** 25 **7** 71 **8** 96 **9** 10

10 20 **11** 0·39, 0·4 **12** 75 921 977, 75 241 119, 75 124 911

13 4 (books) **14** 700 **15** 1 108 paces **16** 4

17 **a** 5 (halves) **b** 12 (quarters) **18** 6 (cm^2)

18:2

1 72 **2** 42 **3** 64 **4** 76 **5** 3 r 2 **6** 6 **7** 7 **8** 18 **9** 175

10 5 r 2 **11** **a** tree **b** hexagon **12** **a** 122 **b** male **c** 398 **13** 1

Activity

12, 42, 18, 48, 60, 36, 24, 54, 30, 0
18, 63, 27, 72, 90, 54, 36, 81, 45, 9

18:3

1 5·86 **2** 10·213 km **3** **a** G **b** L **c** L **d** H **4** **a** 2, 2·6

b 1·2, 1·5 **5** 25·7 m **6** **a** $\frac{9}{4}$ **b** $\frac{18}{5}$ **7** **a** 64 m **b** 84 m^2

18:4

1 800 m^2 **2** **a** 9 **b** 12 **3** **a** $6\frac{1}{3}$ **b** 7 **c** $7\frac{2}{3}$ **d** $8\frac{1}{3}$

4 8, 16, 32, 64 **5** **a** 299 **b** 184

Challenge

Answers will vary. This is not an accurate reflection of your whole suburb because it wasn't a large sample and it is likely that the responses of a variety of people were not included in the survey.

Activity

Answers will vary.

19:1

1 15 **2** 6 **3** 90 **4** 4 **5** 23 **6** 8 **7** 32 **8** 32 **9** 35

10 402 **11** 6 173 211 will be circled. **12** north **13** 36 million

14 7·17 **15** **a** i **b** n **16** **a** 6 cm^2 **b** 10 cm

19:2

1 280 **2** 11 **3** 96 **4** 48 **5** 120 **6** 7 **7** 0 **8** 4 **9** 90

10 300 **11** 700 000 **12** **a** $\frac{19}{5}$ **b** $\frac{17}{8}$ **13** **a** about 10 (people)

b 2 (siblings) **14** 19, 23, 27 **15** **a** $\frac{3}{4}$ **b** $1\frac{1}{8}$ **c** $1\frac{1}{2}$ **d** $2\frac{3}{8}$

16 3·11, 3·12

Activity

14, 42, 7, 28, 70, 49, 21, 63, 35, 56
16, 48, 8, 32, 80, 56, 24, 72, 40, 64

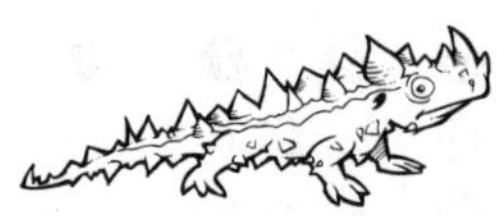

19:3

1 5·591 m **2** 7·798 L

3 **a** Kyrgyzstan **b** Afghanistan **c** E3 **d** B3 **e** 800 km

f Bishkek **g** Amritsar **4** 55

19:4

1 30 **2** **a** 3·6 **b** $3\frac{6}{10}$ (or) $\frac{60}{100}$

3 **a** $\frac{1}{2}$ **b** $\frac{2}{12}$ (or $\frac{1}{6}$) **c** $\frac{4}{12}$ (or $\frac{1}{3}$) **d** $\frac{9}{12}$ (or $\frac{3}{4}$) **4** 12 m

Challenge

Answers will vary. 13·452 is a number greater than 13 and less than 14. It rounds to 13 (to the nearest whole number). It is less than $13\frac{1}{2}$.

Activity

a 2 m **b** 8 cm **c** 10 m **d** 2 cm **e** 20 cm **f** 75 cm **g** 4 m **h** 0·5 cm

20:1

1 0 **2** 17 **3** 8 **4** 9 **5** 2 r 3 **6** 480 **7** 100 **8** 36 **9** 7
10 $2.11 **11** $2.10 **12** $1142.85 **13** 20 000 503 **14** 6
15 18, 21, 24 **16** 80 **17** **a** −7 **b** −13 **18** **a** flower **b** tree

20:2

1 72 **2** 11 **3** 540 **4** 200 **5** 145 **6** 7 **7** 45 **8** 10
9 40 **10** 526 **11** 2·5 km **12** 13, 31 **13** 90 (seeds) **14** **a** west
b north-east **15** 67 **16** **a** west **b** north **17** 20, 200

Activity

1, 2, 3, 4, 5, 6, 7, 8, 9, 10
5, 8, 1, 10, 4, 6, 2, 9, 3, 7

20:3

1 1·27 **2** 0·79 **3** 61·49 **4** 153 **5** 4386 **6** $30.10 **7** 18°C
8 0·06, 0·36, 0·63 **9** 95·2
10 **a** about 21 m **b** east **c** south-westerly **d** Year 1

20:4

1 **a** 15 **b** 30 **2** **a** 2 (counting numbers) **b** 5 (counting numbers)
3 325 BCE (or BC) **4** 60 (packets) **5** 5

Challenge

Answers will vary. One answer could be 12 × 10 − 20 = 100

Activity

a Profit of $12.50 **b** Loss of $7 400 **c** Profit of $6 870

21:1

1 24 **2** 5 **3** 63 **4** 5 **5** 77 **6** 2 **7** 56 **8** 23 **9** 100
10 113c (or $1.13) **11** $1.15 **12** 74 **13** $\frac{5}{16}$ **14** $\frac{75}{100}$ (or $\frac{3}{4}$)
15 yes **16** 367 **17** 85 (days) **18** −8°C

21:2

1 48 **2** 12 **3** 67 **4** 630 **5** 15 r 1 **6** 4 **7** 17 **8** 2
9 30 **10** 11 r 6 **11** 95 **12** 6, 12, 18, 24, 30, 36, 42, 48, 54, 60, 66
13 66, 77, 88 **14** **a** the usher (or man) **b** the exit **c** a spider
d the cinema screen (or claw) **e** the crowd **15** −7°C

Activity

Answers will vary.

21:3

1 53·231 **2** 11·119 **3** 18·771 **4** 129 **5** $18.63 **6** 89·24
7 4 m 4 cm (or 404 cm) **8** **a** 0·02 **b** 0·2 **9** 330° **10** **a** 1 100 km
b 3800 km **c** ACT, Tas, Vic, NSW, SA, NT, Qld, WA **11** 1·5 **12** 20°

21:4

1 175 BCE **2** 53 **3** 5 (birds) **4** **a** $25.80 **b** $2.15 **5** 18
6 1 600 and 420 will be circled.

Challenge

Answers will vary. The sample is very small and all from the same family.

Activity

a 95 cm **b** 175 cm **c** 135 cm **d** 185 cm **e** 65 cm (Answers may vary. Here we measure from the base of the heel.)

22:1

1 4 **2** 13 **3** 11 **4** 4 **5** 17 **6** 45 **7** 84 **8** 103 **9** 100
10 45 **11** 100 807 **12** **a** 21 (cubes) **b** 6 (cubes) **13** 38 095
14 **a** 0·05 **b** 0·5 **15** 365 (days) **16** rhombus
17 9·37, 7·93, 7·39, 3·79

22:2

1 56 **2** 20 **3** 240 **4** 100 **5** 200 r 1 **6** 2·5 **7** 42 **8** 7
9 6 **10** 68 r 2 **11** **a** −$2 **b** −$15 **12** −3
13 **a** 3 **b** 20 ($\frac{1}{6}$ of the throws) **14** 0·01, 0·13, 0·39, 0·4
15 **a** 700 g **b** 5 cm^3 **16** −4

Activity

(4) *parallelogram* (5) *rhombus* (6) *trapezium* (7) *quadrilaterals*
(8) *pentagons* (10) *octagon* (12) *oval* (13) *regular* shapes
(14) *irregular* shapes (15) Shape *B* is rigid.

22:3

1 531 **2** 1 194 **3** $21.84 **4** 12 r 1 **5** 225 r 2 **6** 956
7 40 **8** 30 **9** **a** kite **b** yes **10** A **11** 36 m^3
12 Approximately: **a** 216 km **b** 306 km **c** 360 km **d** 342 km **13** 0

22:4

1 1 CE (or AD). There is no 0 CE (or AD). **2** 65
3

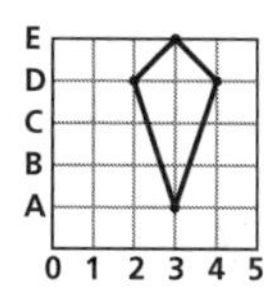

a kite **b** 3D **4** **a** LXXXIX **b** CCCXXIV
5 **a** 8 **b** 3

Challenge

1st row: Volume = 70 cm^3
2nd row: Volume = 48 cm^3
3rd row: Volume = 162 cm^3

Activity

Answers will vary.

23:1

1 42 **2** 38 **3** 6 **4** 5 **5** 78 **6** 36 **7** 9 **8** 64 **9** 360
10 $3.83 **11** $3.85 **12** 17 cm^3 **13**

Squares	1	2	3	4	5
Sides	4	8	12	16	20

14 45 **15** $\frac{5}{4}$ **16** 27, 81, 243 **17** *Unlikely* will be underlined.

23:2

1 300 **2** 21 **3** 90 **4** 60 **5** 22 r 3 **6** 6 **7** 4 **8** 9 **9** 50
10 234 r 1 **11** 821 g
12 **a-d**

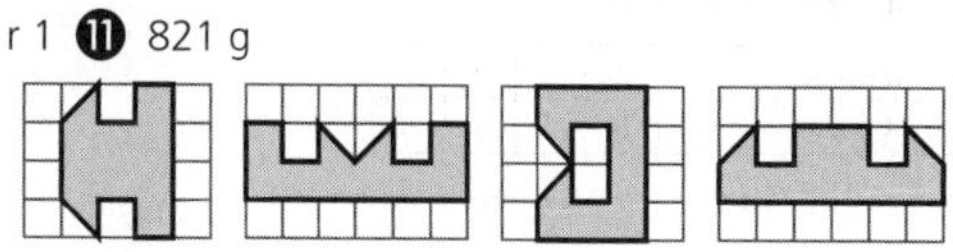

13 12 (dots) **14** 27 cm^3 **15** **a** −$3 **b** −$16

Activity

2, 6, 3, 9, 7, 4, 10, 8, 5, 1

2, 5, 8, 1, 7, 9, 3, 6, 4, 10; □ = 4

23:3

1 12·6 **2** 16·5 **3** $43.26 **4** 16 r 2 **5** 204 r 2 **6** 1 432 r 3

7 72 m³ **8** 0% (impossible) **9** 167 **10** 10 800 (s)

11 60 (5c coins) **12** **a** 9:57 am **b** 7:57 pm **13** 40%

14

Number of years	1	2	3	4	5
Number of months	12	24	36	48	60

a Months = years times 12 **b** 360 (months)

23:4

1 215 BCE (or BC) **2** 67·4 **3** 50 cm³

4

□	15	25	35	44	54
△	54	64	74	83	93

5 **a** 110 **b** 54 **6** 111 **7** **a** 111 222 **b** 847 612

Challenge

Answers will vary. One answer could be:
cm³: the volume of a pencil case, m³: the volume of a room.

Activity

[1] 2	4	[2] 7	0	[3] 5		[4] 8
3		3		[5] 5	4	0
[6] 4	[7] 3	6	8			4
	[8] 1	9		[9] 6	6	9
	3			0		0
	[10] 6	7	4	0	4	1

24:1

1 38 **2** 16 **3** 63 **4** 3 **5** 4 r 1 **6** 3 **7** 36 **8** 9

9 26 **10** 3 r 1 **11** 60 000 000 **12** 5 (Year 6 students)

13

Hexagons	1	2	3	4	5
Sides	6	12	18	24	30

14 13 (halves) **15** C **16** **a** 3 **b** 5

24:2

1 32 **2** 25 **3** 14 **4** 63 **5** 120 **6** 9 **7** 30 **8** 31 **9** 30

10 129 **11** **a** 3 **b** 4 **12** 60 m³ **13** 450 mL **14** **a** mL **b** L **c** mL

15 160 cm³ **16** **a** 62 973 **b** 83 497 **c** 1 082 300

Activity

1, 2, 3, 4, 5, 6, 7, 8, 9, 10

a 7 (grapes) **b** 9 (girls) **c** 5 (rows)

24:3

1 3217 **2** 9345·5 **3** 2080 **4** 609 **5** **a** 12 **b** 4 **c** 6 **d** 18

6 1 000 (mL) **7** **a** true **b** false

8

Number of horses	1	2	3	4	5
Number of legs	4	8	12	16	20

a legs = horses times 4 **b** 2 368 legs

9 **a** 3·527 **b** 8·72162 **c** 9·13824

24:4

1 5 BCE (or BC) **2** 585 cm³

3

□	20	17	32	47	83
△	80	83	68	53	17

4 16

5  **6**

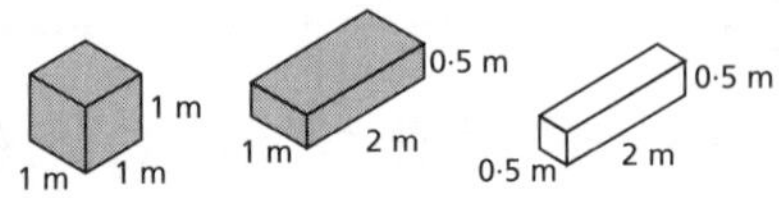

Challenge

Left column: 6 378·9, 4·9028, 8 703·4, 941·6, 310·8, 9·0023, 832·5, 79·32

Right column: 10·23, 324·1, 3·4098, 4·2937, 3 000·2, 5 112·3, 9·0076, 23·1

Activity

	Club	Day
Heather	Gym	Monday
Naomi	Drama	Tuesday
Luke	Tennis	Friday

25:1

1 40 **2** 63 **3** 3 **4** 4 **5** 149 **6** 21 **7** 37 **8** $21

9 54 **10** 24 **11** 2 h **12** **a** $\frac{3}{4}$ **b** $\frac{4}{4}$ (or 1) **13** **a** ML **b** kL

14 1·49 **15** $\frac{6}{8}$ (or $\frac{3}{4}$) **16** L **17** **a** 6 **b** 12 **c** 3 **d** 15

25:2

1 28 **2** 34 **3** 8 **4** 66 **5** 103 **6** 31·724 **7** 314·2

8 8 **9** 46 **10** 109 **11**

Decagons	1	2	3	4	5
Sides	10	20	30	40	50

12 6 (sixths)

13 **a** 7 L 500 mL **b** 385 mL **c** 8 mL **d** 4·32 L **e** 0·9 L

14 **a** $3\frac{1}{2}$ **b** $6\frac{1}{2}$ **15** **a** 0·4 (or 4 tenths) **b** 400 **16** 4

17 3 ML **18** 12 **19** 410·3

Activity

1, 2, 3, 4, 5, 6, 7, 8, 9, 10

a 6 (papers) **b** 8 (teams) **c** 4 (cups of tea)

25:3

1 1633 **2** 1053 **3** **a** 6 **b** 3 **c** 15 **d** yes **4** mL

5 **a** $\frac{5}{6}$ **b** $\frac{5}{12}$ **6** **a** 12 ML **b** 3 000 kL **c** 1·86L

7

Number of cubes	1	2	3	4	5
Number of faces	6	12	18	24	30

a Number of cubes times 6 **b** 1416 (faces)

8 **a** 1·53 **b** 17 476·2 **c** 8·1346

25:4

1 8 times (as big) **2** 16 females **3** 750 mL

4 **a** $\frac{17}{100}$ **b** $\frac{9}{100}$ **c** $\frac{11}{100}$ **d** $\frac{89}{100}$ **5** 6 cm **6** 8 **7** −10

Challenge

Answers will vary.

Activity

a 4 (eighths) **b** $\frac{3}{4}$ **c** $\frac{5}{8}$ **d** $\frac{4}{8}$ (or $\frac{1}{2}$) **e** $\frac{3}{8}$

f $1\frac{1}{8}$ **g** $\frac{1}{8}$ **h** $1\frac{5}{8}$ **i** $1\frac{7}{8}$ **j** $\frac{7}{8}$

 • *AUSTRALIAN SIGNPOST MATHS 6 MENTALS* • ISBN 978 1 4886 2192 5

26:1

1 4 **2** \$21 **3** 10 **4** 36 **5** 41 **6** 22 **7** 6 **8** 80 **9** 49
10 21 **11** a 3 b 2 **12** L **13** 6 (halves) **14** a 1 b 0 **15** true
16 a megalitre b kilolitre **17** a $\frac{4}{5}$ b $\frac{4}{8}$ (or $\frac{1}{2}$)
18 $2\frac{3}{4}$ **19** no **20** 9 + 5 = 14

26:2

1 48 **2** 36 **3** 82 **4** 81 **5** 30 **6** 7 **7** 320 **8** 8 **9** 18
10 40 **11** 5 L **12** a $\frac{5}{8}$ b $\frac{5}{6}$ c $\frac{7}{10}$ d $\frac{5}{12}$ **13** 9000 kL
14 20 (cm^2) **15** 3·047 L **16** triangular prism **17** 18 L **18** 2 L
19 a 4 b 12 c 2 d 14

Activity

1 1 g **2** a 3 kg b 270 g **3** 1300 g (or 1·3 kg)

26:3

1 421·9 (or 421 r 18) **2** 1780·7 (or 1780 r 35) **3** 0·016 L
4 a 6·7 (ML) b 9·37 (ML) **5** $\frac{7}{12}$ **6** 15 cm^3 **7** $\frac{6}{4}$ (or $1\frac{1}{2}$)
8 70 mL **9** a 5 b 10 c 3 d 12 **10** □ + 114 = 539

26:4

1 a 6 b $3\frac{1}{2}$ **2** 500 mL **3** a $\frac{1}{20}$ b $\frac{1}{50}$
4 a $\frac{63}{100}$ b $\frac{43}{100}$ c $\frac{21}{100}$ d $\frac{47}{100}$
5 a 1000 cm^3 b 1000000 cm^3 or 1 m^3 **6**

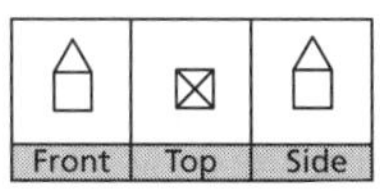

Challenge

a □ − 5 = 87, □ = 92
b (2 × □) − 2 = 28, □ = 15
c 6 × □ = 90, □ = 15

Activity

a Your choice

b

	a	e	i	o	u
Tally	𝍸 I	𝍸 𝍸 III	𝍸 𝍸 I	𝍸 𝍸 II	𝍸 I

c e

27:1

1 5 **2** 56 **3** 52 **4** 7 **5** 0 **6** \$10 **7** 12 **8** 54
9 105 **10** \$160 **11** $6\frac{1}{12}$ **12** a $\frac{7}{10}$ b $\frac{6}{8}$ (or $\frac{3}{4}$) **13** more
14 90 mL **15** a A, C, E b B, D **16** 1 (mL) **17** a 15 b 4 c 8 d 16

27:2

1 21 **2** 32 **3** 65 **4** 54 **5** 34 **6** 4 **7** 129 **8** 55
9 109 **10** 104 **11** 9 × 2 = 18 (or 9 × 2 = □)
12 a 14 b 7 **13** 650 cm^3 **14** 5930 (mL) **15**

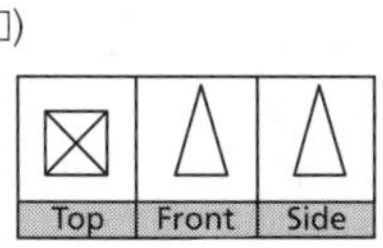

16 square pyramid **17** a 3 (surfaces) b 5 (surfaces) **18** 7 (L) **19** 40

Activity

(1) *metres* (2) *millimetres* (3) *centimetres* (4) *kilometres* (5) *litres* (6) *millilitres* (7) *grams* (8) *kilograms* (9) *seconds* (10) *minutes*

27:3

1 0·42 **2** 2·07 **3** 2·1 **4** a 5 (halves) b 12 (quarters)
5 a 50 mL b 36 mL c 87 mL d 14 mL **6** 6 (faces)
7 Answers will vary, depending on perspective and size.

a 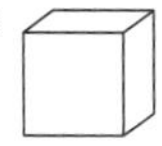 b 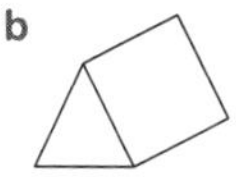 **8** 0·609 L **9** 4800 mL

10 a 7 b $4\frac{1}{2}$ **11** (6 + ____) ÷ 2 = 10

27:4

1 Tanya **2** a $2\frac{1}{4}$ b $\frac{9}{10}$ **3** 1000000 (cm^3)
4 a LXXXVII b CCXCIV **5** 14 (faces) **6** 960

Challenge

Answers will vary.

Activity

a $1\frac{1}{4}$ b $\frac{3}{4}$ c $\frac{1}{4}$ d $\frac{3}{4}$ e $\frac{2}{4}$ (or $\frac{1}{2}$) f $\frac{1}{4}$ g $1\frac{1}{2}$ h $1\frac{1}{4}$ i $1\frac{1}{2}$
j $1\frac{1}{4}$ k $\frac{6}{4}$ (or $1\frac{1}{2}$) l $1\frac{1}{4}$

28:1

1 45 **2** \$13 **3** 5 **4** 4 **5** \$3.75 **6** 101 **7** 64 **8** 91
9 7 **10** \$4.53 **11** a 24 b 240 c 2400 d 24000
12 triangular prism **13** 6 (faces) **14** cylinder
15 a 5000 (cm^3) b 15000 (cm^3) **16** a 21 b 4 c 12 d 20

28:2

1 42 **2** 30 **3** 89 **4** 32 **5** 631 **6** 6 **7** 14 **8** 12 **9** 56
10 82 **11** 1000 (cm^3) **12** a 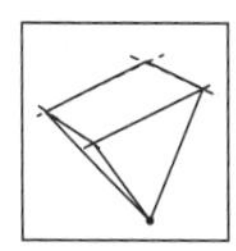 b 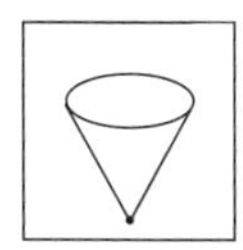

13 16 (quarters) **14** 6 **15** square pyramid **16** 829 mL
17 a $20\frac{1}{2}$ b 11 **18** $\frac{1}{2}$ **19** Answers may vary. Answers could include:
a $\frac{12}{20}$ (or $\frac{3}{5}$) b $\frac{2}{8}$ (or $\frac{3}{12}$) c $\frac{4}{12}$ (or $\frac{1}{3}$)

Activity

1, 2, 3, 4, 5, 6, 7, 8, 9, 10
a 7 (packets) b 5 km c 9 (boxes)

28:3

1 5·4 **2** 3·06 **3** 14·33 **4** 76604 **5** 88268 **6** \$12000
7 a $\frac{2}{4}$ (or $\frac{1}{2}$) b $\frac{3}{4}$ **8** 590 (cm^3) **9**  Drawings may vary.
a 4 (faces) b 6 (edges) c 4 (vertices) **10** 167 **11** 350 mL
12 a $10\frac{1}{2}$ b $10\frac{1}{2}$ **13** a 360 b 3600 c 36000 d 360000

28:4

1 a 900 b 90000 **2** Peter **3** 4 (pizzas)
4 a 200 mL b 1000 mL (or 1L)

Challenge

1/2				1/2			
1/4		1/4		1/4		1/4	
1/8	1/8	1/8	1/8	1/8	1/8	1/8	1/8

Equivalent fractions will be recorded below the table.

Activity

a 0·5 **b** 0·6 **c** 0·35 **d** 0·52 **e** 0·875 **f** 0·0625 **g** 0·625 **h** 0·1875 **i** 0·28 **j** 0·03125 **k** 0·015625 **l** 0·984375

29:1

1 15 **2** 56 **3** 3 **4** 8 **5** 63 **6** 22 **7** $23 **8** 34 **9** 48

10 $9.39 **11** 2068 **12** yes **13** hexagonal prism, cone

14 Answers may vary. **a** $\frac{4}{10}$ **b** $\frac{8}{10}$ **c** $\frac{2}{10}$ **15** 5 oranges **16** 2

17

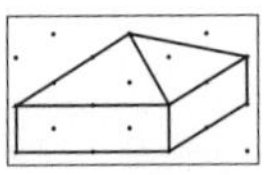

29:2

1 32 **2** 2400 **3** 2500 **4** −10 **5** 1500 **6** 8 **7** 42 **8** 71

9 21 **10** 140 r 3 or 140$\frac{3}{7}$ **11** triangular prism

12 **a** 6 (edges) **b** 4 (vertices) **13**

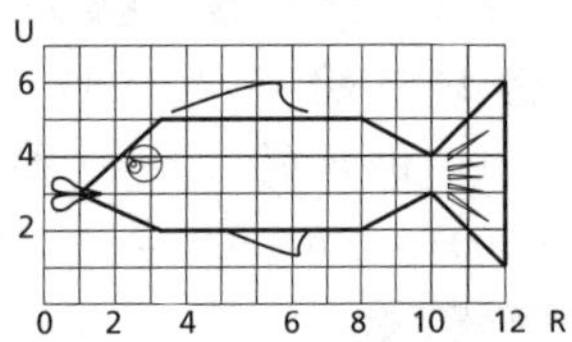

14 12, 30 **15** **a** 3500 **b** 350000 **c** 350000

Activity

1, 2, 3, 4, 5, 6, 7, 8, 9, 10

a $6 **b** 8 (weeks) **c** 5 (tables)

29:3

1 $2 160.84 **2** 31 **3** 1.7 **4** 16.215 **5** 24 000 **6** **a** < **b** >

7 119 m³ **8** $\frac{1}{12}$, $\frac{1}{6}$, $\frac{1}{4}$, $\frac{1}{3}$, $\frac{1}{2}$ **9** 900 (cm³) **10** g and kg will be underlined. **11** 32 **12** **a** 180 **b** 1800 **c** 18000 **d** 180000

29:4

1 **a** 2000 **b** 6000 **c** 10000 **2** 6 (zeros) **3** 50 (or L) **4** 10

5 Svetla **6** 1 500 mL or 1.5 L

Challenge

Equivalent fractions will be recorded below.

1/2				1/2			
1/3		1/3		1/3		1/3	
1/6	1/6	1/6	1/6	1/6	1/6	1/6	1/6

Activity

a 3 (vans) **b** 12 kangaroos, 19 cows

30:1

1 8 **2** 72 **3** 4 **4** 36 **5** $427 **6** 20 **7** 24 **8** 48 **9** 22

10 $6.33 **11** true **12** Answers may vary. Answers could include: **a** $\frac{4}{5}$ **b** $\frac{2}{5}$ **c** $\frac{3}{5}$ **13** 4 L **14** **a** 3 cm³ **b** 6 km **c** 5 kg **d** 9 m³

15 300503 **16** 8 **17** $\frac{3}{8}$ **18** 1600

30:2

1 54 **2** 7 **3** 6.8 **4** 9 **5** 30 r 4 or 30$\frac{4}{6}$ **6** 5600

7 48 000 **8** 8 **9** 55 **10** 771.5 (or 771 r 2 or 771 $\frac{1}{2}$)

11 **a** $\frac{2}{5}$ **b** $\frac{6}{18}$ **12** 204 (cm³) **13** **a** 2 400 **b** 27 000

14 **a** $\frac{3}{4}$ **b** $\frac{3}{4}$ **15** 65 **16** 6000 (cm³) **17** **a** > **b** <

18 (70 × 30) + (2 × 30) = 2 100 + 60 = 2 160 **19** true

Activity

8, 32, 48, 24, 40, 64, 16, 72, 56, 80
6, 24, 36, 18, 30, 48, 12, 54, 42, 60

30:3

1 640 + 192 = 832 **2** 24·1 **3** 11·84

4 **a** 1:50 **b** 1·5 m (or 150 cm) **c** almost 1 m (or 100 cm) **d** bed **e** desk **f** J1 or J2 **g** Answers may vary. One answer could be D2.

5 Answers may vary. Answers could include: **a** $\frac{2}{12}$ **b** $\frac{4}{16}$ (or $\frac{1}{4}$) **c** $\frac{8}{20}$ (or $\frac{2}{5}$) **d** $\frac{10}{10}$ (or $\frac{1}{1}$) **e** $\frac{2}{6}$ **f** $\frac{8}{10}$ **6** (40 × 52) + (3 × 52)

30:4

1 3500 **2** six hundred and thirty thousand **3** □ = 7, △ = 2

4 **a** 65·5 kg **b** 34·5 kg

5 **a** about 800000 km² **b** about 2500000 km²

Challenge

Answers will vary. When completing a chance experiment, we repeat the event often so that we can observe the overall likelihood of each outcome.

Activity

a true **b** true **c** true

31:1

1 1 **2** 75 **3** 0 **4** 720 **5** 45 **6** 48 **7** 80 **8** 23 **9** 125

10 1379 **11** 1400 **12** Answers may vary. Answers could include: **a** $\frac{4}{10}$ **b** $\frac{2}{4}$ **c** $\frac{6}{8}$ **13** C (6 kg) will be circled. **14** **a** 40000 **b** 300

15 **a** 48 m² **b** 28 m **16** $\frac{3}{10} + \frac{5}{10} = \frac{8}{10}$ **17** 1 kg 375 g **18** 1000 (cm³)

31:2

1 30 **2** $240 **3** 11·3 **4** 63 **5** 281 **6** 7 **7** 64 **8** 15000

9 40000 **10** 126 **11** (20 × 20) + (4 × 20) = 400 + 80 = 480

12 **a** (2, 2) **b** (−2, 1) **c** (−2, −2) **d** (0, −1) **e** (2, 0) **f** (0, 0)

13 **a** < **b** > **14** **a** 3201 **b** 3003

Activity

9, 17, 10, 14, 18, 12, 16, 11, 15, 13
odd + odd = *even*, even + odd = *odd*

31:3

1 **a** 1820 + 637 = 2457 **b** 510 + 153 = 663 **2** **a** $\frac{4}{5}$ **b** $\frac{3}{12}$

3 **a** 12 years **b** 5 years **c** 16 years **4** 2·97 **5** 492 (cm³)

6 $\frac{4}{6} - \frac{1}{6} = \frac{3}{6}$ (or $\frac{1}{2}$) **7** 4 (L) **8** **a** 350 **b** 35000 **c** 350000

31:4

❶ 48 (people) ❷ a about 18 cm^2 b about 260 m^2

❸ a 18 b 27 ❹ a 18·2 t b 91 t ❺ 37
(This is one more than the product of the other two numbers.)

Challenge

Answers will vary.

Activity

a 2000 **b** 6300 **c** 4800 **d** 16000 **e** 1600 **f** 32000
g 490000 **h** 630000

32:1

❶ 200 ❷ 35 ❸ 6 ❹ 10 ❺ 2·7 (or $2\frac{7}{10}$ or 2 r 7) ❻ $98

❼ 18000 ❽ 1200 ❾ 600 ❿ $10\frac{3}{4}$ (or 10 r 3 or 10·75)

⓫ Answers may vary. Answers could include: **a** $\frac{18}{20}$ **b** $\frac{2}{6}$ **c** $\frac{2}{2}$

⓬ 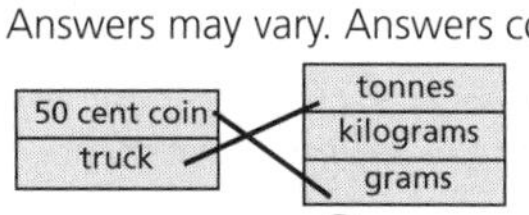

⓭ 81 ⓮ a 24 m^2 b 28 m

⓯ a 30 g b 23 m ⓰ 10 (birds) ⓱ 768 ⓲ 10 (cm^3)

32:2

❶ 75 ❷ 63000 ❸ 54 ❹ −7 ❺ $42.35 ❻ 6 ❼ 4

❽ 20000 ❾ 16 ❿ $34.05 ⓫ 9 ⓬ 65 ($cm^3$)

⓭ $\frac{3}{6} + \frac{2}{6} = \frac{5}{6}$ ⓮ a 2 (t) b 6500 (kg) ⓯ a $\frac{7}{8}$ b $\frac{1}{8}$

⓰ a 12 cm b 40 kg c 5 mL ⓱ 0·2 (or 2 tenths) ⓲ a $\frac{1}{5}$ b $\frac{9}{15}$

Activity

(19) Side view is *3*. (20) Front view is *1*. (21) Top view is *2*.
(22) *19:30* (or 1930) (23) *5:40* am (24) *protractor* (25) *compass*
(26) *coordinates* (27) *picture* graph (28) *tally*

32:3

❶ 253 ❷ 903 ❸ 2 795 ❹ 7 ❺ $\frac{8}{10} - \frac{2}{10} = \frac{6}{10}$

❻ 175 min (or 2h 55 min) ❼ 7 ❽ a $\frac{20}{28}$ b $\frac{8}{28}$ c $\frac{7}{28}$ d $\frac{21}{28}$

❾ 14 ❿ 3000 (kg) ⓫ 8 (L) ⓬ a < b >

32:4

❶ 1 and 14; 2 and 7 ❷ 8 (boats) ❸ a 2·4 t b 4 t ❹ 5

❺ 9 (horses) as Sue has at least one emu. ❻ 4

Challenge

a 9 **b** 85 **c** 49 **d** 63 **e** 13 **f** 8

Activity

Answers will vary.

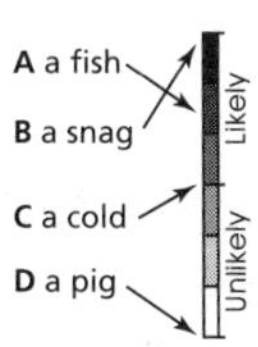

33:1

❶ 71 ❷ $9 ❸ 66 ❹ 7 ❺ 2 488 ❻ 8 ❼ 16 ❽ 17 ❾ 27

❿ 90 ⓫ 2 ⓬ 790 and 85 will be circled. ⓭ $\frac{4}{8}$, $\frac{5}{10}$ ⓮ 5 (pages)

⓯ 7730 ⓰ $\frac{30}{100}$ or $\frac{3}{10}$ ⓱ $1\frac{3}{8}$, $3\frac{1}{8}$, 4, $5\frac{1}{4}$ ⓲ factors

33:2

❶ 360 ❷ −1 ❸ 108 ❹ 4 ❺ 206 ❻ 9 ❼ 1 800 ❽ 37

❾ 9 ❿ 105 r 1 (or $105\frac{1}{5}$ or 105·5) ⓫ $\frac{6}{8} + \frac{1}{8} = \frac{7}{8}$

⓬ 9·803 (kg) ⓭ a 4 m b 3 m ⓮ 7 (apples)

⓯ a 5000 (kg) b 2000 (kg) c 20000 (kg) d 4025 (kg)

⓰ a $\frac{3}{5}$ b $\frac{3}{24}$ ⓱ 30 and 600 will be circled. ⓲ 4

Activity

a yes **b** yes **c** yes

33:3

❶ 462 ❷ 780 ❸ 732 ❹ a 16 b 18 ❺ 2002 (g) ❻ 945 km

❼ a 700 b 0·7 or $\frac{7}{10}$ ❽ 7·21, 54, 67·25, 72 ❾ 9

❿ 5·5 t ⓫ $\frac{7}{10} - \frac{2}{10} = \frac{5}{10}$ ⓬ $1\frac{1}{2}$ ⓭ a 37 b 60 c 124

33:4

❶ a 345 + 511 = 856 b 518 − 345 = 173 ❷ a 5 b 6

❸ a 10 min b 1 h 40 min ❹ a 1·2 t b 3 t

Challenge

Answers will vary. 45 284 309 has 8 digits. In words it is forty-five million two hundred and eighty-four thousand three hundred and nine. It is an odd number that is greater than 10 million. It rounds to 45 million when rounding to the nearest million.

Activity

1 4, 36, 16, 81, 49, 100

2 a 35, 21, 49, 14 **b** 35, 45, 100 **c** 4, 36, 16, 14, 100

34:1

❶ $240 ❷ 125 ❸ 207 ❹ 210 ❺ 83 ❻ 8 ❼ 186

❽ 1000 ❾ 115 ❿ $24 ⓫ 1, 18, 2, 9, 3, 6

⓬ 800 110 will be circled. ⓭ kg ⓮ 6 ⓯ 21·01 ⓰ 9 (t)

⓱ 6530 (grams) ⓲ a 10 (halves) b 20 (quarters)

34:2

❶ 8100 ❷ 71 ❸ 240 ❹ 74 ❺ 3500 ❻ 0 ❼ 98 ❽ 8

❾ 9 ❿ 8·01 ⓫ a $\frac{20}{100}$ (or $\frac{2}{10}$ or $\frac{1}{5}$) b $\frac{75}{100}$ (or $\frac{3}{4}$)

⓬ a 10·375 t b 3·845 t c 0·8 t d 7.07 t ⓭ 11 cm ⓮ 70 cm^2

⓯ a 9000 (mg) b 2 (g) ⓰ 4 ⓱ 230 and 352 will be circled.

Activity

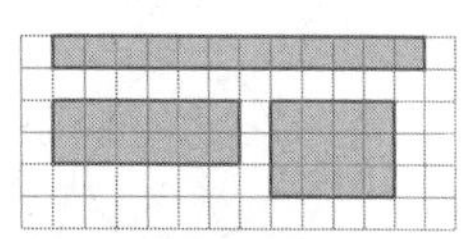

Factors of 12 are 1, 12, 2, 6, 3 and 4.

34:3

❶ 6300 ❷ 13075 ❸ 22464 ❹ 2 and 4 ❺ 250 (grams) ❻ 6

❼ a 100 m b 700 m ❽ 2·307 (kg) ❾ $20 ❿ a 3 × 7 = 21
b 9 × 7 = 63 c 27 − 13 = 14 ⓫ 1, 42, 2, 21, 3, 14, 6, 7

34:4

❶ a 3·2 t b 4 t ❷ a 12 b $\frac{1}{2}$ c $\frac{1}{12}$ ❸  ❹ $\frac{1}{5}$

Challenge

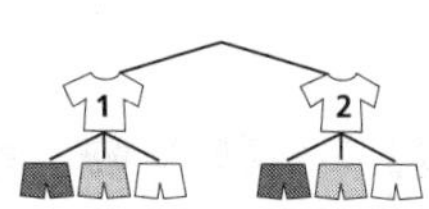

Activity

	a	b	c	d	e	f	g	h
10 kg	2	2	2	2	1	1	0	0
5 kg	1	1	0	0	3	3	4	4
2 kg	1	0	3	2	1	0	3	2
1 kg	0	2	1	3	0	2	1	3

35:1

1 0 **2** $58 **3** 28 **4** 1 **5** 86 **6** $24 **7** 37 **8** 180

9 39 **10** $0.39 **11** 127 **12** **a** 2 **b** 3 **c** 2 **d** 1 **13**

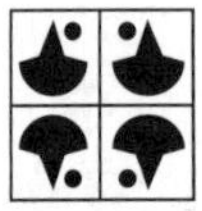

14 **a** yes **b** yes **c** $\frac{7}{10}$ **d** $\frac{7}{10}$

15 15 and 18 will be circled. **16** 6 (times) **17** 5 127 g

35:2

1 56 **2** 32 **3** 80 **4** 5 400 **5** 2·15 **6** 3 **7** 512 **8** 0

9 81 **10** 5·45 **11** $8.35 **12** 4·726 (kg) **13** 5 (groups)

14 84 **15** The words "an eyelash" will be circled. **16** 180 (km)

17 **a** 0·16 cm² **b** 0·25 cm² **18** **a** 202 **b** 706 **19** 33

Activity

[1] 2	3	[2] 5	6	[3] 2	■	[4] 5
4	■	1	■	[5] 5	4	6
[6] 4	[7] 5	9	3	■	■	9
■	[8] 1	3	■	[9] 8	6	5
■	8	■	■	0	■	4
■	[10] 4	5	5	6	2	5

35:3

1 176 **2** 1 700 **3** 63 **4** **a** 287 582 **b** 211 305 **5** 68·04

6 2 500 (grams) **7** **a** 5 000 (mg) **b** 9 (g) **8** 312

9 3 ÷ 3 + 3 (or 3 + 3 ÷ 3) **10** 9 932 (g)

11 **a** 30 ÷ 6 = 5 **b** 16 ÷ 8 = 2 **12** **a** 10 × 6 = 60
b 13 + 30 = 43 **c** 53 − 31 = 22 **d** 42 × 3 = 126

35:4

1 17 (trips) **2** 8 (times) **3** **a** 200 (squares) **b** 2 400 (squares)

4 $76

Challenge

Answers will vary.

Activity

a 10:00 **b** no **c** no **d** yes

36:1

1 67 **2** 140 **3** 70 **4** $360 **5** 31 **6** 16 **7** 6

8 60 **9** 106 **10** 34 **11** $\frac{70}{100}$ = 70% **12** 50 **13** **a** 3 **b** 1

14 **a** flip **b** turn **15** 4 (squared) **16** 15 (square tiles)

17 **a** 7.1 ha **b** 20 m² **18** 9000 (g)

36:2

1 5 **2** 82 **3** 48 **4** 210 **5** 60·3 **6** 8c **7** 3 **8** 9 **9** 41

10 10·05 **11** 10 **12** 2 370 (grams) **13** **a** 15 (outfits) **b** 84 (outfits)

14 6 (ways) **15** 38 **16** 90 000 m² **17** 5 (times)

18 **a** 0·04 cm² **b** 0·64 cm²

Activity

0, 3, 7, 8, 6, 4, 2, 5, 1, 9
7, 5, 9, 2, 8, 6, 4, 10, 3, 1

36:3

1 186 **2** 846 210 **3** 736 **4** 871 **5** 823 **6** more **7** C

8 9 (pairs) **9** 48 **10** 6 382 **11** 12 500 (g)

12 **a** 54 ÷ 6 = 9 **b** 36 ÷ 9 = 4

36:4

1 **a** 3 600 kg **b** 12 000 kg **2** 48 (small squares)

3 9 **4** 18 **5** **a** 5 **b** 10 **c** 10 **d** 20 **6** 8

Challenge

Answers will vary. Some answers are: In words it is five point two three one. There are 2 tenths, it rounds to 5 (to the nearest whole number) and it is more than 5·2.

Activity

a 20 m (per second) **b** 48 km (per hour)
c 245 km (per day) **d** 12 mm (per second)

37:1

1 350 **2** 5 **3** 50 **4** 32 **5** $630 **6** 30 **7** 320 **8** $111

9 130 **10** $99.47 **11** $99.45 **12** 700 (ha) **13** $5 **14** 104, 112, 120, 128 **15** five thirds **16** **a** 14:44 (or 1444) **b** 15:02 (or 1502)

17 **a** 7:32 am **b** 9:32 pm **c** 6:40 pm **d** 9:47 am

18 **a** 50 × 20 = 1 000 **b** 40 × 40 = 1 600 **c** 20 × 60 = 1 200

19 20 000 (m²)

37:2

1 720 **2** 0 **3** 3 **4** 104 **5** 95·45 **6** 80 **7** 9 **8** 6

9 49 **10** 32 800 **11** 6 (ha) **12** 8 (outfits) **13** 6 (square kilometres)

14 **a** $4\frac{1}{2}$ cm² **b** $4\frac{1}{2}$ cm² **15** 58 **16** $1.60

17 **a** 5 000 (m²) **b** 2 500 (m²) **18** 3 497 (grams)

Activity

(11) *circle* (16) *centre* (17) *radius* (18) *diameter* (19) *circumference* (20) *quadrant* (21) semi-*circle* (22) *sector* (23) *segment* (24) *diagonals*

37:3

1 4 397 926 **2** 6 591 092 **3** 1 318 500 **4** 9 341 880

5 **a** 2 ha **b** 4 ha **6** 2 (km²) **7** 65 will be circled. **8** 35

9 $2.35 **10** 700 (ha) **11** **a** 75 kg **b** 150 kg

37:4

1 **a** 2 000 m² **b** 924 m² **2** $801 **3** 16 (times) **4** 90

5 6 (different choices)

Challenge

Answers will vary. One answer could be 8 × 3 = 24.

Activity

Answers will vary.

17:3 — out of 9

1
$$\begin{array}{r} 83921 \\ 35032 \\ +\ \ 2115 \\ \hline \end{array}$$

2
$$\begin{array}{r} 730{\cdot}93 \\ 143{\cdot}71 \\ +\ \ 21{\cdot}30 \\ \hline \end{array}$$

3 The 24-hour time, one hour after:

a 12:30 am _______ **b** 12:30 pm _______

4 **a** What is the main ingredient used in making a quiche? _______

Quiche Recipe by Weight

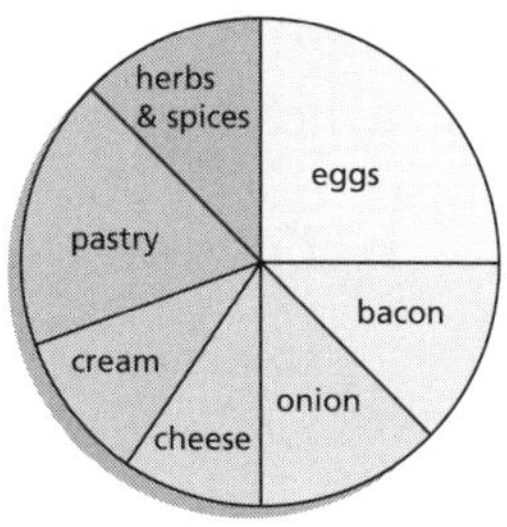

b What fraction of the final quiche is made from eggs? _______

c If the quiche weighs 400 g, how many 50 g eggs were used in the recipe? _______

Which would we use more of:

d bacon or cheese? _______

e pastry or onion? _______

5 Sides on a pentagon. _______

6 Write $3\frac{4}{5}$ as an improper fraction. _______

7 Opposite sides of a rectangle are e _______ and p _______.

8 How long will it take to travel 900 km at an average speed of 90 km/h? _______

9 **a** 15 − (9 − 6) _______

b 100 × 2 − 10 × 2 _______

17:4 — Extension — out of 3

1 Cara begins with $95.50. She buys:

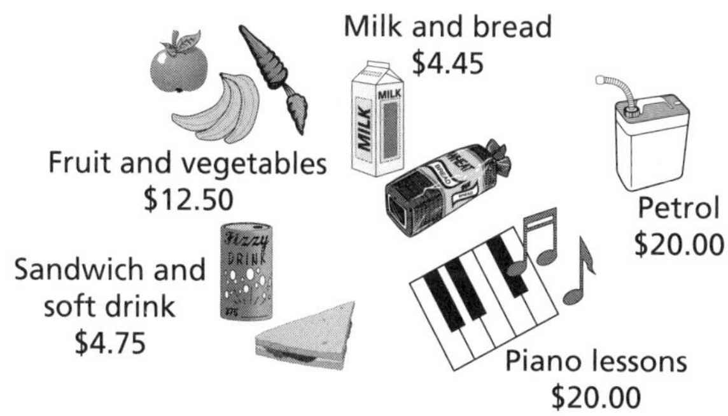

a What is Cara's total cost? _______

b How much money is left? _______

2 **How $50 was spent**

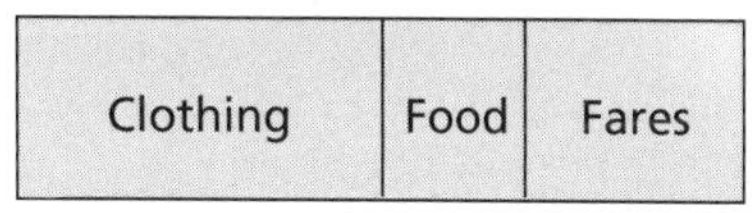

Divided bar graph

a What % was spent on fares? _______

b What % was spent on food? _______

3

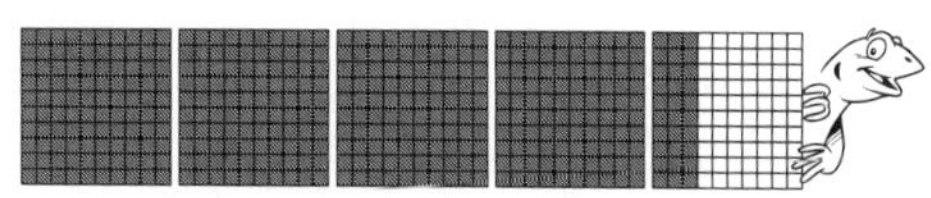

Write this number as a:

a mixed number _______

b decimal _______

Challenge

Write decimal addition sentences that are equal to 1, e.g. 0·75 + 0·25.

____

____

Turn to ID Card B on page 7.

Give the answers for these numbers.

(9) _______ lines (13) _______ of an angle

(20) _______ (21) _______

(22) _______ (23) _______

(24) _______ (26) _______ of symmetry

(28) _______ (29) 1: _______

18:1 ☐ out of 18

1. 6 × 5 ____
2. 9 + 7 ____
3. 11 − 5 ____
4. 12 ÷ 6 ____
5. $2\overline{)400}$
6. 5 squared. ____
7. 80 minus 9. ____
8. 8 more than 88. ____
9. Divide 60 by 6. ____
10. $3\overline{)60}$
11. Complete the pattern.
    0·36, 0·37, 0·38, ______, ______
12. Arrange in descending order
    75 124 911, 75 241 119, 75 921 977
    ____
13. If I had $35, how many of these books could I buy?
    ______

14. What is the value of the 7 in 3 411 723? ______
15. What is the difference between walking straight to school (9 072 paces) or going via the shops (10 180 paces)? ______
16. Is 2 132 a multiple of 3, 4 or 5? ______
17. **a** How many halves in $2\frac{1}{2}$? ______
    b How many quarters in 3? ______
18. What is the area of the shaded shape?
    ______ cm^2

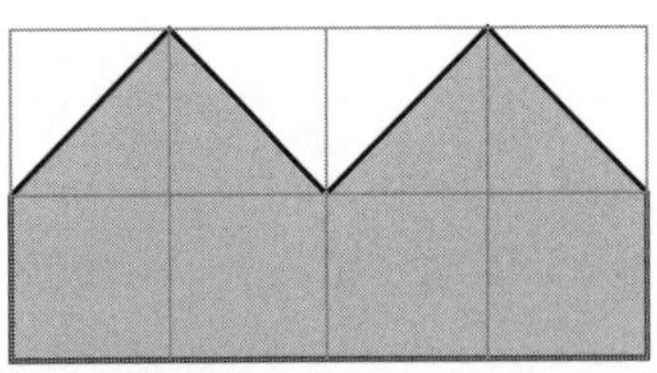

18:2 ☐ out of 13

1. 9 × 8 ____
2. 48 − 6 ____
3. 8 × 8 ____
4. 12 + 64 ____
5. $6\overline{)20}$ r
6. 36 ÷ 6 ____
7. 6 + 3 ÷ 3 ____
8. ☐ + 81 = 99, ☐ = ____
9. 180 − ☐ = 5, ☐ = ____
10. $3\overline{)17}$ r
11. From **A**, what is:
    a north-east? ______
    b south-west? ______

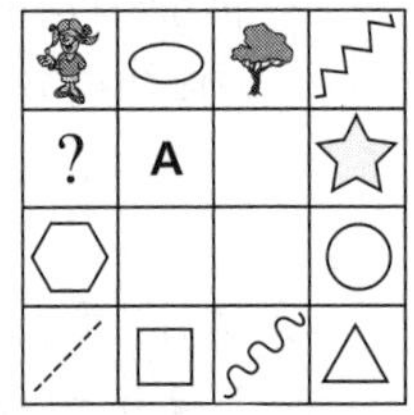

12. 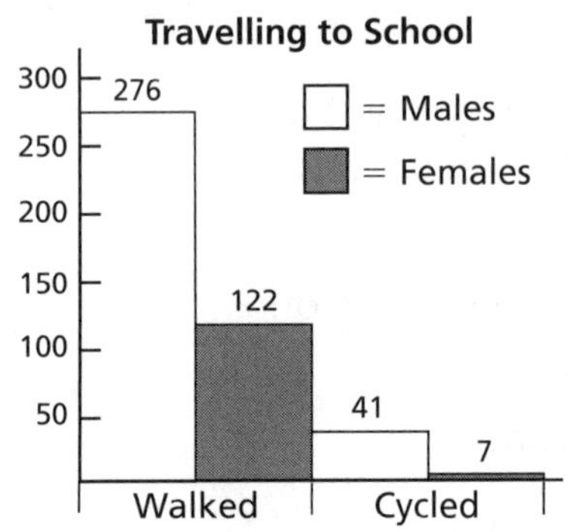

    a How many people who walked were females? ______
    b Is it more likely that the next person to arrive at school by walking will be male or female? ______
    c How many people walked altogether? ______
13. 0·6 + 0·4 ______

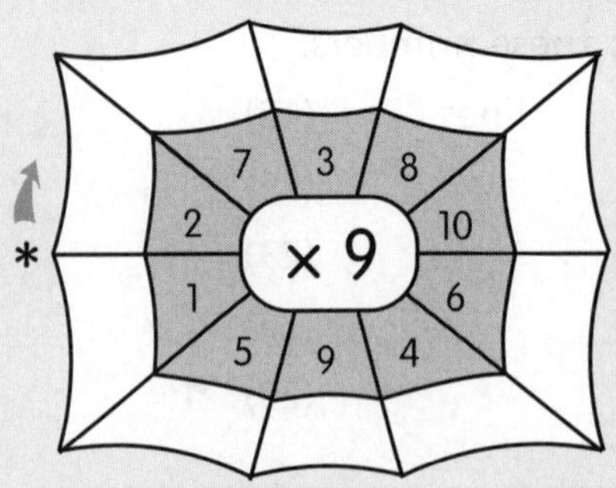

9	18	27	36	45
54	63	72	81	90

1 3·512 + 2·348

2 6·999 km + 3·214 km

3 Which island is at:

a D2? ______

b B4? ______

Which island is:

c north of the ship? ______

d south-east of the ship? ______

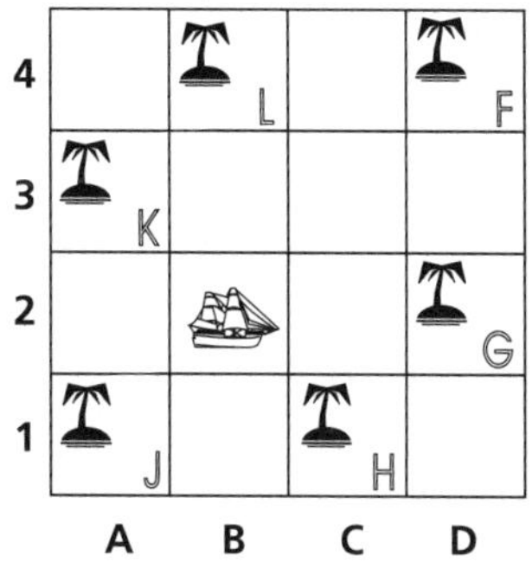

4 Complete each pattern.

a 0·2, 0·8, 1·4, ____, ____

b 0·3, 0·6, 0·9, ____, ____

5 A stone is kicked 5·8 m then 7·8 m and finally 12·1 m. How far has it been kicked altogether? ______

6 Write as an improper fraction:

a $2\frac{1}{4}$ ______ **b** $3\frac{3}{5}$ ______

7 For this shape find the:

a perimeter ______

b area ______

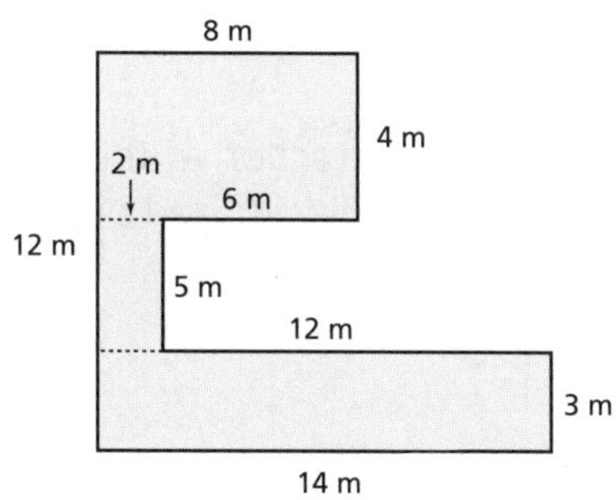

1 The Foster family used 5 tins of paint for walls upstairs, and 3 tins of paint in the study downstairs. 1 tin of paint covers 100 m^2. What area was covered? ______

2 One sixth of a whole is 3. Write the value of each shaded part.

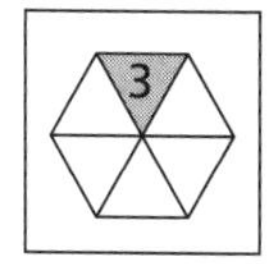

a 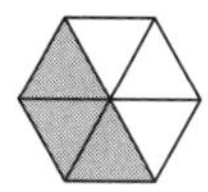 ______

b 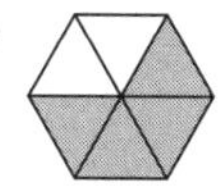 ______

3 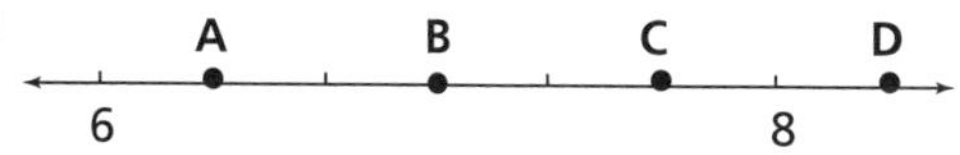

Give the value at the letter:

a A ______ **b** B ______

c C ______ **d** D ______

4 Which factors of 64 are also multiples of 8? ______

5 The numeral for:

a CCXCIX ______ **b** CLXXXIV ______

Challenge

Ask 5 people to tell you their favourite hobby. Record the results below. Do you think this is an accurate reflection of your whole suburb? Why or why not?

______

______

______

Conduct a survey to find out which sport is the most popular.

a How many people will you ask? ______

b Who will you ask? ______

______

c How will you collect the information? ______

______

______

19:1 ☐ out of 16

1. 7 + 8 ____
2. 13 − 7 ____
3. 9 × 10 ____
4. 12 ÷ 3 ____
5. $3\overline{)69}$
6. 6 less than 14. ____
7. 8 times 4. ____
8. Sum of 26 and 6. ____
9. 7 groups of 5. ____
10. $2\overline{)804}$
11. Circle the largest number.

    6 167 189   6 173 211   6 099 999

12. What is the opposite direction of south? ____
13. Is 35 763 842 closer to 35 million or 36 million? ____
14. Which is the smallest, 7·77, 7·17 or 7·7? ____
15.

h	i	j
k	l	m
n	o	p

a What letter is north of "o" and east of "h"? ____

b What letter is south of "h" and west of "p"? ____

16. What is:

a the area? ____

b the perimeter? ____

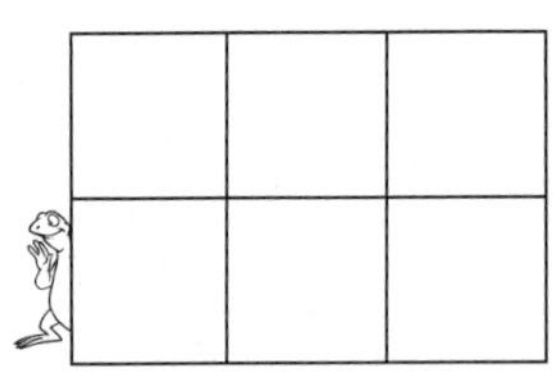

19:2 ☐ out of 16

1. 7 × 40 ____
2. 14 − 3 ____
3. 5 + 91 ____
4. 8 × 6 ____
5. $\begin{array}{r} 40 \\ \times\ 3 \\ \hline \end{array}$
6. 42 ÷ 6 ____
7. 8 × (6 − 6) ____
8. 90 − ☐ = 86, ☐ = ____
9. ☐ − 40 = 50, ☐ = ____
10. $\begin{array}{r} 50 \\ \times\ 6 \\ \hline \end{array}$

11. Round 744 680 to the nearest hundred thousand. ____
12. Write the improper fraction for:

    a $3\frac{4}{5}$ ____   b $2\frac{1}{8}$ ____

13. **Number of Siblings**

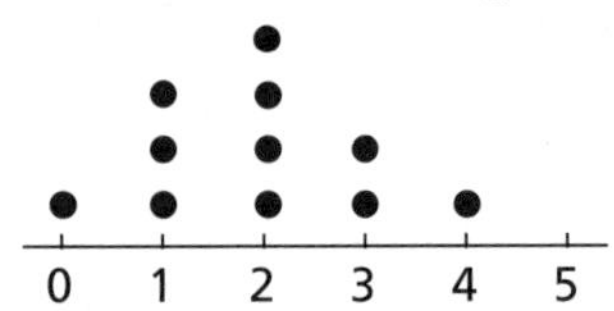

Key: ● = 10 people
(Data is rounded to the nearest 10.)

a How many people had 4 siblings? ____

b Which number of siblings was the most common? ____

14. Continue this pattern.
    7, 11, 15, ____, ____, ____
15.

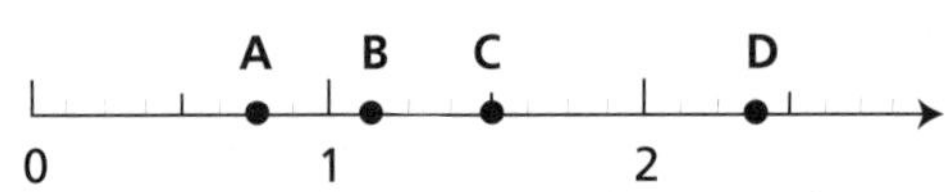

Give the fraction at the letter, as its simplest mixed numeral.

a A ____   b B ____

c C ____   d D ____

16. 3·08, 3·09, 3·1, ____, ____

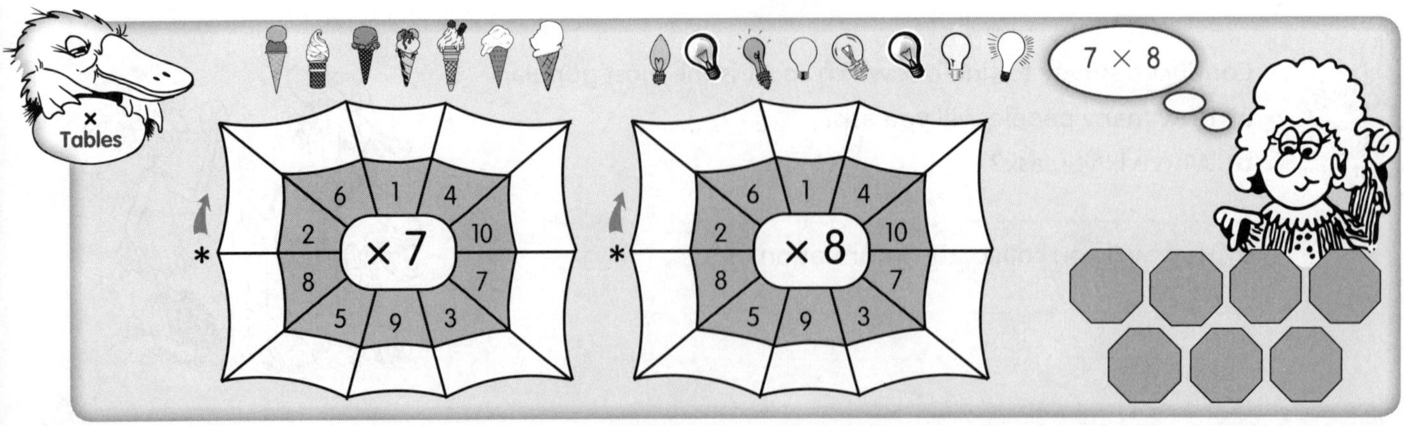

 ISBN 978 1 4886 2192 5

19:3 ☐ out of 4

1.
$$\begin{array}{r} 3{\cdot}472\,m \\ +\ 2{\cdot}119\,m \\ \hline \end{array}$$

2.
$$\begin{array}{r} 6{\cdot}458\,L \\ +\ 1{\cdot}34\ \ L \\ \hline \end{array}$$

3. Each grid square is 400 km by 400 km.

What country has coordinates of:

a **G4** ____________

b **D1** ____________

What coordinates would be used for:

c Dushanbe? ____________

d Ashkhabad? ____________

e What is the distance (to the nearest 100 km) between Kabul and Amritsar? ____________

What city is about:

f 800 km north-east of Dushanbe? ____________

g 200 km south-east of Lahore? ____________

4. If 1^2 means 1 squared (1×1), find:

$1^2 + 2^2 + 3^2 + 4^2 + 5^2$ ____________

19:4 Extension ☐ out of 4

1. The shaded part has a value of 12. What is the value of the whole? ____________

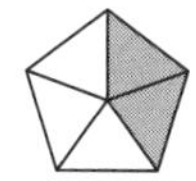

2. 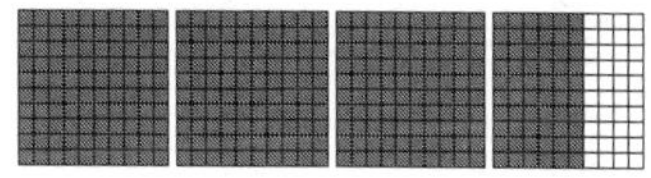

Show this number as a:

a decimal ____________

b mixed number ____________

3. 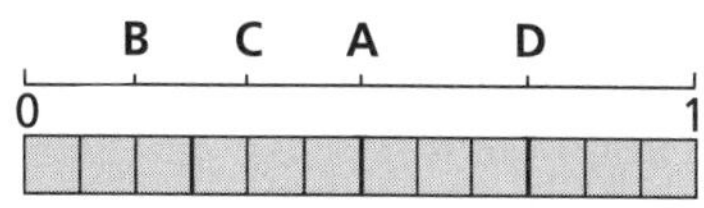

On this number line what fraction is at:

a **A**? ____ **b** **B**? ____

c **C**? ____ **d** **D**? ____

4. I painted 5·78 m of my fence on the first day, 2·67 m on the next and 3·55 m to finish. How long is my fence? ____________

Challenge

Write facts about the number 13·452.

____

____

____

____

Estimation

Choose a measurement from the table as an estimate for the length of a:

a bed ____________ **b** mouse ____________

c bus ____________ **d** paperclip ____________

e shoe ____________ **f** cricket bat ____________

g car ____________ **h** ant ____________

2 cm	10 m
0·5 cm	0·5 km
2 m	50 m
2 km	4 m
100 km	8 cm
20 cm	10 km
1 mm	75 cm

20:1  ☐ out of 18

1. 7×0 ______
2. $8 + 9$ ______
3. $16 - 8$ ______
4. $27 \div 3$ ______
5. $6\overline{)15}$ r ______
6. 80 times 6. ______
7. Increase 94 by 6. ______
8. 9 rows of 4. ______
9. Take 19 from 26. ______
10. $4\overline{)\$8.44}$ ______
11. Round off the answer to Question 10, correct to the nearest 5 cents. ______

12. $8 000 is shared by 7 women. How much does each get? (Round off correct to the nearest 5 cents.) ______
13. Write the numeral for twenty million five hundred and three. ______
14. In how many different ways can you make 30c using silver coins? ______
15. 9, 12, 15, ______, ______, ______
16. 4×20 ______
17. Write the number for:
    - **a** minus seven ______
    - **b** negative thirteen ______
18. Which object is:
    - **a** north of **A** and west of **B**? ______
    - **b** east of **D** and south of **C**? ______

20:2 ☐ out of 17

1. 8×9 ______
2. $19 - 8$ ______
3. 6×90 ______
4. $110 + 90$ ______
5. $137 + 8$ (written in columns) ______
6. $42 \div 6$ ______
7. $6 \times 9 - 9$ ______
8. $60 \div \square = 6$, $\square =$ ______
9. $\square \div 8 = 5$, $\square =$ ______
10. $600 - 74$ (written in columns) ______
11. Adua drives 1·25 km on concrete and 1·25 km on bitumen. How far has she driven altogether? ______

12. 7, ______, 19, 25, ______, 37
13. How many seeds are in a packet if half are used to plant 5 rows of 9 seeds? ______
14. A bus travels east for 4 blocks, north for 2 blocks, west for 2 blocks, then stops.

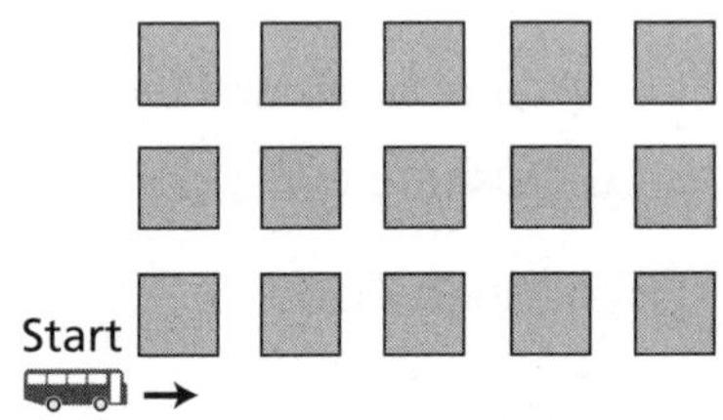

    - **a** What direction is it now facing? ______
    - **b** What direction is it now from the starting point? ______
15. $100 - 32{\cdot}8 - 0{\cdot}2$ ______
16. If you are facing north-west, what direction is to your:
    - **a** left? ______
    - **b** right? ______
17. 0·02, 0·2, 2, ______, ______

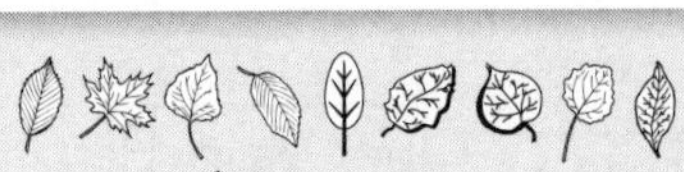

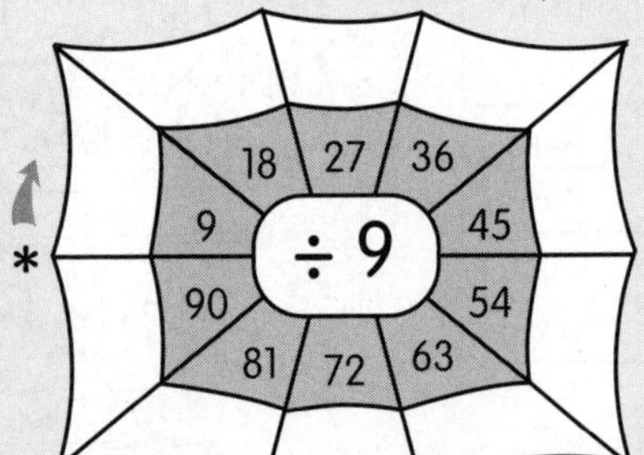

If 9 will divide the sum of the digits, it will divide the number itself.

$108 \div 9$

$1 + 0 + 8 = 9$

$108 \div 9 = 12$

out of 10

1. $\begin{array}{r} 3.7 \\ -\,2.43 \\ \hline \end{array}$

2. $\begin{array}{r} 2.4 \\ -\,1.61 \\ \hline \end{array}$

3. $\begin{array}{r} 73.9 \\ -\,12.41 \\ \hline \end{array}$

4. $\begin{array}{r} 51 \\ \times\;\;3 \\ \hline \end{array}$

5. $\begin{array}{r} 731 \\ \times\;\;6 \\ \hline \end{array}$

6. $\begin{array}{r} \$6.02 \\ \times\;\;5 \\ \hline \end{array}$

7. The difference between –6°C and 12°C. ______

8. Arrange in ascending order: 0·06, 0·63, 0·36 ______

9. 100 – 3·7 – 1·1 ______

10. On Makayla's first day at her new school, she studies the map at the front gate. Fill in the distance and directions using the scale.

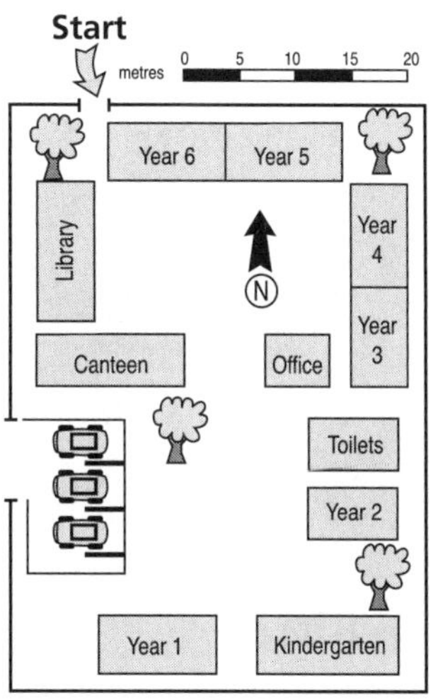

a She walks ______ m south to order her lunch.

b She then walks 15 m ______ to the office.

c She then walks 15 m in a ______ direction to rest under a shady tree.

d If she then walks south to her classroom, what year is she in? ______

out of 5

1. One seventh of the whole is 5. Write the value of the shaded part.

a 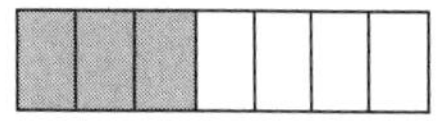 ______

b 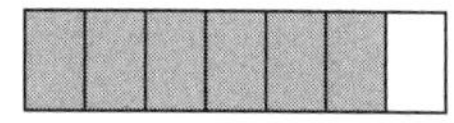 ______

2. 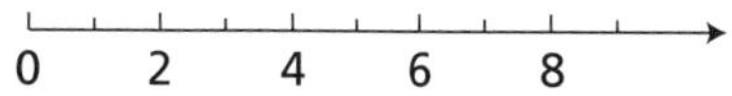

How many counting numbers are:

a 2 units away from 4? ______

b less than 3 units from 4? ______

3. A man born in 365 BCE died 40 years later. The year he died was: ______

4. How many packets can fit in the box? ______

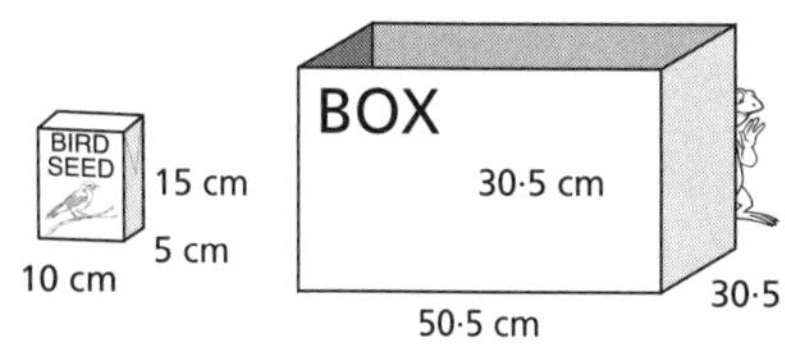

5. Which one-digit number when multiplied by 7·79 gives an answer closest to 40? ______

Challenge

Write number sentences that are equal to 100.

______

______

______

______

Profit and Loss

When we sell something for more than we paid for it, we make a **profit**.
When we sell something for less than we paid for it, we make a **loss**.

Give the profit or loss, if an item:

a bought for \$137.50 is then sold for \$150. Profit of ______

b bought for \$18 250 is then sold for \$10 850. ______ of ______

c bought for \$9 380 is then sold for \$16 250. ______ of ______

21:1 ☐ out of 18

1. 6×4 ____
2. $12 - 7$ ____
3. 9×7 ____
4. $45 \div 9$ ____
5. $\begin{array}{r} 70 \\ +\ \ 7 \\ \hline \end{array}$
6. Divide 18 by 9. ____
7. Seven eights. ____
8. 28 take away 5. ____
9. Total of 45 and 55. ____
10. $\begin{array}{r} 74\text{c} \\ +\ 39\text{c} \\ \hline \end{array}$

11. Round off the answer to Question 10, correct to the nearest 5 cents. ____
12. $0{\cdot}74 \times 100$ ____
13. Write the fraction that has numerator 5 and denominator 16. ____
14. What fraction is covered? ____

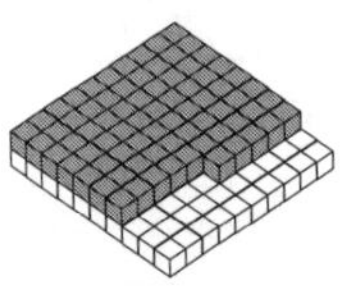

15. Is 7995 divisible by 5? ____
16. A bag of marbles was dropped and 70 marbles were lost. If 297 remained, how many marbles were in the bag before it was dropped? ____

17. Jose worked for 5 days each week for 17 weeks. For how many days did he work? ____

18. A temperature of 2°C dropped 10 degrees. What was it then? ____

21:2 ☐ out of 15

1. 6×8 ____
2. $17 - 5$ ____
3. $3 + 64$ ____
4. 9×70 ____
5. $7\overline{)1\,0\,6}$ r ____
6. $36 \div 9$ ____
7. $3 + 7 \times 2$ ____
8. $26 - 3 \times 8$ ____
9. $\square - 14 = 16$, $\square =$ ____
10. $9\overline{)1\,0\,5}$ r ____
11. $110 - 20 + 10 - 5$ ____
12. The first eleven multiples of 6. ____
13. 33, 44, 55, ____, ____, ____
14.

What is found at the coordinates:

a **F3**? ____

b **J4**? ____

c **A5**? ____

d **F5**? ____

e **C2**? ____

15. The temperature on Monday was 5° C. What is the temperature if it was 12 degrees colder the following week? ____

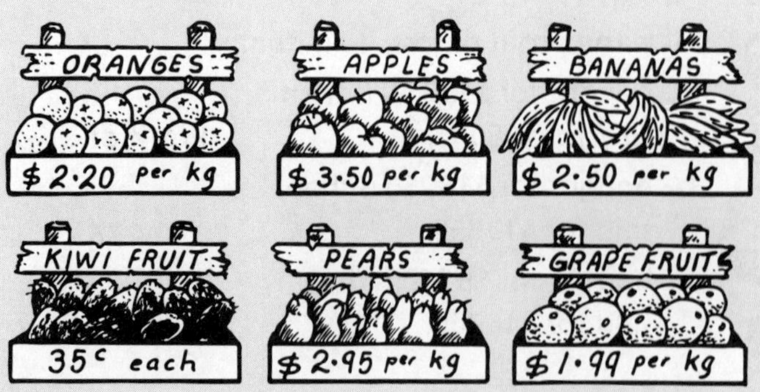

____
____
____
____
____

21:3 ☐ out of 12

1
$$\begin{array}{r} 74.931 \\ -21.7 \\ \hline \end{array}$$

2
$$\begin{array}{r} 24.715 \\ -13.596 \\ \hline \end{array}$$

3
$$\begin{array}{r} 3.971 \\ +14.8 \\ \hline \end{array}$$

4
$$\begin{array}{r} 43 \\ \times\ 3 \\ \hline \end{array}$$

5
$$\begin{array}{r} \$6.21 \\ \times\ \ \ 3 \\ \hline \end{array}$$

6
$$\begin{array}{r} 22.31 \\ \times\ \ \ 4 \\ \hline \end{array}$$

7 I jumped 95 cm, 98 cm, 1 m and 1 m 11 cm. What was the sum of the jumps? ________

8 The value of the 2 in:

a 6·32 ________ b 70·25 ________

9 Find the size of the reflex angle. ________

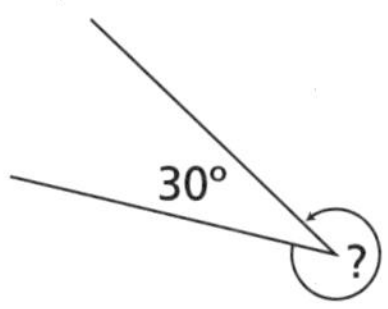

10 Use the scale to find the distance from Sydney to:

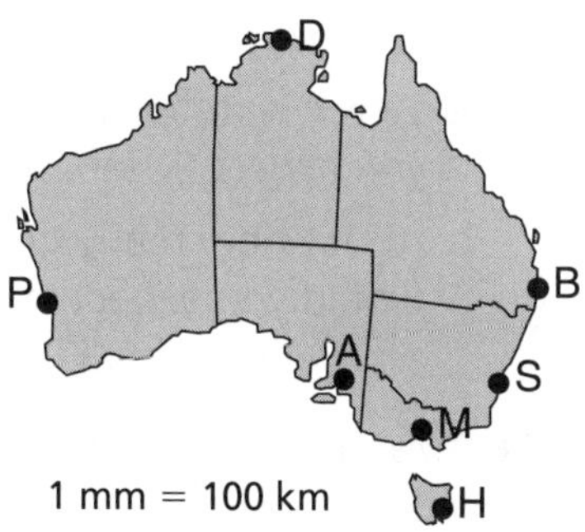

a Hobart ________

b Perth ________

c List the states and territories of Australia in order of area size.
ACT, Tas, ________

11 18 − 9 + 5 − 12·5 ________

12 Maximum temperature = 18°
Minimum temperature = −2°
The difference = ________

21:4 ☐ out of 6

Extension

1 A man, born in 210 BCE, died 35 years later. The year he died was: ________

2 The average of ten numbers is 5·3. What is their sum? ________

3 I keep rabbits and birds. There are 9 heads and 26 feet. How many birds do I have? ________

4 3 lunches cost $6.45. How much would:

a 12 lunches cost? ________

b 1 lunch cost? ________

5 The number of parallelograms of any size in this figure. ________

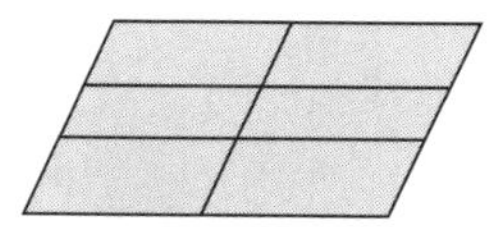

6 Circle the numbers that are divisible by both 4 and 5.

610 305 1444 1600 420

Challenge

I surveyed all the members of my family and created this sector graph. How is this information misleading?

____
____
____
____

Australians Who Have Visited Uluru

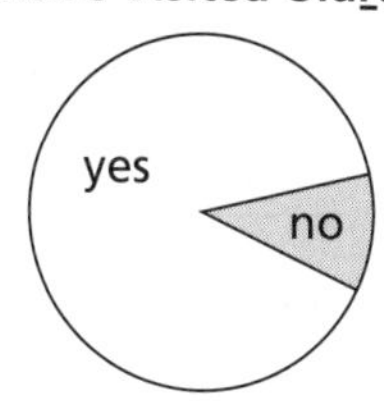

Concept

Heather is the youngest person in her family. This drawing has a scale of 1:50. Measure the heights in this picture using millimetres, and then find, correct to the nearest 5 cm, the real height of:

a Heather ________ b her mother ________

c her brother ________ d her father ________

e Heather's dog, Shasta ________

22:1 — out of 17

1. 13 − 9 ____
2. 4 + 9 ____
3. 77 ÷ 7 ____
4. 24 ÷ 6 ____
5. $\begin{array}{r} 13 \\ +\ 4 \\ \hline \end{array}$
6. Product of 9 and 5. ____
7. Increase 70 by 14. ____
8. 111 subtract 8. ____
9. 10 squared. ____
10. $\begin{array}{r} 60 \\ -\ 15 \\ \hline \end{array}$
11. 100 000 + 800 + 7 ____
12. 

   a How many cubes were used to build this model? ____
   b How many cubes cannot be seen in the picture above? ____
13. Write the numeral for thirty-eight thousand and ninety-five. ____
14. The value of 5 in:
   a 0·752 ____ b 6·5 ____
15. How many days in 2010? ____
16. Name this shape.

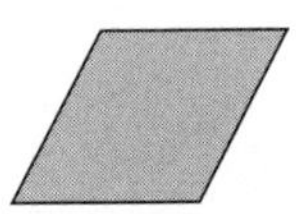

____
17. Arrange from the largest to smallest:
   7·93, 7·39, 9·37, 3·79

____

22:2 — out of 16

1. 8 × 7 ____
2. 24 − 4 ____
3. 8 × 30 ____
4. 20 + 80 ____
5. $4\overline{)8\,0\,1}$
6. 5 ÷ 2 ____
7. (10 − 3) × 6 ____
8. □ × 7 = 49, □ = ____
9. 6 ÷ □ = 1, □ = ____
10. $5\overline{)3\,4\,2}$

11. William had $5 in his bank account. What would his new balance be if he spent:
   a $7? ____ b $20? ____
12. Write the integer for a loss of 3. ____
13. Stickers were stuck on a dice so that the faces showed three 3s, two 5s and one 6. The dice was thrown 120 times.

   a Which number would you expect to see most often? ____
   b About how many times would you expect to see an even number? ____
14. Arrange from smallest to largest.
   0·39, 0·4, 0·13, 0·01

____
15. Write the short form of:
   a seven hundred grams ____
   b five cubic centimetres ____
16. −7 + 3 ____

Turn to ID Card C on page 8.
Give the answers for these numbers.

(4) ____ (5) ____
(6) ____ (7) ____
(8) ____ (10) ____
(12) ____ (13) ____ shapes
(14) ____ shapes (15) Shape ____ is rigid.

Make a study card: Put questions on one side and answers on the other.

1. $\begin{array}{r} 59 \\ \times \ 9 \\ \hline \end{array}$

2. $\begin{array}{r} 597 \\ \times \quad 2 \\ \hline \end{array}$

3. $\begin{array}{r} \$2.73 \\ \times \quad\ 8 \\ \hline \end{array}$

4. $2\overline{)25}$

5. $3\overline{)677}$

6. $6\overline{)5736}$

7. 100 − 35·3 − 24·7 ______

8. If 5 dice are rolled, what is the highest possible score? ______

9. a Name this shape. ______

   b Is this shape a quadrilateral? ______

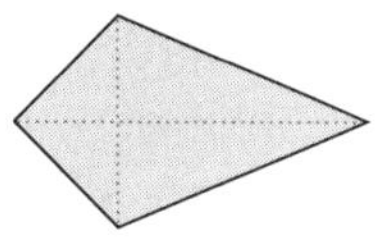

10. 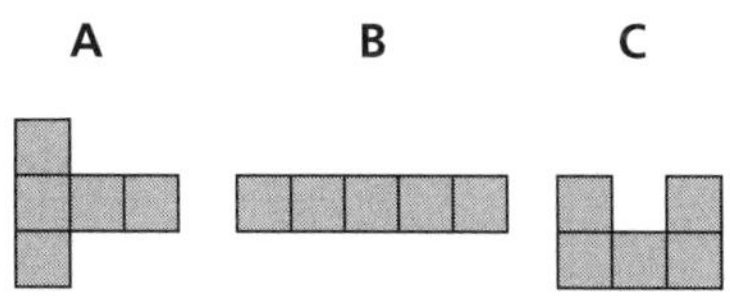

Which of these is the net of an open cube? ______

11. Calculate the volume of a rectangular prism 3 m long, 2 m wide and 6 m high. ______

12. What is the distance from Hobart to:

   a A? ______

   b B? ______

   c C? ______

   d D? ______

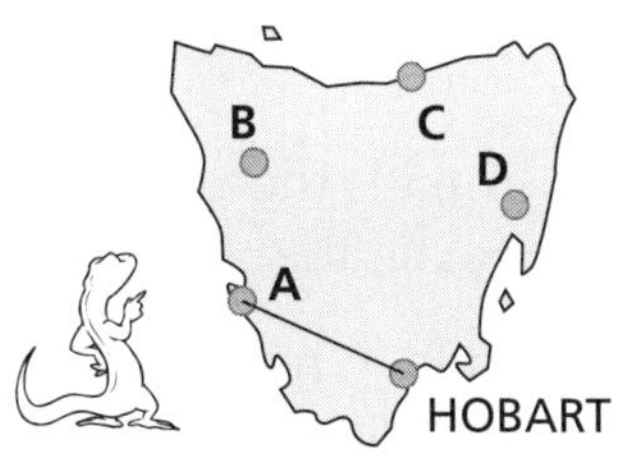

Scale: 1 mm = 18 km

13. 14 − 7 × 4 ÷ 2

______

1. A girl was born in 5 BCE and died 5 years later. In which year did she die? ______

2. 100 − 7 − 7 − 7 − 7 − 7 ______

3. Plot these points and join them in the order given.
   3A, 4D, 3E, 2D, 3A

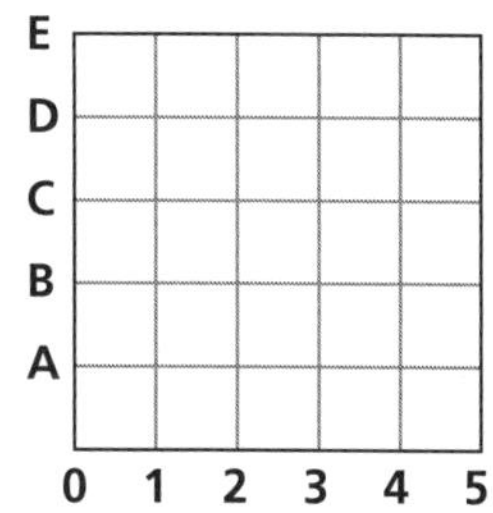

   a What shape have you drawn?

   ______

   b The diagonals intersect at:

   ______

4. The Roman numeral for:

   a 89 ______   b 324 ______

5. The whole outside of this model was painted. How many blocks have only:

   a 3 sides painted? ______

   b 2 sides painted? ______

Challenge

Complete this table.

Volume of a box = length × width × height

Length	Width	Height	Volume
5 cm	2 cm	7 cm	
8 cm	3 cm	2 cm	
9 cm	6 cm	3 cm	

______

______

______

______

______

 • *AUSTRALIAN SIGNPOST MATHS 6 MENTALS* • ISBN 978 1 4886 2192 5

23:1

out of 17

1. 6 × 7 ____
2. 29 + 9 ____
3. 14 − 8 ____
4. 40 ÷ 8 ____
5. $\begin{array}{r} 13 \\ \times \quad 6 \\ \hline \end{array}$
6. Double 18. ____
7. 13 minus 4. ____
8. 9 more than 55. ____
9. 4 times 90. ____
10. $\begin{array}{r} \$1.38 \\ + \ \$2.45 \\ \hline \end{array}$
11. Round off the answer to Question 10, correct to the nearest 5 cents. ____
12. Each cube represents one cubic centimetre. What is the volume of this shape. ____

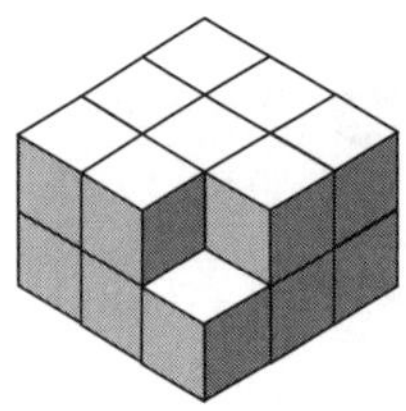

13. Complete this pattern:

Squares	1	2	3	4	5
Sides	4	8			

14. The sum of the consecutive numbers 14, 15 and 16. ____
15. The improper fraction modelled here. ____

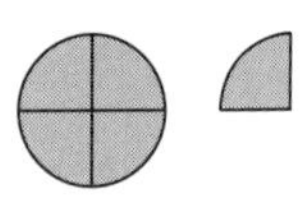

16. 1, 3, 9, ____, ____, ____
17. A dice was made from this net. Underline the word below that describes the chance of throwing an even number.

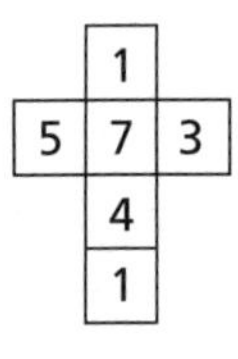

certain   impossible   unlikely   likely

23:2

out of 15

1. 6 × 50 ____
2. 28 − 7 ____
3. 7 + 83 ____
4. 600 ÷ 10 ____
5. $6\overline{)135}$
6. 48 ÷ 8 ____
7. 4 × 32 ÷ 32 ____
8. □ + 41 = 50, □ = ____
9. □ − 41 = 9, □ = ____
10. $4\overline{)937}$

11. Grams in 0·821 kg. ____
12. This shape has already been folded along either a vertical or horizontal axis of symmetry. Draw all four possible original shapes.

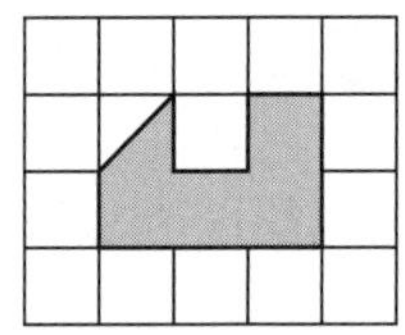

a

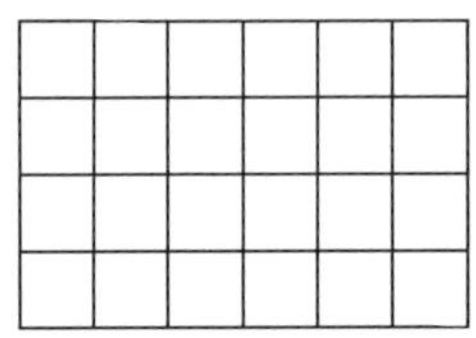

b

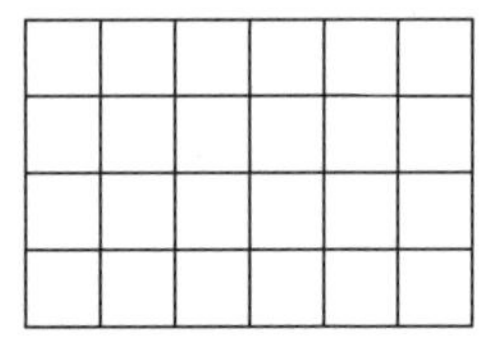

c

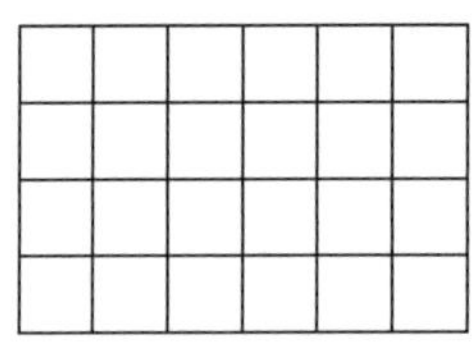

d

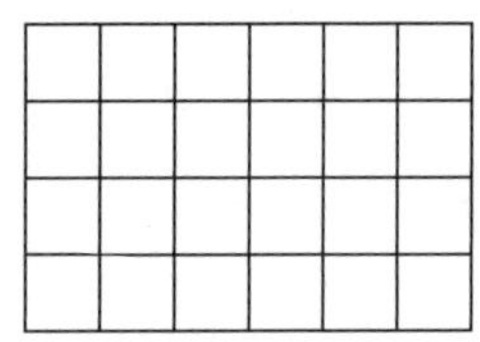

13. How many dots would be in the 6th row? ____

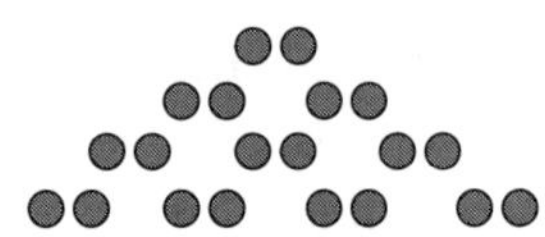

14. What is the volume of a cube that has sides 3 m long? ____
15. Hannah has $11 in her bank account. What would her new balance be if she spent:
a $14? ____   **b** $27? ____

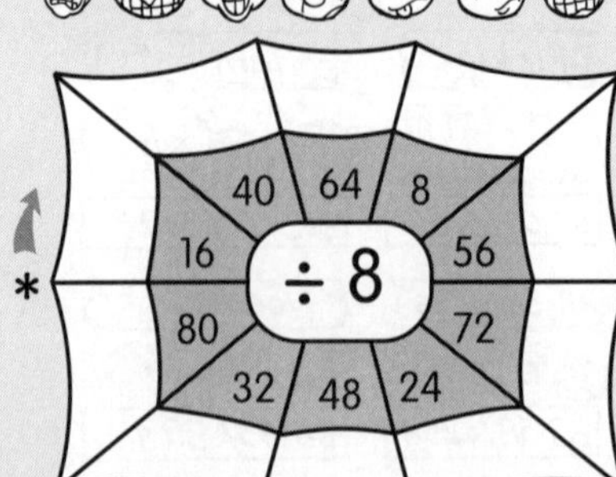

February

1	2	3	4	5	6	7
8	9	10	11	12	13	14
15	16	17	18	19	20	21
22	23	24	25	26	27	28

23:3 ☐ out of 14

1 $\begin{array}{r} 2 \cdot 1 \\ \times \quad 6 \\ \hline \end{array}$

2 $\begin{array}{r} 3 \cdot 3 \\ \times \quad 5 \\ \hline \end{array}$

3 $\begin{array}{r} \$7.21 \\ \times \quad 6 \\ \hline \end{array}$

4 $5\overline{)82}$

5 $3\overline{)614}$

6 $4\overline{)5731}$

7 What is the volume of a container 4 m long, 3 m wide, and 6 m high? ______

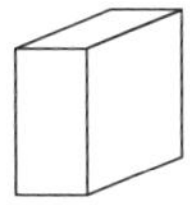

8 What is the chance as a percentage of throwing an even number using a dice made from this net? ______

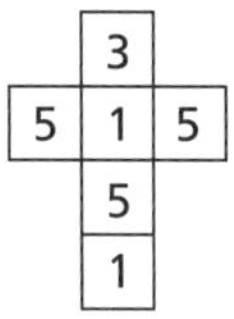

9 (2 × 100) − (3 × 11) ______

10 How many seconds in 3 hours? ______

11 How many 5 cent coins make $3? ______

12 Use am or pm to write:

a 09:57 ______ **b** 19:57 ______

13 Our school has 10 soccer balls. 6 of them were used today. What percentage were not used? ______

14 Complete:

Number of years	1	2	3	4	5
Number of months	12				

a Write a rule to describe the pattern.

______

b How many months in 30 years? ______

23:4 Extension ☐ out of 7

1 A 35-year-old Greek woman died in 180 BCE. When was she born? ______

2 80 − (6·3 × 2) ______

3 Is the volume of a hen's egg closest to 5 cm³, 50 cm³, 500 cm³ or 0·5 cm³? ______

4 Complete this table if △ = □ + 39.

□	15	25	35	44	54
△					

5 Write the numeral for:

a CX ______

b LIV ______

6 To the total of 14, 18 and 37, add the product of 6 and 7. ______

7 111 222, 108 715, 847 612, 81 410
Which number above is divisible by:

a 3? ______ **b** 4? ______

Challenge

List volumes you would measure in:

cm^3	m^3

Calculator Crossnumber Puzzle

Across

1 81 × 305
5 9743 − 9203
6 6^2 + 4332
8 475 ÷ 25
9 223 × 3
10 821^2

Down

1 4446 ÷ 19
2 9000 − 1631
3 275 ÷ 5
4 701 391 + 103 510
7 56^2
9 25 × 24

24:1 — out of 16

1. 18 + 20 ____
2. 21 − 5 ____
3. 9 × 7 ____
4. 27 ÷ 9 ____
5. $2\overline{)9}$ r ____
6. Divide 21 by 7. ____
7. 6 squared. ____
8. 5 less than 14. ____
9. Add 7 to 19. ____
10. $9\overline{)28}$ r ____

11. What is the value of the 6 in 69 121 744? ____
12. Into a cubic metre, would you be most likely to fit 2, 5 or 25 Year 6 students? ____
13. Complete this pattern:

Hexagons	1	2	3	4	5
Sides	6	12			

14. Halves in $6\frac{1}{2}$? ____
15. A B C

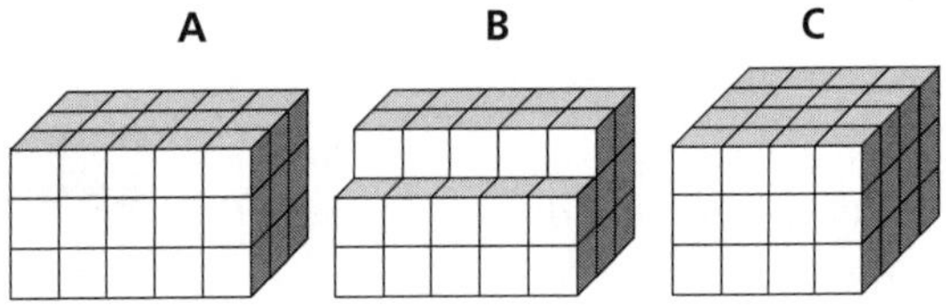

Which uses the most cubes? ____

16. a $\frac{1}{5}$ of 15 ____
    b $\frac{1}{3}$ of 15 ____

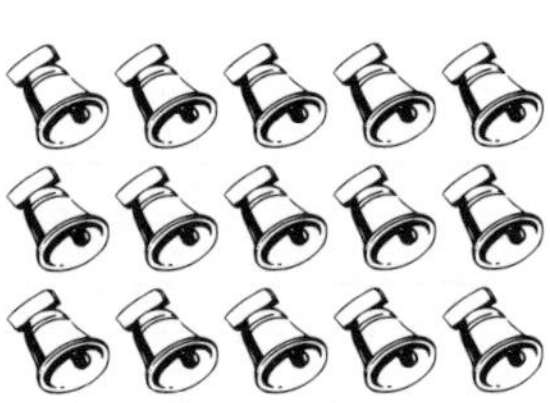

24:2 — out of 16

1. 4 × 8 ____
2. 14 + 11 ____
3. 26 − 12 ____
4. 7 × 9 ____
5. $\begin{array}{r} 40 \\ \times\ 3 \\ \hline \end{array}$
6. 54 ÷ 6 ____
7. 6 × 3 + 4 × 3 ____
8. □ − 23 = 8, □ = ____
9. □ + 14 = 44, □ = ____
10. $\begin{array}{r} 43 \\ \times\ 3 \\ \hline \end{array}$

11. a $\frac{1}{4}$ of 12 ____
    b $\frac{1}{3}$ of 12 ____

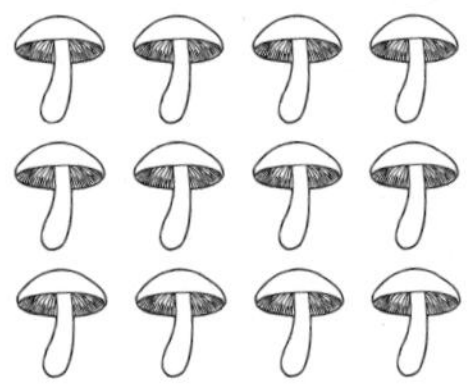

12. Write the short form of 60 cubic metres. ____
13. Use the short form to write 450 millilitres. ____
14. Which measure (L or mL) has been left off each label?

a b c

____ ____ ____

15. Find the volume in cm^3 of a block 2 cm high, 8 cm wide and 10 cm long. ____

16. a 6297·3 × 10 ____
    b 834·97 × 100 ____
    c 1082·3 × 1000 ____

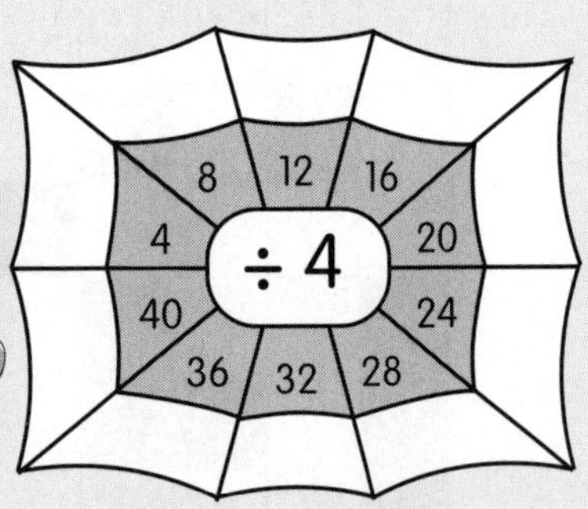

a Naomi, Alana, Luke and Greg shared 28 grapes. How many did each receive? ____

b 36 Year 5 girls were put into 4 equal teams. How many were put in each team? ____

c How many rows of 4 can be made with 20 mugs? ____

24:3 [ ] out of 9

1. $10\overline{)32170}$

2. $10\overline{)93455}$

3. $3\overline{)6240}$

4. $6\overline{)3654}$

5. a $\frac{1}{2}$ of 24 ____

   b $\frac{1}{6}$ of 24 ____

   c $\frac{1}{4}$ of 24 ____

   d $\frac{3}{4}$ of 24 ____

6. How many millilitres in a litre? ____

7. True or false?

   a A glass holds about 250 mL of water. ____

   b Three glasses could be filled using 550 mL of water. ____

8. Complete:

Number of horses	1	2	3	4	5
Number of legs	4				

   a Write a rule to describe the pattern.

   ____

   b How many legs on 592 horses? ____

9. a 35·27 ÷ 10 ____

   b 872·162 ÷ 100 ____

   c 9138·24 ÷ 1000 ____

24:4 Extension [ ] out of 6

1. A man, born in 80 BCE, died 75 years later. The year he died was: ____

2. Find the volume of a rectangular prism of length 19·5 cm, breadth 10 cm and height 3 cm. ____

3. Complete the table if △ = 100 − □.

□	20	17	32	47	83
△					

4. There are 24 pupils in 4F. $\frac{1}{3}$ are girls. How many are boys? ____

5. Draw the missing part of this pattern.

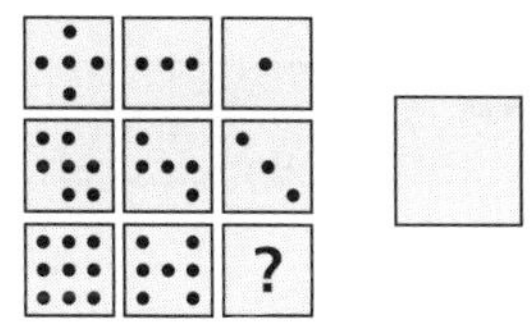

6. Colour the models that represent one cubic metre.

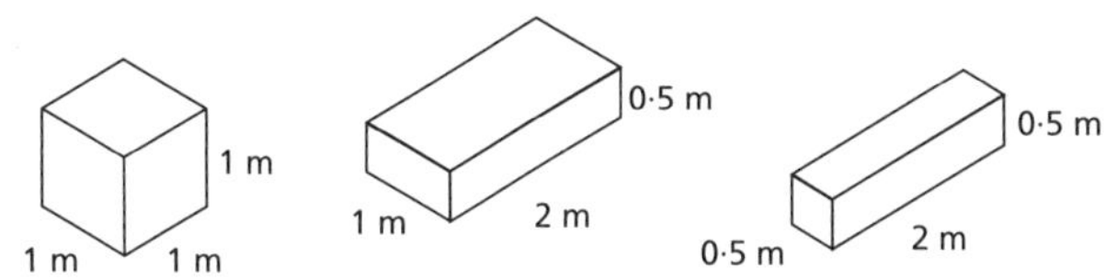

Challenge

Complete:

63·789 × 100	____	102·3 ÷ 10	____
49·028 ÷ 10	____	32·41 × 10	____
8·7034 × 1000	____	3409·8 ÷ 1000	____
9·416 × 100	____	429·37 ÷ 100	____
31·08 × 10	____	30·002 × 100	____
9002·3 ÷ 1000	____	5·1123 × 1000	____
8·325 × 100	____	9007·6 ÷ 1000	____
793·2 ÷ 10	____	2·31 × 10	____

Use the clues to fill in the tables.

Put a tick for YES ☑
Put a cross for NO ☒

	Drama	Gym	Tennis	Monday	Tuesday	Friday
Heather						
Naomi						
Luke						

Heather, Naomi and Luke are in different clubs. One of the girls goes to gym on Monday. Naomi goes to her club on Tuesday. Luke does not do drama. His club meets on Friday.

ANSWERS	Club	Day
Heather		
Naomi		
Luke		

25:1 out of 17

1. 5×8 ____
2. 9×7 ____
3. $24 \div 8$ ____
4. $28 \div 7$ ____
5. $\begin{array}{r} 140 \\ +\ \ 9 \\ \hline \end{array}$
6. Triple 7. ____
7. Take 13 from 50. ____
8. \$12 plus \$9. ____
9. 6 rows of 9. ____
10. $\begin{array}{r} 36 \\ -\ 12 \\ \hline \end{array}$
11. Round 100 minutes to the nearest number of hours. ____
12. 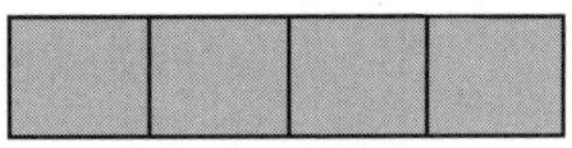

    a $\frac{1}{4} + \frac{2}{4} = \frac{\square}{\square}$ b $\frac{2}{4} + \frac{2}{4} = \frac{\square}{\square}$
13. Write the abbreviation for:
    a megalitres ____ b kilolitres ____
14. Write one and forty-nine hundredths as a decimal. ____
15. $\frac{3}{8} + \frac{1}{8} + \frac{2}{8}$ ____
16. Would you use litres (L) or millilitres (mL) to measure water in a bath? ____

17. a $\frac{1}{3}$ of 18 ____
    b $\frac{2}{3}$ of 18 ____
    c $\frac{1}{6}$ of 18 ____
    d $\frac{5}{6}$ of 18 ____

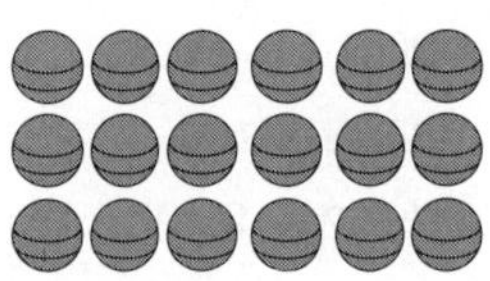

25:2 out of 19

1. 4×7 ____
2. $37 - 3$ ____
3. $64 \div 8$ ____
4. $23 + 43$ ____
5. $4\overline{)412}$
6. $317{\cdot}24 \div 10$ ____
7. $10 \times 31{\cdot}42$ ____
8. $36 - \square = 28$, $\square =$ ____
9. $\square - 9 = 37$, $\square =$ ____
10. $5\overline{)545}$
11. Complete this pattern:

Decagons	1	2	3	4	5
Sides	10	20			

12. How many sixths in a whole? ____
13. a Write 7·5 L as litres and millilitres.
    ____
    Write as millilitres:
    b 0·385 L ____ c 0·008 L ____
    Write as litres using decimals:
    d 4 320 mL ____ e 900 mL ____
14. a $4 - \frac{1}{2}$ ____ b $8 - 1\frac{1}{2}$ ____
15. The value of 4 in:
    a 8·45 ____ b 427·09 ____
16. $(6 - 3 \times 2) + 4$ ____
17. Write 3 000 kL as megalitres. ____
18. Melanie has 15 peaches, but $\frac{1}{5}$ of them were bad. How many were good? ____
19. $4{\cdot}103 \times 100$ ____

a Jim buys 36 papers in 6 weeks. How many does he buy each week? ____

b How many teams of 6 can be formed with 48 players? ____

c For each cup of tea, I use 6 g of sugar. How many cups of tea would use up to 24 g of sugar? ____

25:3 ☐ out of 8

1. $40\overline{)65320}$

2. $60\overline{)63180}$

3. a $\frac{1}{3}$ of 18 ______

b $\frac{1}{6}$ of 18 ______

c $\frac{5}{6}$ of 18 ______

d Is $\frac{1}{6}$ less than $\frac{1}{3}$? ______

4. Would you use litres (L) or millilitres (mL) to measure water in a cup? ______

5. a $\frac{4}{6} + \frac{1}{6}$ ______ b $\frac{10}{12} - \frac{5}{12}$ ______

6. a Write 12 000 kL as megalitres. ______

b 3 ML = ______ kL

c Write 1 860 mL as litres. ______

7. Complete this pattern:

Number of cubes	1	2	3	4	5
Number of faces	6	12			

a Write a rule to describe the pattern.

______

b How many faces on 236 cubes? ______

8. a $15{\cdot}3 \div 10$ ______

b $174{\cdot}762 \times 100$ ______

c $8134{\cdot}6 \div 1\,000$ ______

25:4 ☐ out of 7

Extension

1. If you double the length, breadth and height of this shape, how many times as big will its volume be?

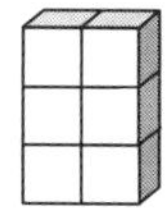

______

2. $\frac{1}{5}$ of 20 kangaroos are male. How many are female? ______

3. $\frac{3}{4}$ of 1 litre. ______

4. a $\frac{13}{100} + \frac{4}{100}$ ______ b $\frac{18}{100} - \frac{9}{100}$ ______

c $\frac{6}{100} + \frac{5}{100}$ ______ d $\frac{99}{100} - \frac{10}{100}$ ______

5. A bird's head is $\frac{1}{3}$ as long as its body and $\frac{1}{4}$ as long as its tail. The bird is 48 cm long. How long is its head? ______

6. How many triangles can be found on this figure? ______

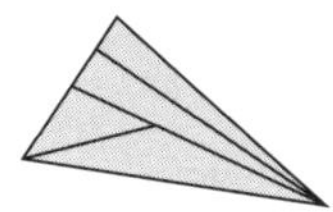

7. 20 − 30 ______

Challenge

Survey 20 people. Ask them how many siblings (brothers and sisters) they have. Tally the results in the table.

Siblings		Total
0		
1		
2		
3		
4		
other		

Use the diagram to answer these questions.

a How many eights in one half? ______

b $1 - \frac{1}{4}$ ______ c $\frac{1}{2} + \frac{1}{8}$ ______ d $\frac{5}{8} - \frac{1}{8}$ ______

e $\frac{3}{4} - \frac{3}{8}$ ______ f $\frac{1}{2} + \frac{5}{8}$ ______ g $\frac{7}{8} - \frac{3}{4}$ ______

h $1\frac{7}{8} - \frac{1}{4}$ ______ i $2 - \frac{1}{8}$ ______ j $1\frac{1}{2} - \frac{5}{8}$ ______

26:1  out of 20

1. $14 - 10$ ____
2. \$18 + \$3 ____
3. $70 \div 7$ ____
4. 9×4 ____
5. $3\overline{)123}$
6. Sum of 19 and 3. ____
7. Take 9 from 15. ____
8. Half of 160. ____
9. 7 squared. ____
10. $4\overline{)84}$
11. **a** $\frac{1}{2}$ of 6 ____ **b** $\frac{1}{3}$ of 6 ____
12. The abbreviation for "litre". ____
13. How many halves in 3 apples? ____

14. For a sphere, how many:
    a surfaces? ____
    b edges? ____
15. True or false? 1 cm^3 has the same volume as 1 mL of water. ____
16. **a** ML stands for ____.
    b kL stands for ____.
17. **a** $\frac{1}{5} + \frac{3}{5} =$ ____ **b** $\frac{5}{8} - \frac{1}{8} =$ ____
18. 4 take away $1\frac{1}{4}$. ____
19. Does a can of soft drink hold more than one litre? ____
20. Write a number sentence for "5 more than 9 is 14" ____

26:2 out of 19

1. 8×6 ____
2. $39 - 3$ ____
3. $71 + 11$ ____
4. 9×9 ____
5. $30\overline{)900}$
6. $49 \div 7$ ____
7. 20×16 ____
8. $\square \times 8 = 64$, $\square =$ ____
9. $\square + 72 = 90$, $\square =$ ____
10. $40\overline{)1600}$
11. Write 5000 mL in litres. ____
12. **a** $\frac{7}{8} - \frac{2}{8}$ ____ **b** $\frac{3}{6} + \frac{2}{6}$ ____
    c $\frac{3}{10} + \frac{4}{10}$ ____ **d** $\frac{7}{12} - \frac{2}{12}$ ____
13. 9 ML = ____ kL
14. How many cm^3 in 20 mL? ____
15. Write 3 L 47 mL in decimal form. ____
16. 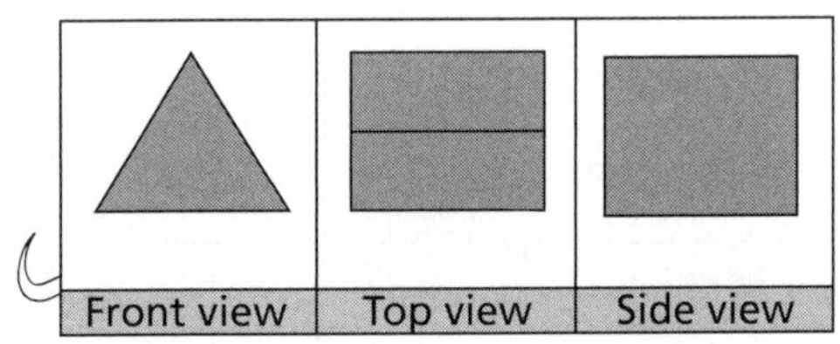

    This object is a ____
17. Litres in 18000 cm^3. ____
18. Would a jug of water hold: 2 L, 2 mL or 2 kL? ____
19. **a** $\frac{1}{4}$ of 16 ____ **b** $\frac{3}{4}$ of 16 ____
    c $\frac{1}{8}$ of 16 ____ **d** $\frac{7}{8}$ of 16 ____

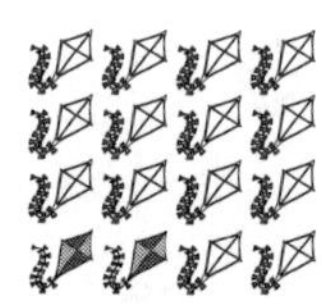

One litre of water exactly balances one kilogram.

1. If one litre of water has a mass of one kilogram what is the mass of one millilitre of water? ____
2. What is the mass of:
   a 3 L of water ____ **b** 270 mL of water? ____
3. A one-litre bottle has a mass of 300 g when empty. What is its mass when it is full of water? (The bottle has a capacity of 1 L.) ____

 ISBN 978 1 4886 2192 5

26:3 ☐ out of 10

1. $20\overline{)8438}$

2. $50\overline{)89035}$

3. Write 16 mL as litres. ______

4. Use the decimal form to write these measurements as megalitres.
   a 6700 kL = ________ ML
   b 9370 kL = ________ ML

5. Colour $\frac{1}{3}$ of this shape red and $\frac{1}{4}$ blue.
   How much is shaded altogether? ________

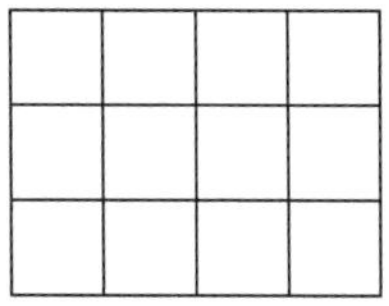

6. What is the volume of 15 mL of water? ______

7. $\frac{3}{4}$ plus $\frac{3}{4}$. ______

8. If you filled your cupped hands with water, would they hold about 12 mL, 2 L, 70 mL or 700 mL? ______

9. **a** $\frac{1}{3}$ of 15 ______
   b $\frac{2}{3}$ of 15 ______
   c $\frac{1}{5}$ of 15 ______
   d $\frac{4}{5}$ of 15 ______

10. Write a number sentence for 114 more than a certain number gives 539.

____

26:4 Extension ☐ out of 6

1. **a** Four lots of $1\frac{1}{2}$ ______ **b** Seven lots of $\frac{1}{2}$ ______

2. $\frac{1}{4}$ of two litres. ______

3. What fraction of $1 is:
   a 5c? ______ **b** 2c? ______

4. **a** $\frac{41}{100} + \frac{22}{100}$ ______ **b** $\frac{50}{100} - \frac{7}{100}$ ______
   c $\frac{32}{100} - \frac{11}{100}$ ______ **d** $\frac{6}{100} + \frac{41}{100}$ ______

5. 1 mL of a liquid has a volume of $1 cm^3$. What is the volume of:
   a 1 L? ______ **b** 1 kL? ______

6. Draw the elevations for this shape.

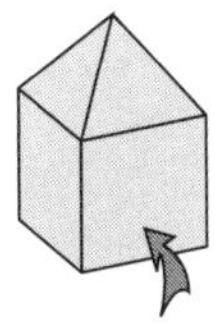

front

Front	Top	Side

Challenge

Construct a number sentence to match the problem, then find the value of the missing number.

a *Five less than a number is 87.* ______________

b *Twice a number, minus 2 makes 28.* ______________

c *The product of a number and 6 is 90.* ______________

Chance

Which vowel is used the most?

a Which vowel do you think is used the most? ______

b Use this tally to record the vowels in this activity.

	a	e	i	o	u
Tally					

c Which vowel was used the most? ______

27:1

[ ] out of 17

1. 25 ÷ 5 ____
2. 8 × 7 ____
3. 43 + 9 ____
4. 70 ÷ 10 ____
5. $\begin{array}{r} 0 \\ \times\ 10 \\ \hline \end{array}$
6. \$50 ÷ 5 ____
7. Halve 24. ____
8. 9 groups of 6. ____
9. 10 more than 95. ____
10. $\begin{array}{r} \$1\,2\,0 \\ +\ \$4\,0 \\ \hline \end{array}$
11. Which is larger $5\frac{1}{2}$ or $6\frac{1}{2}$? ____
12. **a** $\frac{3}{10} + \frac{4}{10}$ ____ **b** $\frac{2}{8} + \frac{4}{8}$ ____
13. Is the space occupied by a car, more or less than 1 m^3? ____

14. Use the short form to write 90 millilitres. ____
15.

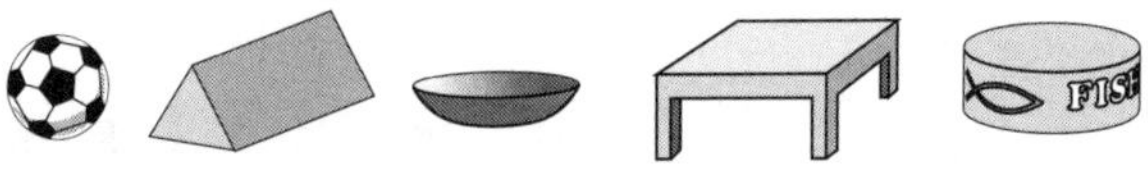

A B C D E

Which have a top view that is:

a a circle? ____

b a rectangle? ____

16. Complete: 1 cm^3 = ____ mL
17. **a** $\frac{3}{4}$ of 20 ____

b $\frac{1}{5}$ of 20 ____

c $\frac{2}{5}$ of 20 ____

d $\frac{4}{5}$ of 20 ____

27:2

[ ] out of 19

1. 25 − 4 ____
2. 4 × 8 ____
3. 23 + 42 ____
4. 9 × 6 ____
5. $3\overline{)1\,0\,2}$
6. 32 ÷ 8 ____
7. 3 × 43 ____
8. □ − 14 = 41, □ = ____
9. □ + 71 = 180, □ = ____
10. $5\overline{)5\,2\,0}$
11. Write a number sentence about the product of 9 and 2. ____
12. **a** $\frac{1}{2}$ of 28 ____ **b** $\frac{1}{4}$ of 28 ____
13. What volume will a container hold if its capacity is 650 mL? ____
14. 5·93 L = ____ mL
15. Draw the top, front and side elevations of this solid.

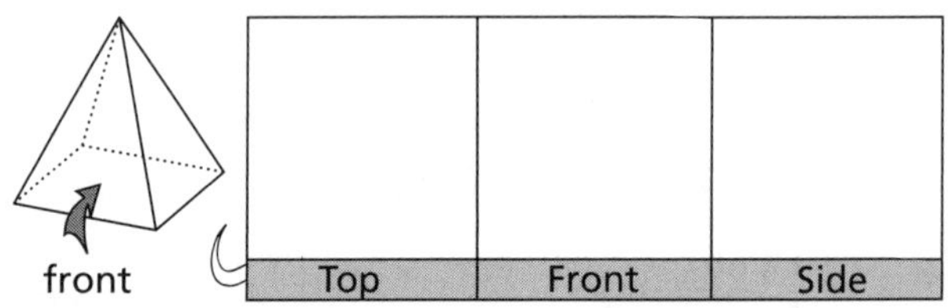

16. What 3D shape can be made from these faces?

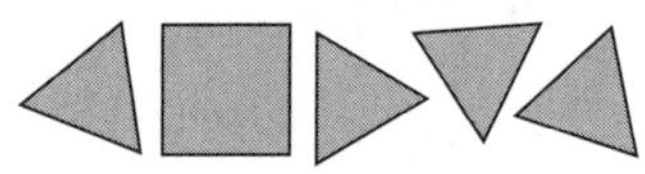

____

17. How many surfaces has a:

a cylinder? ____

b square pyramid? ____

18. Litres in 7 000 cm^3. ____
19. Ten is a quarter of ____.

Turn to ID Card A on page 6.

Give the answers for these numbers.

(1) ____	(2) ____
(3) ____	(4) ____
(5) ____	(6) ____
(7) ____	(8) ____
(9) ____	(10) ____

27:3
 out of 11

1 $2\overline{)0 \cdot 8\,4}$

2 $5\overline{)1\,0 \cdot 3\,5}$

3 $3\overline{)6 \cdot 3}$

4 **a** Halves in $2\frac{1}{2}$. ______

b Quarters in 3. ______

5 Find the capacity (in mL) of a container with a volume of:

a 50 cm^3 ______ **b** 36 cm^3 ______

c 87 cm^3 ______ **d** 14 cm^3 ______

6 How many faces has a cube? ______

7 Draw:

a a cube **b** a triangular prism

8 Write 609 mL as litres in decimal form. ______

9 What is the capacity (in mL) of 12 yogurt containers if each has a volume of 400 cm^3? ______

10 **a** $2\frac{1}{2} + 4\frac{1}{2}$ ______

b $3\frac{1}{4} + 1\frac{3}{4}$ ______

11 Write a number sentence for "the average of 6 and a certain number is 10". ______

27:4
Extension

out of 6

1 Tanya and Karyn took 20 cakes each to the cake stall. If Tanya sold $\frac{6}{10}$ of her cakes and Karyn sold $\frac{1}{2}$ of her cakes, who sold the most cakes?

______

2 **a** $2\frac{3}{4}$ take away $\frac{1}{2}$. ______

b From 1 whole, take away $\frac{1}{10}$. ______

3 How many cm^3 in 1 m^3? ______
(100 cm × 100 cm × 100 cm = 1 m^3)

4 The Roman numeral for:

a 87 ______ **b** 294 ______

5 A corner has been cut off this block. How many faces would the block have if each of the corners were cut off? ______

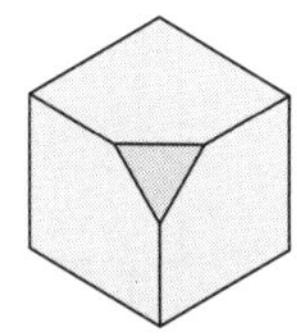

6 (96 × 2) + (96 × 8) ______

Challenge

Survey 20 people. Ask them what country they would most like to visit out of Canada, Fiji, South Africa and China. Tally the results in the table.

		Total
Canada		
Fiji		
South Africa		
China		

Discuss the results with your family.

Use the diagram to answer these questions.

a $1 + \frac{1}{4} =$ ______ **b** $\frac{1}{2} + \frac{1}{4} =$ ______ **c** $\frac{1}{2} - \frac{1}{4} =$ ______

d $1 - \frac{1}{4} =$ ______ **e** $\frac{3}{4} - \frac{1}{4} =$ ______ **f** $\frac{3}{4} - \frac{1}{2} =$ ______

g $2 - \frac{1}{2} =$ ______ **h** $2 - \frac{3}{4} =$ ______ **i** $2 - \frac{1}{2} =$ ______

j $\frac{3}{4} + \frac{1}{2} =$ ______ **k** $\frac{3}{4} + \frac{3}{4} =$ ______ **l** $2 - \frac{3}{4} =$ ______

28:1 — out of 16

1. 5 × 9 ____
2. $7 + $6 ____
3. 14 − 9 ____
4. 40 ÷ 10 ____
5. $2.50 + $1.25 = ____
6. 9 more than 92. ____
7. 8 squared. ____
8. Increase 82 by 9. ____
9. 15 subtract 8. ____
10. $8.00 − $3.47 = ____
11. **a** 3 × 8 ____ **b** 3 × 80 ____
    c 30 × 80 ____ **d** 300 × 80 ____
12. 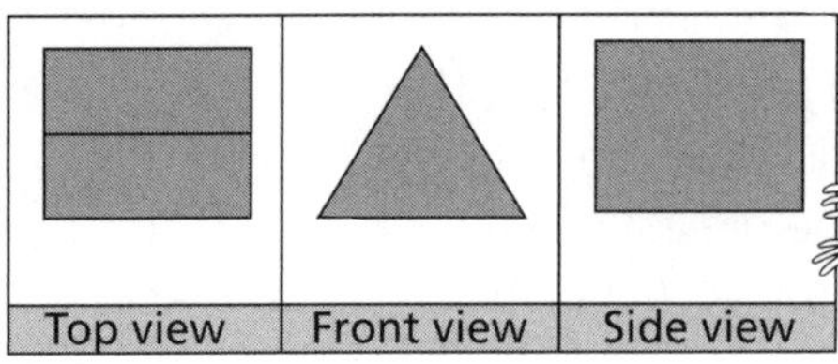

Do these views show a triangular pyramid or a triangular prism?
____
13. How many faces on a cube? ____
14. What solid would a stack of 5 cent coins form? ____
15. Cubic centimetres in:
    a 5 L ____ **b** 15 L ____
16. **a** $\frac{3}{4}$ of 28 ____
    b $\frac{1}{7}$ of 28 ____
    c $\frac{3}{7}$ of 28 ____
    d $\frac{5}{7}$ of 28 ____

28:2 — out of 19

1. 7 × 6 ____
2. 42 − 12 ____
3. 17 + 72 ____
4. 8 × 4 ____
5. 604 + 27 = ____
6. 54 ÷ 9 ____
7. 50 − 4 × 9 ____
8. 18 ÷ 3 + 6 ____
9. □ ÷ 7 = 8, □ = ____
10. 991 − 909 = ____

11. How many cm^3 in 1 litre? ____
12. Draw a copy of each solid.
    a 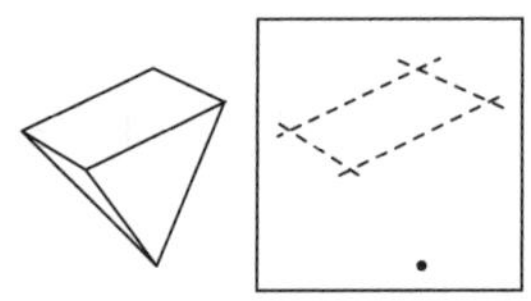
    b 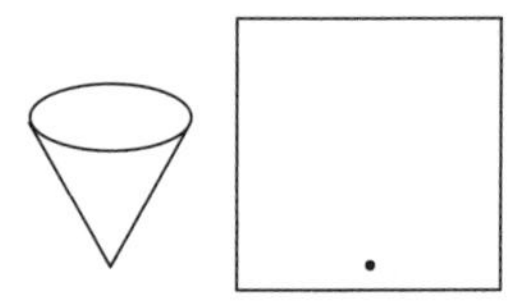
13. Quarters in 4 oranges. ____
14. 5 × 6 − □ = 24, □ = ____
15. What shape can be made from this net?
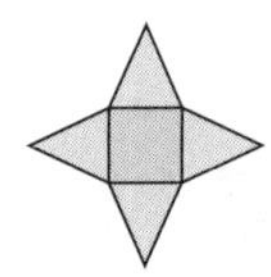
____
16. 0·829 L = ____ mL
17. **a** $11\frac{1}{2} + 9$ ____
    b $7\frac{1}{2} + 3\frac{1}{2}$ ____
18. What fraction of a metre is 50 cm? ____
19. Write a fraction equal to:
    a $\frac{6}{10}$ = ____ **b** $\frac{1}{4}$ = ____ **c** $\frac{2}{6}$ = ____

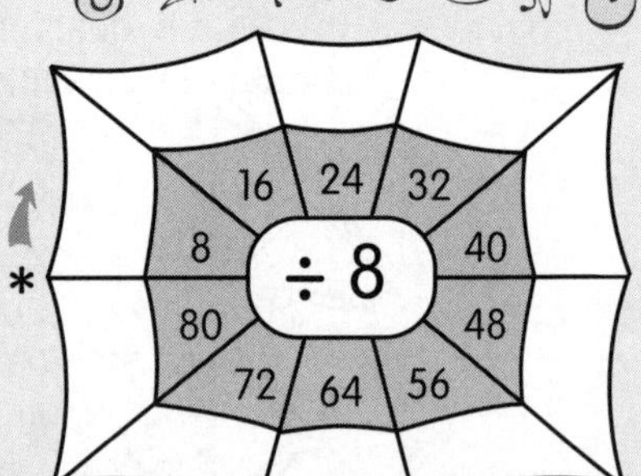

a How many packets holding 8 pencils could I fill using 56 pencils? ____

b In 8 hours I walked 40 km. What was the average distance covered each hour? ____

c Eight globes fill one box. How many boxes are needed for 72 globes? ____

28:3 — ☐ out of 13

1. $2\overline{)10 \cdot 8}$
2. $6\overline{)18 \cdot 36}$
3. $4\overline{)57 \cdot 32}$
4. $\begin{array}{r} 43076 \\ 31204 \\ +\ 2324 \\ \hline \end{array}$
5. $\begin{array}{r} 24790 \\ 13402 \\ +\ 50076 \\ \hline \end{array}$
6. 600 children were each given $20. How much money was given altogether? ______
7. **a** $\frac{1}{4}$ plus $\frac{1}{4}$ ______

   b $\frac{1}{4}$ plus $\frac{1}{2}$ ______
8. Cubic centimetres in 0·59 L. ______
9. Draw a triangular pyramid. How many:

   a faces? ______

   b edges? ______

   c vertices? ______
10. ☐ − 47 = 120, ☐ = ______
11. What is the capacity (in mL) of a can of volume 350 cm³? ______
12. **a** $7 + 3\frac{1}{2}$ ______ **b** $6 + 4\frac{1}{2}$ ______
13. **a** 90 × 4 ______

    b 90 × 40 ______

    c 90 × 400 ______

    d 90 × 4000 ______

28:4 — Extension — ☐ out of 4

1. **a** 30 squared. ______

   b 300 squared. ______
2. In a test, Luis scored $\frac{3}{4}$ of the possible marks, while Peter scored $\frac{4}{5}$ of the possible marks. Which of the two boys scored the higher mark? ______
3. Jodie ordered $\frac{1}{4}$ of a pizza for each of her 14 friends. How many pizzas did she order? ______

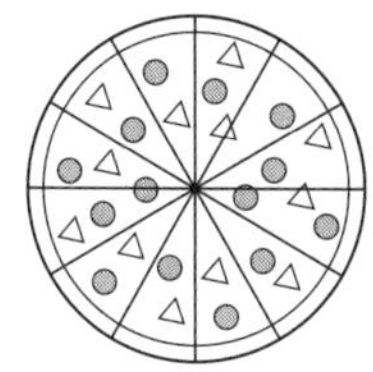

4. How much water (in mL) can be poured into a container with volume:

   a 200 cm³? ______

   b 1 000 cm³? ______

Challenge

Complete this fraction wall. Record equivalent fractions below.

$\frac{1}{2}$				$\frac{1}{2}$			
$\frac{1}{4}$							
$\frac{1}{8}$							

Note: $\frac{2}{4} = \frac{4}{8}$

Concept

Fractions to Decimals Using a Calculator

Use a calculator to change these to decimals.

a $\frac{1}{2}$ ______ **b** $\frac{3}{5}$ ______ **c** $\frac{7}{20}$ ______

d $\frac{13}{25}$ ______ **e** $\frac{7}{8}$ ______ **f** $\frac{1}{16}$ ______

g $\frac{5}{8}$ ______ **h** $\frac{3}{16}$ ______ **i** $\frac{7}{25}$ ______

j $\frac{1}{32}$ ______ **k** $\frac{1}{64}$ ______ **l** $\frac{63}{64}$ ______

29:1 ☐ out of 17

1. 8 + 7 ____
2. 7 × 8 ____
3. 12 − 9 ____
4. 24 ÷ 3 ____
5. $\begin{array}{r} 9 \\ \times\ 7 \\ \hline \end{array}$
6. Half of 44. ____
7. Total $18 and $5. ____
8. 40 minus 6. ____
9. Multiply 6 by 8. ____
10. $\begin{array}{r} \$2.18 \\ +\ \$7.21 \\ \hline \end{array}$
11. The Olympic Games are held every 4 years. If they were held in 2000, will they be held in 2065, 2066, 2067 or 2068? ____

12. Does 35 mL of water have a volume of 35 cm^3? ____
13. Name the 3D shapes that are part of this pencil.

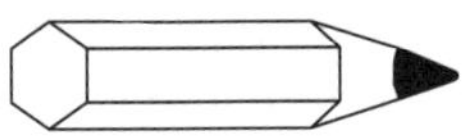

____

14. Write a fraction equal to:
    a $\frac{2}{5}$ ☐ b $\frac{4}{5}$ ☐ c $\frac{1}{5}$ ☐

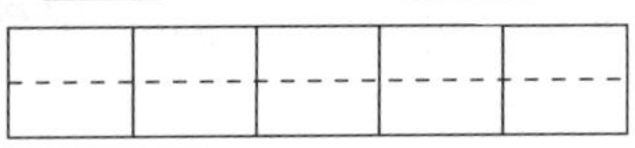

15. $\frac{1}{4}$ of 20 oranges. ____
16. 14 − (3 × 4) ____
17. Complete the drawing of this shape.

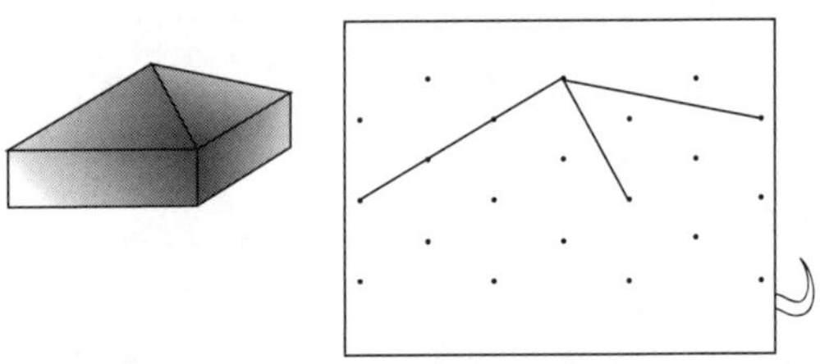

29:2 ☐ out of 15

1. 36 − 4 ____
2. 60 × 40 ____
3. 50 × 50 ____
4. 5 − 15 ____
5. $\begin{array}{r} 30 \\ \times\ 50 \\ \hline \end{array}$
6. 56 ÷ 7 ____
7. 7 × 8 − 14 ____
8. 90 − ☐ = 19, ☐ = ____
9. 42 ÷ ☐ = 2, ☐ = ____
10. $7\overline{)983}$
11. Name this solid. ____

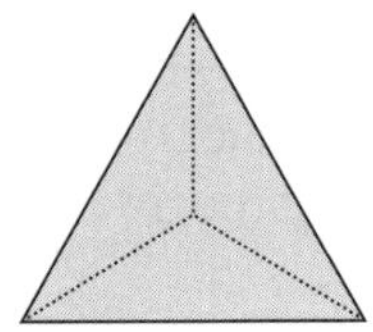

12. For the shape above:
    a how many edges? ____
    b how many vertices? ____
13.

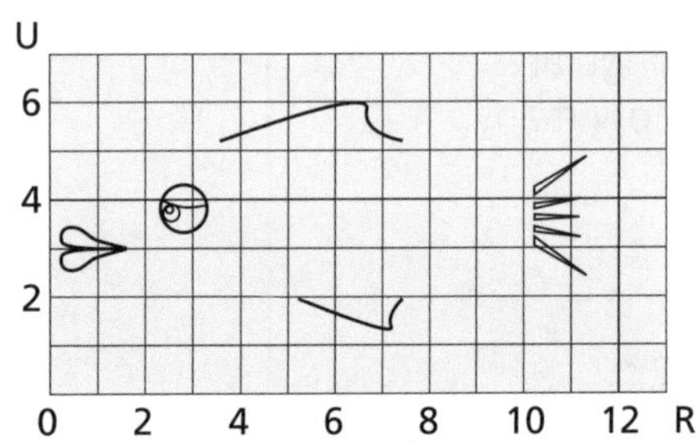

(1R, 3U) is the point 1 right and 3 up from zero. Join the coordinates in order, to complete the picture above.
(1R, 3U), (3R, 5U), (8R, 5U), (10R, 4U), (10R, 3U), (12R, 6U), (12R, 1U), (10R, 3U), (8R, 2U), (3R, 2U), (1R, 3U)

14. 6, ____, 18, 24, ____, 36
15. a 7 × 500 ____
    b 700 × 500 ____
    c 7000 × 50 ____

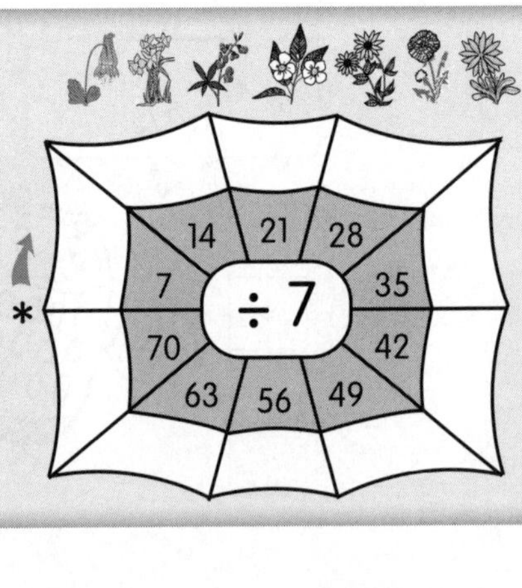

a Heather is paid one seventh of $42. How much is she paid? ____

b How many weeks are in 56 days? ____

c Seven people sit at each table. How many tables are needed for 35 people? ____

29:3 ☐ out of 12

1. $\$540.21 \times 4$

2. $3 \cdot 875 \times 8$

3. $6\overline{)10 \cdot 2}$

4. $2\overline{)32 \cdot 43}$

5. The best estimate of 784 × 32: 2400, 24 000 or 240 000? ______

6. < or >?

   a $\frac{1}{5}$ ☐ $\frac{3}{10}$ b $\frac{7}{10}$ ☐ $\frac{2}{5}$

7. The short form of 119 cubic metres. ______

8. 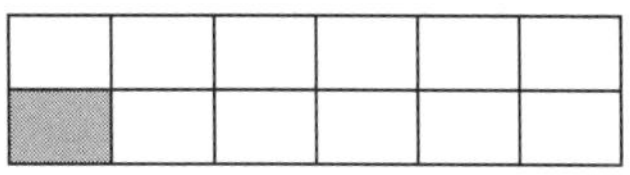

   Write in order, from smallest to largest:

   $\frac{1}{2}$, $\frac{1}{12}$, $\frac{1}{3}$, $\frac{1}{6}$, $\frac{1}{4}$ ______

9. 900 mL = ______ cm^3

10. Underline the units that have been correctly written.

    KG G gm g. Kg
    g kg. kg G. kG

11. How many cm^3 are in 32 mL? ______

12. a 3 × 60 ______

    b 30 × 60 ______

    c 300 × 60 ______

    d 3000 × 60 ______

29:4 ☐ out of 6 **Extension**

1. Find the estimate by rounding each number to the nearest 10.

   a 21 × 99 ______

   b 48 × 121 ______

   c 504 × 21 ______

2. How many zeros has the product of 3 thousand and 16 thousand? ______

3. CXX – LXX ______

4. The product of 3 numbers is 630. Two of them are 7 and 9. What is the third number? ______

5. If → means "is taller than", who is the tallest? ______

   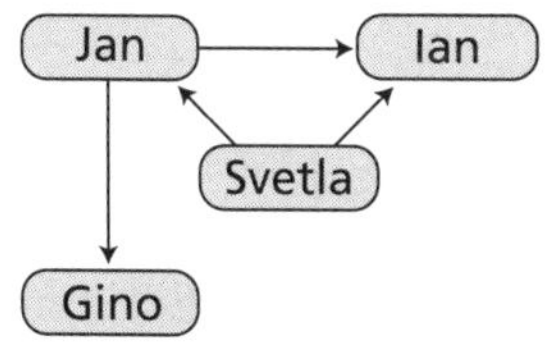

6. $\frac{3}{4}$ of 2 litres. ______

Challenge

Complete this fraction wall. Record equivalent fractions below.

<table>
<tr><td colspan="3">$\frac{1}{2}$</td><td colspan="3">$\frac{1}{2}$</td></tr>
<tr><td colspan="2">$\frac{1}{3}$</td><td colspan="2"></td><td colspan="2"></td></tr>
<tr><td>$\frac{1}{6}$</td><td></td><td></td><td></td><td></td><td></td></tr>
</table>

Note: $\frac{2}{3} = \frac{4}{6}$

a To get to camp, Year 5 used 8-seater vans and 5-seater cars. There were 10 vehicles used. If there were 59 seats, how many vans were used? ______

b In the paddock, kangaroos and cows grazed together. The 31 animals had 100 legs altogether. How many of each type of animal were in the paddock?

kangaroos: ______ cows: ______

30:1 — out of 18

1. 17 − 9 ____
2. 9 × 8 ____
3. 20 ÷ 5 ____
4. 29 + 7 ____
5. $6 1 × 7
6. 200 ÷ 10 ____
7. Add 18 and 6. ____
8. 6 lots of 8. ____
9. 7 less than 29. ____
10. $10.00 − $3.67
11. 4 × 315 = (4 × 300) + (4 × 10) + (4 × 5)
    Is the above true or false? ____
12. Write a fraction equal to:
    a $\frac{8}{10}$ = $\frac{\square}{\square}$ **b** $\frac{4}{10}$ = $\frac{\square}{\square}$ **c** $\frac{6}{10}$ = $\frac{\square}{\square}$

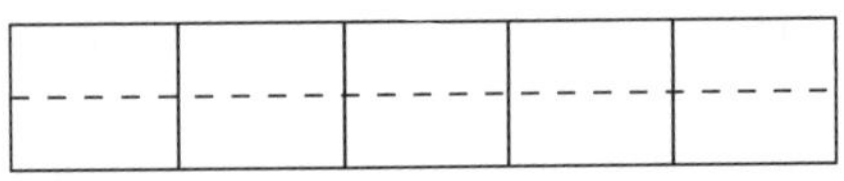

13. 4000 cm³ = ____ L
14. Use the short form to write:
    a 3 cubic centimetres ____
    b 6 kilometres ____
    c 5 kilograms ____
    d 9 cubic metres ____
15. 300 000 + 500 + 3 ____
16. Round off 8·4 to the nearest whole number. ____
17. Which is the smallest fraction, $\frac{1}{2}$ or $\frac{3}{8}$? ____
18. Circle the closest estimate to 326 × 5.
    1400 1600 1500 1700

30:2 — out of 19

1. 58 − 4 ____
2. 63 ÷ 9 ____
3. 8 − 1·2 ____
4. 72 ÷ 8 ____
5. 6)184
6. 7 × 800 ____
7. 80 × 600 ____
8. □ × 8 = 64, □ = ____
9. 35 + □ =90, □ = ____
10. 4)3086
11. **a** $\frac{4\ (\div 2)}{10\ (\div 2)}$ = $\frac{\square}{\square}$ **b** $\frac{2\ (\times 3)}{6\ (\times 3)}$ = $\frac{\square}{\square}$
12. The capacity of a container that can hold 204 mL is ____ cm³.
13. Round off each number to its first digit and multiply to find an estimate.
    a 38 × 63 ____
    b 894 × 27 ____
14. Which fraction is bigger:
    a $\frac{3}{4}$ or $\frac{1}{3}$? ____ **b** $\frac{3}{4}$ or $\frac{2}{3}$? ____
15. 15 ÷ 3 + 10 × 2 × 3 ____
16. 6 L = ____ cm³

17. < or >?
    a $\frac{8}{10}$ □ $\frac{3}{5}$ **b** $\frac{2}{6}$ □ $\frac{2}{3}$
18. 72 × 30 = (70 × ____) + (____ × ____)
    = ____ + ____
    = ____
19. True or false? 4 × 300 = 3 × 400 ____

30:3 ☐ out of 6

1. $13 \times 64 = \underset{\_\_\_\_}{\begin{array}{r}64\\ \times\ 10\end{array}} + \underset{\_\_\_\_}{\begin{array}{r}64\\ \times\ 3\end{array}} = \_\_\_\_$

2. $3\overline{)7\,2\cdot 3}$

3. $7\overline{)8\,2\cdot 8\,8}$

4. 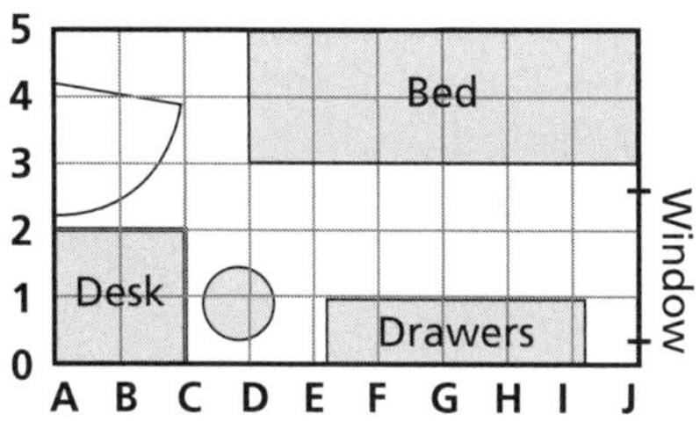

Scale:
1 cm
represents
50 cm

a The scale of this drawing. ____ : ____

What is the actual length of:

b the bed? ____

c the drawers? ____

What is at the coordinate position:

d **G4**? ____ **e** **B1**? ____

Which coordinates could be used for:

f the window? ____

g the floor? ____

5. Write a fraction equal to:

a $\frac{1}{6}$ $\frac{\square}{\square}$ **b** $\frac{2}{8}$ $\frac{\square}{\square}$ **c** $\frac{4}{10}$ $\frac{\square}{\square}$

d $\frac{5}{5}$ $\frac{\square}{\square}$ **e** $\frac{1}{3}$ $\frac{\square}{\square}$ **f** $\frac{4}{5}$ $\frac{\square}{\square}$

6. Complete: $43 \times 52 = (40 \times \_\_\_) + (3 \times \_\_\_)$

30:4 ☐ out of 5 **Extension**

1. Find an estimate for 68×47 by rounding off each number and then multiplying. ____

2. Write in words the answer to 900×700.

____

3. $\frac{7}{10} + \frac{1}{5} = \frac{\square}{10} + \frac{\triangle}{10}$ $\square =$ ____, $\triangle =$ ____

4. Linda weighs 57 kg. She was holding $8\frac{1}{2}$ kg of groceries when she stepped onto the scales.

a What was the total weight? ____

b How much less than 100 kg is the total weight? ____

5. Tasmania has an area of 68 330 km². Estimate (to the nearest 100 000 km²) the area of:

a NSW ____ **b** WA ____

Challenge

Toss a coin 40 times and record your results in the table.

		Total
Heads		
Tails		

When completing a chance experiment, why do we repeat the event so often?

____

____

Codes

Use the code to write "true" or "false" for each code statement.

A	B	C	D	E	F	G	H	I	J	K	L	M	N	O	P	R	S	T	U	V	W	Y
1	*	9	&	4	?	0	/	2	(	+	7	<	5	#	)	3	$	=	8	@	>	6

a 1 7#50 (#83546 $=13=$ >2=/ (8$= #54 $=4). ____

b $8994$$ &4)45&$ 7130476 #5 /13& >#3+. ____

c <156 34942@4 1&@294, =/4 >2$4)3#?2= ?3#< 2=. ____

31:1 ☐ out of 18

1. 9 ÷ 9 ____
2. 72 + 3 ____
3. 0 ÷ 10 ____
4. 8 × 90 ____
5. $\begin{array}{r} 27 \\ +\ 18 \\ \hline \end{array}$
6. Halve 96. ____
7. 4 rows of 20. ____
8. Total of 16 and 7. ____
9. 5 × 5 × 5 ____
10. $\begin{array}{r} 856 \\ +\ 523 \\ \hline \end{array}$

11. Round the answer to Question 10, correct to the nearest 100. ________
12. Write a fraction equal to:
    a $\frac{2}{5}$ $\frac{\square}{\square}$ **b** $\frac{1}{2}$ $\frac{\square}{\square}$ **c** $\frac{3}{4}$ $\frac{\square}{\square}$
13. Circle the correctly written measure.
    A 6 KG **B** 6 kG **C** 6 kg **D** 6 kgs
14. The value of the bold digit:
    a 7**4**1 865 ________
    b 989 **3**50 ________
15. **a** Area = ________
    b Perimeter = ________

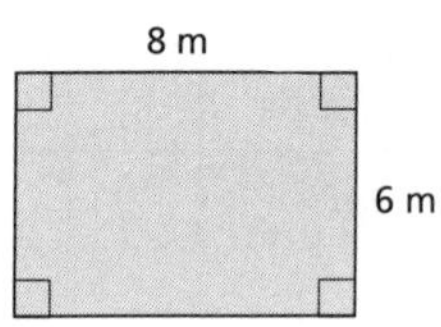

16. $\frac{3}{10} + \frac{1}{2} = \frac{\square}{\square} + \frac{\square}{\square} = \frac{\square}{\square}$

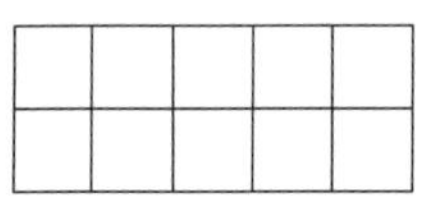

17. Use the short form to write one kilogram three hundred and seventy-five grams. ________
18. 1L = ________ cm^3

31:2 ☐ out of 14

1. 37 − 7 ____
2. 4 × $60 ____
3. 13 − 1·7 ____
4. 7 × 9 ____
5. $\begin{array}{r} 189 \\ +\ 92 \\ \hline \end{array}$
6. 56 ÷ 8 ____
7. 4 × 4 × 4 ____
8. 500 × 30 ____
9. 80 × 500 ____
10. $\begin{array}{r} 314 \\ -\ 188 \\ \hline \end{array}$

11. 24 × 20 = (20 × ____) + (____ × ____)
    = ____ + ____
    = ____
12. 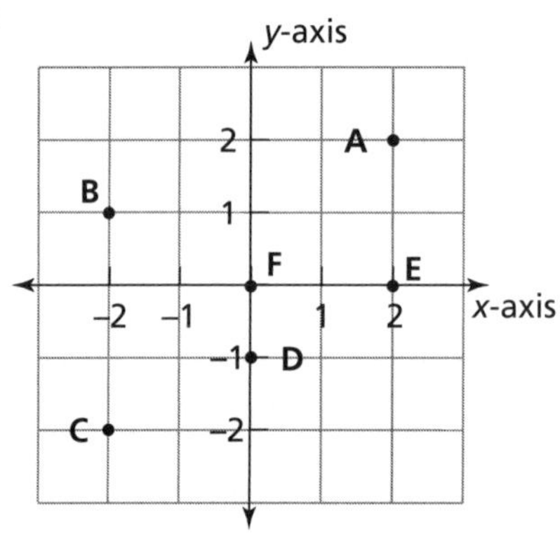

    Write the coordinates for:
    a **A** ____ **b** **B** ____
    c **C** ____ **d** **D** ____
    e **E** ____ **f** **F** ____
13. < or >?
    a $\frac{1}{2}$ ☐ $\frac{4}{6}$ **b** $\frac{3}{4}$ ☐ $\frac{3}{8}$
14. **a** $4\overline{)12804}$ **b** $5\overline{)15015}$

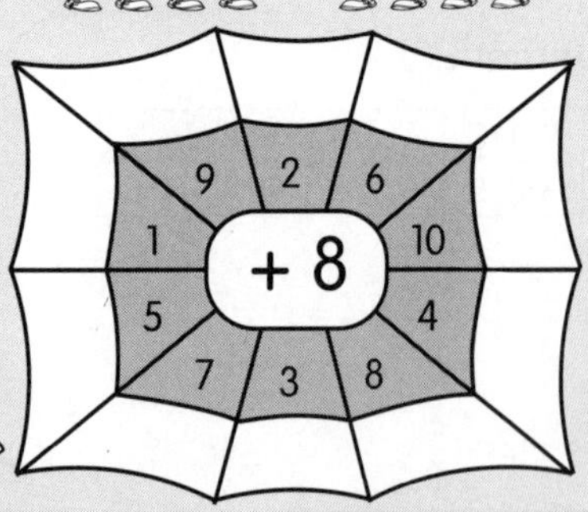

If you add an even number:
- ☐ the answer will be even if the other number is even.
- ☐ the answer will be odd if the other number is odd.

What happens when you add an odd number?
odd + odd = ________
even + odd = ________

 ISBN 978 1 4886 2192 5

31:3 ☐ out of 8

1 **a**

$27 \times 91 = \begin{array}{r} 91 \\ \times\ 20 \\ \hline \_\_\_\_ \end{array} + \begin{array}{r} 91 \\ \times\ 7 \\ \hline \_\_\_\_ \end{array} = \_\_\_\_$

b

$39 \times 17 = \begin{array}{r} 17 \\ \times\ 30 \\ \hline \_\_\_\_ \end{array} + \begin{array}{r} 17 \\ \times\ 9 \\ \hline \_\_\_\_ \end{array} = \_\_\_\_$

2 **a** $\frac{8\ (\div 2)}{10\ (\div 2)}$ $\frac{\square}{\square}$ **b** $\frac{1\ (\times 3)}{4\ (\times 3)}$ $\frac{\square}{\square}$

3

1997 — Felicity is born.
2002 — First swimming lesson
2009 — First tennis lesson
2013 — First guitar lesson

How old was Felicity when she had her:

a first tennis lesson? ______

b first swimming lesson? ______

c first guitar lesson? ______

4 Write two point nine seven as a numeral. ______

5 The capacity of a container that can hold 492 mL is ____ cm^3.

6 $\frac{2}{3} - \frac{1}{6} = \frac{\square}{\square} + \frac{\square}{\square} = \frac{\square}{\square}$

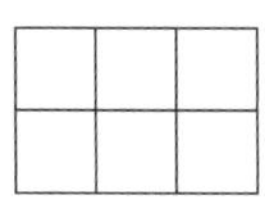

7 4000 cm^3 = ____ L

8 **a** 5 × 70 ______

b 5 × 7000 ______

c 50 × 7000 ______

31:4 ☐ out of 5

Extension

1 1 boat weighs the same as 8 people. How many people would weigh the same as 6 boats? ______

2 Estimate the area of:

a the top of a matchbox ______

b a tennis court ______

3 One fifth of a whole is 9. Write the value of the shaded part. ______

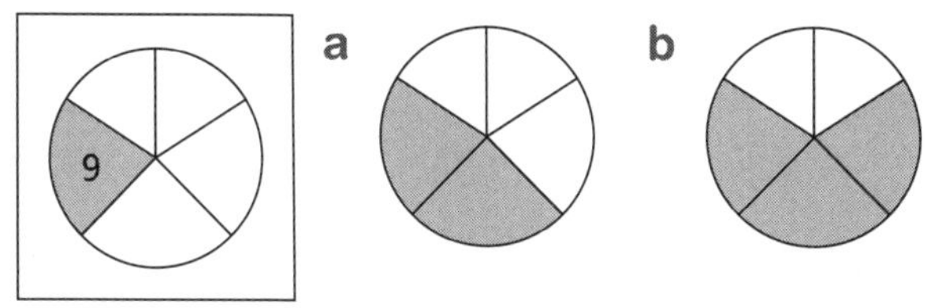

a ______ **b** ______

4 The mass of 3 trucks is 9·1 t. What is the mass of:

a 6 trucks? ______

b 30 trucks? ______

5 3 over 2 | 7; 2 over 7 | 15; 8 over 7 | 57; 9 over 4 | ?

What is the missing number? ______

Challenge

Record a time line for your life.
Fit in as many events and dates as you can.

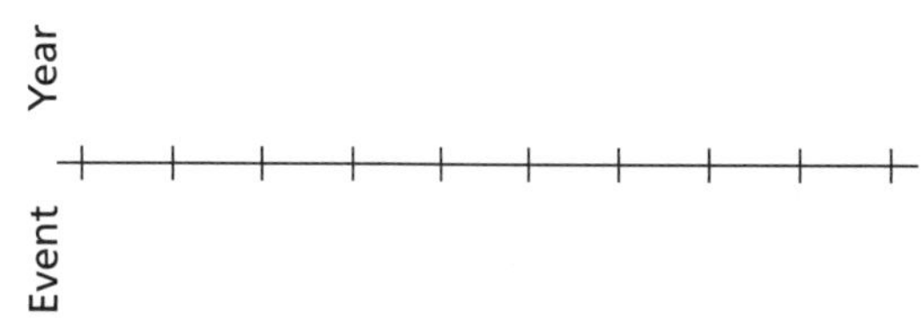

Estimate the Product

86 × 225

Round off each number.

Estimate = 90 × 200
= 18000

Calculator check

86 × 225 = 19360

Round each number to its leading figure to estimate the answer.

a 38 × 47 ______ **b** 72 × 91 ______

c 57 × 83 ______ **d** 83 × 176 ______

e 38^2 ______ **f** 391 × 76 ______

g 693^2 ______ **h** 714 × 911 ______

32:1 ☐ out of 18

1. 5×40 ____
2. $19 + 16$ ____
3. $24 - 18$ ____
4. $80 \div 8$ ____
5. $10\overline{)27}$
6. $9 less than $107. ____
7. 900×20 ____
8. 40×30 ____
9. 10 times 60. ____
10. $4\overline{)43}$
11. Write a fraction equal to:
    a $\frac{9}{10}$ $\frac{\square}{\square}$ b $\frac{1}{3}$ $\frac{\square}{\square}$ c $\frac{4}{4}$ $\frac{\square}{\square}$
12. Match the best unit of measure for each mass.

50 cent coin
truck

tonnes
kilograms
grams

13. Nine squared. ____
14. 12 m

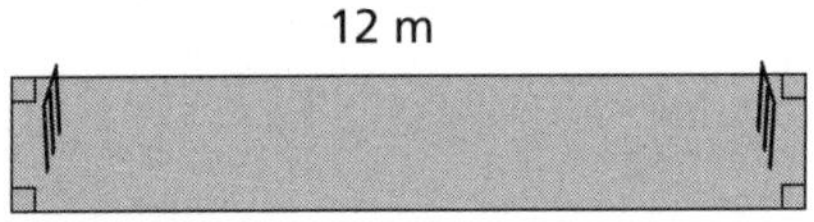

2 m

For this cricket pitch find the:
a area ____ b perimeter ____
15. Use the short form to write:
    a thirty grams ____
    b twenty-three metres ____
16. 15 birds are in a flock. One third fly away. How many are left? ____

17. 700 plus 60 plus 8. ____
18. How many cm^3 in 10 mL? ____

32:2 ☐ out of 18

1. $42 + 33$ ____
2. 900×70 ____
3. 6×9 ____
4. $3 - 10$ ____
5. $6.05 $\times$ 7
6. $42 \div 7$ ____
7. 2 squared. ____
8. 40×500 ____
9. 50s in 800. ____
10. $11.35 $\times$ 3
11. $17 - \square = 47 - 39$, $\square =$ ____
12. 65 mL = ____ cm^3
13. $\frac{3}{6} + \frac{1}{3} = \frac{\square}{\square} + \frac{\square}{\square} = \frac{\square}{\square}$

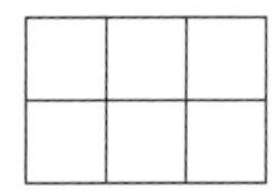

14. a Tonnes in 2 000 kg. ____
    b Kilograms in 6·5 tonnes. ____
15. 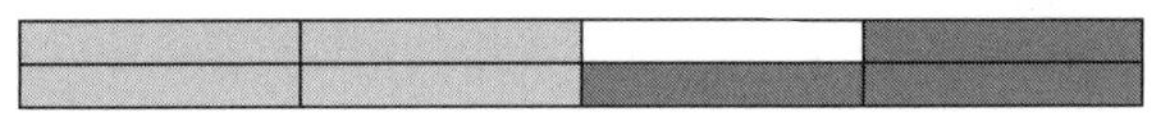

    a $\frac{1}{2} + \frac{3}{8}$ ____ b $1 - \frac{7}{8}$ ____
16.

5 g	50 g	500 g	40 kg	
5 mL	200 mL	20 mL	45 m	12 cm

Choose the best answer above for the:
a height of a glass ____
b mass of a boy ____
c capacity of a teaspoon ____
17. What is the value of the 2 in 5·21? ____
18. a $\frac{2\ (\div 2)}{10\ (\div 2)}$ $\frac{\square}{\square}$ b $\frac{3\ (\times 3)}{5\ (\times 3)}$ $\frac{\square}{\square}$

Turn to ID Card D on page 9.
Give the answers for these numbers.

(19) ____ (20) ____
(21) ____ (22) ____
(23) ____ (24) ____
(25) ____ (26) ____
(27) ____ graph (28) ____

32:3  ☐ out of 12

1. $\begin{array}{r} 23 \\ \times\ 11 \\ \hline \\ \hline \\ \hline \end{array}$

2. $\begin{array}{r} 43 \\ \times\ 21 \\ \hline \\ \hline \\ \hline \end{array}$

3. $\begin{array}{r} 65 \\ \times\ 43 \\ \hline \\ \hline \\ \hline \end{array}$

4. $9 \times 2 + \square = 25$, $\square =$ ____

5. $\frac{4}{5} - \frac{2}{10} = \frac{\square}{\square} - \frac{\square}{\square} = \frac{\square}{\square}$

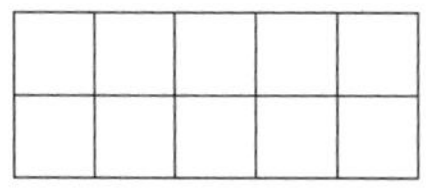

6. My painting time totalled 525 minutes over 3 days. On average, how long did I paint for each day? ____

7. 14, 28 and 49 are multiples of ____.

8. a $\frac{5}{7} = \frac{\square}{28}$, $\square =$ ____

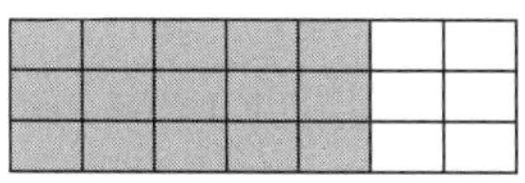

   b $\frac{2}{7} = \frac{\square}{28}$, $\square =$ ____

   c $\frac{1}{4} = \frac{\square}{28}$, $\square =$ ____

   d $\frac{3}{4} = \frac{\square}{28}$, $\square =$ ____

9. The chance of Melissa scoring a goal at netball is about 1 in 3. About how many did she miss if she scored 7 goals? ____

10. Kilograms in 3 t. ____

11. $8000\ cm^3 =$ ____ L

12. < or >?

    a $\frac{1}{10}\ \square\ \frac{4}{5}$ b $\frac{5}{6}\ \square\ \frac{2}{3}$

32:4 ☐ out of 6

Extension

1. Write all possible pairs of counting numbers that make this sentence true.

   $31 - 17 = \triangle \times \square$

   ____

2. If one boat has the same weight as 9 people, how many boats would have the same weight as 72 people? ____

3. The mass of 10 men is 0·8 t. What is the mass of:

   a 30 men? ____ **b** 50 men? ____

4. $\square - \triangle + \square = 20$

   If $\square - \triangle = 13$ and $\square + \square = 25$, find the value of $\triangle$. ____

5. Sue has emus and horses. These have 40 legs altogether. What is the greatest number of horses possible? ____

6. $128 \div \square = 32$, $\square =$ ____

Challenge

Complete:

a $\triangle + 7 = 16$ so $\triangle =$ ____

b $\square - 62 = 23$ so $\square =$ ____

c $2 \times \triangle = 98$ so $\triangle =$ ____

d $\square \div 9 = 7$ so $\square =$ ____

e $\triangle + 84 = 106 - 9$ so $\triangle =$ ____

f $8 \times \square = 45 + 19$ so $\square =$ ____

Estimating Chance

Estimate the chance of each event by using an arrow to connect the event to a position on the given scale.

The next time I go fishing I'll catch:

A a fish

B a snag

C a cold

D a pig

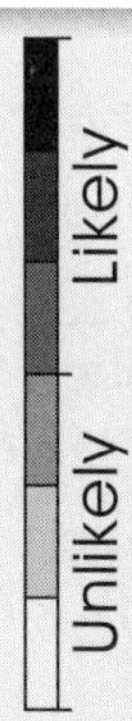

33:1 — ☐ out of 18

1. $27 + 44$ ____
2. $\$14 - \$5$ ____
3. 1×66 ____
4. $28 \div 4$ ____
5. $\begin{array}{r} 311 \\ \times \quad 8 \\ \hline \end{array}$
6. 15 minus 7. ____
7. 4 squared. ____
8. 8 more than 9. ____
9. Nine threes. ____
10. $\begin{array}{r} 146 \\ - \quad 56 \\ \hline \end{array}$
11. $(3 + \triangle) \times 7 = 35,\quad \triangle =$ ____
12. Circle the numbers that are divisible by 5.

    852 790 555231 85
13. Complete: $\frac{1}{2} = \frac{2}{4} = \frac{\square}{8} = \frac{5}{\square}$
14. In a newspaper there are 50 pages. If $\frac{1}{10}$ of the newspaper contains comics, how many pages of comics are there? ____

15. $7000 + 700 + 30$ ____
16. What fraction of \$1 is 30c? ____

17. Arrange these in descending order:

    $5\frac{1}{4},\ 1\frac{3}{8},\ 4,\ 3\frac{1}{8}$ ____
18. 1, 2, 4, 8, 16 and 32 are all of the ____ of 32.

33:2 — ☐ out of 18

1. 4×90 ____
2. $88 - 89$ ____
3. $61 + 47$ ____
4. $4 \times 22 \div 22$ ____
5. $4\overline{)824}$
6. $63 \div 7$ ____
7. 60×30 ____
8. $5 \times 5 + 12$ ____
9. $\square \times 9 = 81,\ \square =$ ____
10. $5\overline{)526}$
11. $\frac{3}{4} + \frac{1}{8} = \frac{\square}{\square} + \frac{\square}{\square} = \frac{\square}{\square}$

12. Kilograms in 9803 g. ____
13. Find the real length of:

    a the kitchen ____

    b the lounge room ____

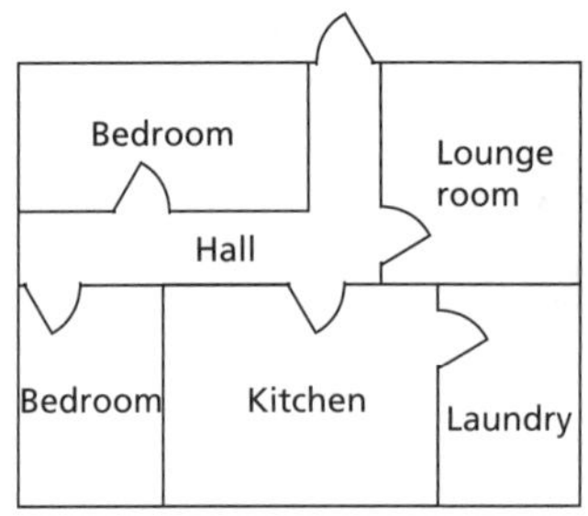

Scale: 1 cm = 2 m

14. I ate one quarter of an apple each day. How many apples did I eat after 4 weeks? ____

15. Kilograms in:

    a 5 t ____ b 2 t ____

    c 20 t ____ d 4 t 25 kg ____
16. a $\frac{6\ (\div 2)}{10\ (\div 2)}$ $\frac{\square}{\square}$ b $\frac{1\ (\times 3)}{8\ (\times 3)}$ $\frac{\square}{\square}$
17. Circle the numbers divisible by 6.

    44 30 16 600 68
18. $7 + \triangle \times 2 = 10 + 5,\quad \triangle =$ ____

Testing Divisibility Rules Using a Calculator

a Choose any 10 large numbers ending in 0 or 5. Is each one divisible by 5? ____

b Choose any 10 large numbers whose last digits are divisible by 4 (like 810912). Is each one divisible by 4? ____

c Choose any 10 large numbers whose sum of digits is divisible by 3 (like 411441). Is each one divisible by 3? ____

One number is divisible by another if the answer is a whole number when you divide.

33:3 ☐ out of 13

1 $\begin{array}{r} 21 \\ \times\ 22 \\ \hline \\ \hline \end{array}$ **2** $\begin{array}{r} 52 \\ \times\ 15 \\ \hline \\ \hline \end{array}$ **3** $\begin{array}{r} 61 \\ \times\ 12 \\ \hline \\ \hline \end{array}$

4 How many quarters in:

a 4? ____ **b** $4\frac{1}{2}$? ____

5 Grams in 2 kg 2 g. ______

6 On a scale drawing, 1 cm represents 300 km. What distance does 3·15 cm represent? ______

7 What is the value of the underlined digit?

a 6<u>7</u>30 ______ **b** 4·<u>7</u>5 ______

8 Arrange from smallest to largest:

67·25, 54, 7·21, 72

____

9 What number squared gives 81? ______

10 Write 5 500 kg as tonnes. ______

11 $\frac{7}{10} - \frac{1}{5} = \frac{\square}{\square} - \frac{\square}{\square} = \frac{\square}{\square}$

12 Write three halves as a mixed numeral. ______

13 **a** ☐ + 56 = 93, ☐ = ____

b ☐ − 13 = 47, ☐ = ____

c ☐ × 8 = 992, ☐ = ____

33:4 Extension ☐ out of 4

1 Fill in the boxes.

a $\begin{array}{r} 3\ 4\ \square \\ +\ \square\ \square\ 1 \\ \hline 8\ 5\ 6 \end{array}$ **b** $\begin{array}{r} \square\ 1\ 8 \\ -\ 3\ \square\ \square \\ \hline 1\ 7\ 3 \end{array}$

2 Which of the numbers 5, 6 or 7 is a factor of:

a 8 145? ______ **b** 2 172? ______

3 **a** I took one hour to do my homework. Alana took half as long. Heather took one third as long as Alana. How long did Heather take? ______

b In part a, how much time was spent on homework altogether? ______

4 Each boat has a mass of 0·3 tonnes. What is the mass of:

a 4 boats? ______

b 10 boats? ______

Challenge

Write facts about the number 45 284 309.

____

____

____

____

____

____

4, 45, 16, 21, 23, 100, 35, 36, 81, 49, 14

1 Which of the numbers above are square numbers? ______________

2 Which are multiples of:

a 7? ______________

b 5? ______________

c 2? ______________

34:1 [ ] out of 18

1. 6 × $40 ____
2. 74 + 51 ____
3. 215 − 8 ____
4. 210 × 1 ____
5. $3\overline{)2\,4\,9}$
6. Divide 32 by 4. ____
7. Double 93. ____
8. 10 × 10 × 10 ____
9. 107 plus 8. ____
10. $5\overline{)\$1\,2\,0}$
11. List the factors of 18.

    ____, ____, ____, ____, ____, ____
12. Circle the number that is divisible by 10.

    2307   800010   410054
13. A person's mass is measured in ________.
14. How many pairs of parallel edges has this triangular prism?

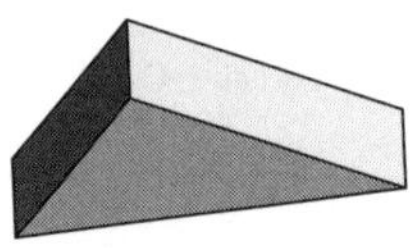

    ____
15. Write the numeral for twenty-one point zero one. ____
16. 9000 kg = ____ t
17. Grams in 6·53 kg. ____
18. a Halves in 5 wholes.

    ____

    b Quarters in 5 wholes.

    ____

34:2 [ ] out of 17

1. 90 × 90 ____
2. 76 − 5 ____
3. 3 × 80 ____
4. 14 + 60 ____
5. $\begin{array}{r} 5\,0 \\ \times\ 7\,0 \\ \hline \end{array}$
6. 81 ÷ 9 − 9 ____
7. 7 × 7 × 2 ____
8. 2 × 2 × 2 ____
9. 3 squared. ____
10. $\begin{array}{r} 8 \cdot 4 \\ -\ 0 \cdot 3\,9 \\ \hline \end{array}$
11. What fraction of $1 is:

    a 20c? ____

    b 75c? ____
12. Write in tonnes as a decimal.

    a 10 t 375 kg ____

    b 3 t 845 kg ____

    c 800 kg ____

    d 7 t 70 kg ____
13. If 1 cm on a map represents 5 km, what measurement represents 55 km? ____
14. Calculate the area of a rectangle with a length of 10 cm and a breadth of 7 cm. ____
15. a 9 g = ________ mg

    b 2000 mg = ________ g
16. Round 3·6 to the nearest whole. ____
17. Circle the numbers that are divisible by 2.

    230   351   5607   107   352

Example of Factors

Draw the rectangles that have an area of 6 units^2.

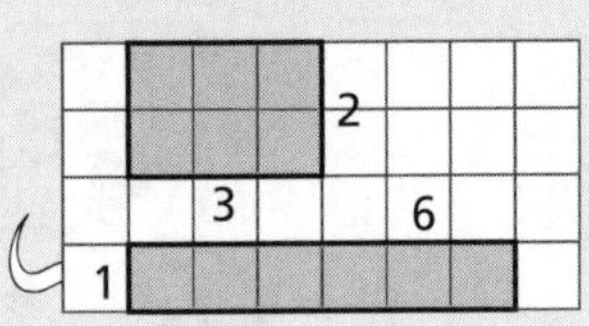

Draw rectangles of area 12 units^2.

List the factors. ____________

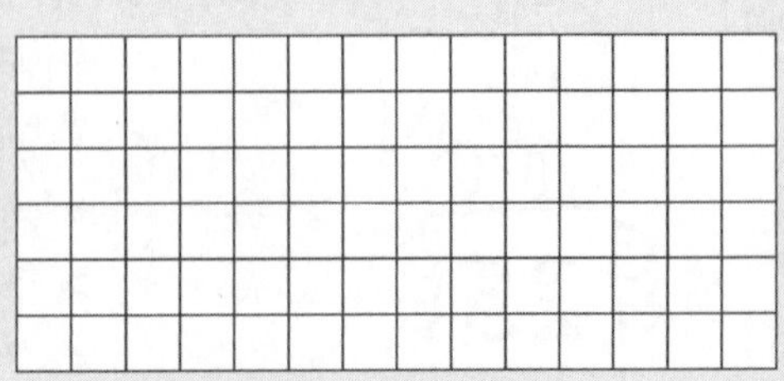

 ISBN 978 1 4886 2192 5

34:3 out of 11

1. 420 × 15 = ______

2. 523 × 25 = ______

3. 624 × 36 = ______

4. 16, 20, 24 and 28 are all divisible by ______.

5. Grams in $\frac{1}{4}$ of a kilogram. ______

6. Indu, Rajiv and Taya sit for a test. In how many ways could they be placed 1st, 2nd and 3rd? ______

7. On a map 1 cm represents 200 m. What is represented by:
   a 0·5 cm? ______
   b 3·5 cm? ______

8. Kilograms in 2 307 g. ______

9. Asha spent $100 on party decorations. Tye only spent two tenths of what Asha spent. How much did Tye spend? ______

10. Round each number to the nearest whole then estimate the answer.
    a 3·4 × 7·2 ______
    b 9·3 × 6·9 ______
    c 26·8 − 13·1 ______

11. Write all the factors of 42.
    ______

34:4 out of 4

Extension

1. The mass of a horse is 0·4 tonnes. Find the mass of:
   a 8 horses ______
   b 10 horses ______

2. 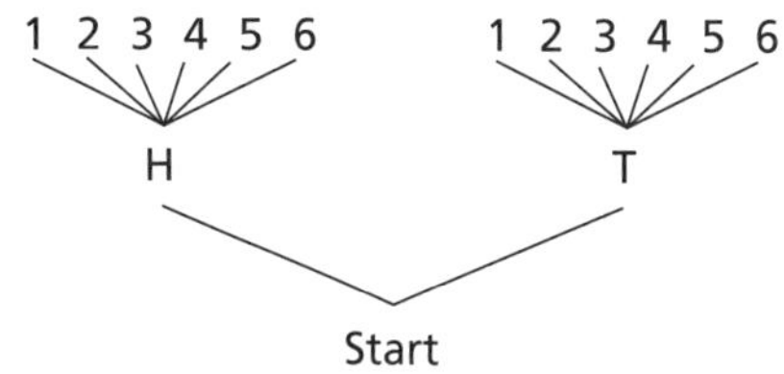

   I tossed a coin, then rolled a dice. Use this tree diagram to find:
   a the number of possible outcomes ______
   b the chance of a tail ______
   c the chance of a head and 3 ______

3. Draw the missing part of this pattern.

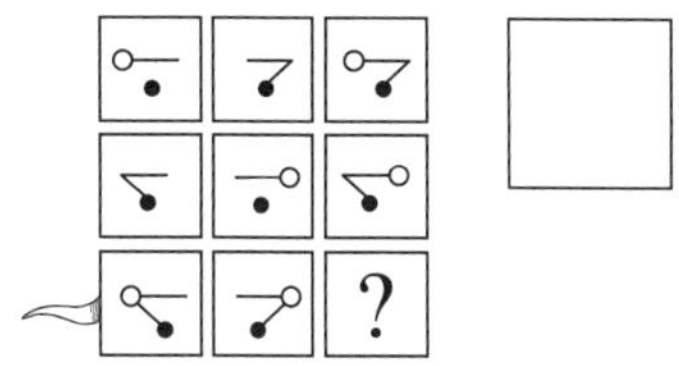

4. Which is not equivalent to 0·5?
   $\frac{1}{2}$, $\frac{1}{5}$, $\frac{5}{10}$, 50%? ______

Challenge

Draw a tree diagram to show possible combinations if I have the choice of wearing 2 T-shirts and 3 pairs of shorts.

Can you balance this 27 kg mass using only the masses shown below?
Use the columns in the table to show as many answers as you can.

One answer is given here. Other answers have been started.

(2 × 10) + (1 × 5) + (1 × 2)

	a	b	c	d	e	f	g	h
10 kg	2	2	2	2	1			
5 kg	1	1	0					
2 kg	1	0						
1 kg	0							

 • *AUSTRALIAN SIGNPOST MATHS 6 MENTALS* • ISBN 978 1 4886 2192 5

35:1 ☐ out of 17

1. 0×83 ____
2. \$64 − \$6 ____
3. 7×4 ____
4. $10 \div 10$ ____
5. $78 + 8$ ____
6. Half of \$48. ____
7. Add 29 and 8. ____
8. 3 times 60. ____
9. 46 take away 7. ____
10. \$0.89 − \$0.50 ____
11. $192 - \square = 65$, $\square =$ ____
12. How many decimal places in each number?
    a 5·16 ____ b 38·502 ____
    c 22·91 ____ d 4103·4 ____
13. Create a pattern by flipping the tile in both directions.

14. a Is $\frac{2}{10}$ the same as $\frac{1}{5}$? ____
    b Is $\frac{5}{10}$ the same as $\frac{1}{2}$? ____
    c $\frac{2}{10} + \frac{5}{10}$ ____
    d $\frac{1}{5} + \frac{1}{2}$ ____

15. Circle the multiples of 3.
    15 16 17 18 19 20
16. How many times will this shape match its original position as it rotates through one complete revolution? ____

17. Grams in 5 kg 127 g. ____

35:2 ☐ out of 19

1. 8×7 ____
2. $65 - 33$ ____
3. $8 + 72$ ____
4. 6×900 ____
5. $0 \cdot 95 + 1 \cdot 2$ ____
6. $33 \div 11 - 6 \times 0$ ____
7. $8 \times 8 \times 8$ ____
8. Zero squared. ____
9. 9 squared. ____
10. $6 \cdot 9 - 1 \cdot 45$ ____
11. Round off \$8.33 correct to the nearest 5 cents. ____
12. Kilograms in 4726 g. ____
13. 4 out of 5 friends will fit in a small boat. How many different groups of 4 could be chosen? ____
14. 10 squared take away 4 squared. ____
15. Circle the item you would weigh in milligrams.
    a giraffe an eyelash a pencil
16. A scale length of 1 cm represents 40 km. How many kilometres are represented by 4·5 cm? ____
17. Find the area of a square of length:
    a 0·4 cm ____ b 0·5 cm ____
18. a $9\overline{)1818}$ b $7\overline{)4942}$
19. Round 32·6 to the nearest whole. ____

Calculator Crossnumber Puzzle

Across
1 714 × 33
5 6463 − 5917
6 975 + 3618
8 7384 ÷ 568
9 $25^2 + 240$
10 675^2

Down
1 4148 ÷ 17
2 6000 − 807
3 625 ÷ 25
4 328600 + 240945
7 72^2
9 6000 − 5194

35:3 ☐ out of 12

1. $\begin{array}{r} 22 \\ \times\ 8 \\ \hline \end{array}$

2. $\begin{array}{r} 340 \\ \times\ 5 \\ \hline \end{array}$

3. $\begin{array}{r} 21 \\ \times\ 3 \\ \hline \end{array}$

4. a $\begin{array}{r} 264000 \\ +\ 23582 \\ \hline \end{array}$ b $\begin{array}{r} 281813 \\ -\ 70508 \\ \hline \end{array}$

5. Insert a decimal point in the answer to make this number sentence correct.
   7·56 × 9 = 6804 ______

6. Grams in $2\frac{1}{2}$ kilograms. ______

7. a 5 g = ______ mg   b 9000 mg = ______ g

8. How many pairs can I make using one of six different colours and a number from 1 to 52? ______

9. Which of +, −, × and ÷ will make 3 □ 3 △ 3 = 4 true?   □ = ______, △ = ______

10. 9·932 kg = ______ g

11. Divide or multiply each part by a number to make each question easier to solve.
    a 300 ÷ 60
    ____ ÷ ____ = ____
    b 0·16 ÷ 0·08
    ____ ÷ ____ = ____

12. Round each number to the nearest whole, then estimate the answer.
    a 10·2 × 5·9 ______
    b 12·5 + 29·8 ______
    c 52·6 − 30·5 ______
    d 42 × 3·4 ______

35:4 ☐ out of 4 Extension

1. A truck can carry 8 tonnes of sand. What is the least number of trips needed to shift 135 tonnes of sand? ______

2. How many times will a tracing of this shape match itself as the tracing is rotated through one revolution about the centre point? ______

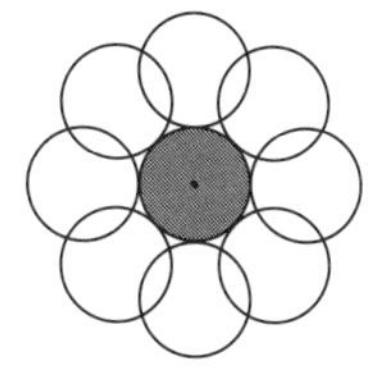

3. a How many small squares are in this rectangle? ______
   b How many are in an area 4 times as long and 3 times as wide? ______

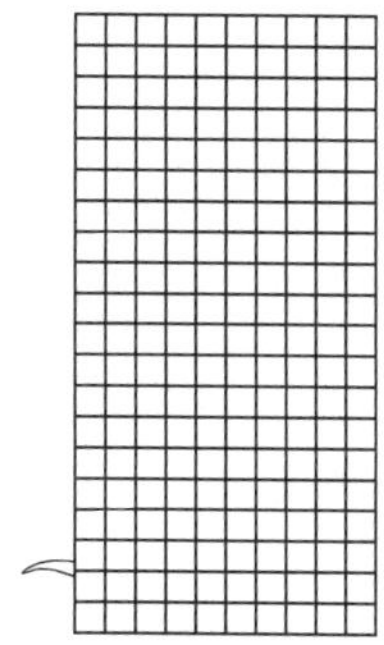

4. After losing $54 and finding only $20, I had $42 left. How much did I start with? ______

Challenge

Create a design on the grid by flipping, sliding and turning this pattern.

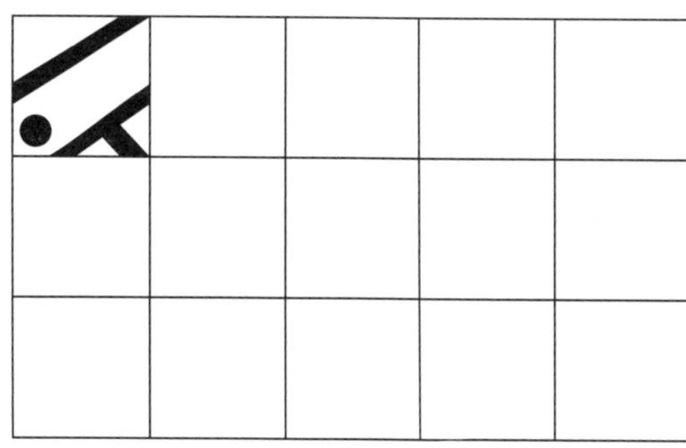

Reflections

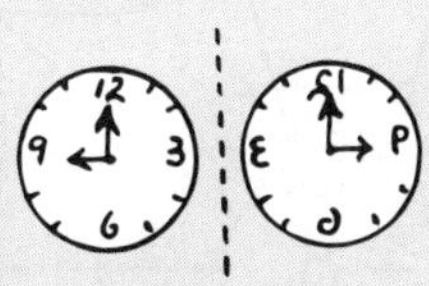

A reflection is a flip.

a I saw the clock in the mirror. It looked like 2 o'clock but it was really ______.

Refer to the flip on the left.

b Do the lengths of the arms change? ______

c Does the angle between arms change? ______

d Do things face the opposite direction? ______

36:1 out of 18

1. 74 − 7 ____
2. 60 + 80 ____
3. 350 ÷ 5 ____
4. 9 × $40 ____
5. $4\overline{)124}$
6. 9 less than 25. ____
7. 36 ÷ 6 ____
8. 3 × 4 × 5 ____
9. 16 more than 90. ____
10. $3\overline{)102}$
11. $0{\cdot}7 = \frac{\square}{100} =$ ____ %
12. □ × 4 = 200, □ = ____
13. How many decimal places in each number?
    a 32·941 ____ **b** 958·4 ____
14. Was each pattern made using flip, slide or turn?
    a
    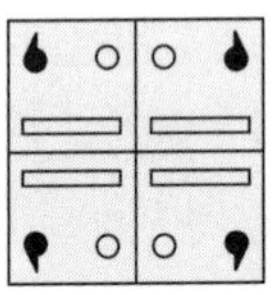
    ____
    b
    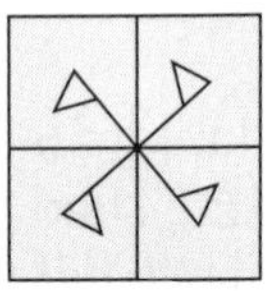
    ____
15. 16 = ____ squared
16. 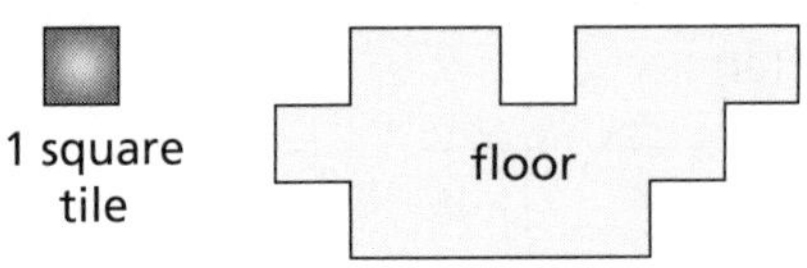

    How many of the square tiles are needed to cover the floor? ____
17. The short form for:
    a 7·1 hectares ____
    b 20 square metres ____
18. 9 kg = ____ g

36:2 out of 18

1. 300 ÷ 60 ____
2. 52 + 30 ____
3. 6 × 8 ____
4. 230 − 20 ____
5. $\begin{array}{r} 6{\cdot}7 \\ \times\ \ 9 \\ \hline \end{array}$
6. 56c ÷ 7 ____
7. 1·8 ÷ 0·6 ____
8. 810 ÷ 90 ____
9. 65 − 3 × 8 ____
10. $\begin{array}{r} 13{\cdot}85 \\ -\ \ 3{\cdot}8 \\ \hline \end{array}$
11. Round off the answer to Question 10, correct to the nearest whole. ____
12. Grams in 2 kg 370 g. ____
13. How many outfits can be chosen from:
    a 3 shirts and 5 pants? ____
    b 12 shirts and 7 pants? ____
14. 
    How many different ways can I choose a pair of creatures from those above? ____
15. 6 squared plus 2. ____
16. Square metres in 9 ha. ____
17. How many times will a tracing of this shape match itself, as the tracing is rotated through one revolution about the centre point?

    ____
18. Find the area of a square of length:
    a 0·2 cm ____ **b** 0·8 cm ____

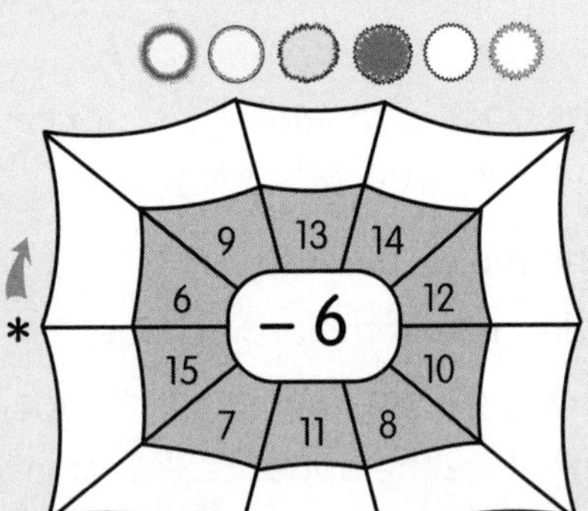

36:3 ☐ out of 12

1. $\begin{array}{r} 31 \\ \times\ 6 \\ \hline \end{array}$

2. $10\overline{)8462100}$

3. $\begin{array}{r} 335 \\ +401 \\ \hline \end{array}$

4. $\begin{array}{r} 658 \\ +213 \\ \hline \end{array}$

5. $\begin{array}{r} 529 \\ +294 \\ \hline \end{array}$

6. Is the mass of most men more or less than 50 kg? ______

7. To move the picture from start to finish, which of the following would you choose?

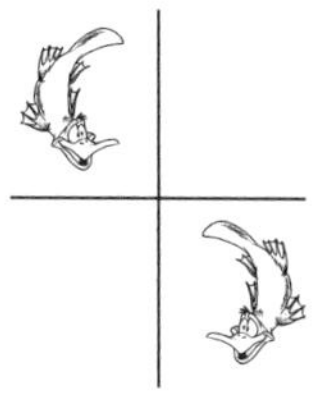

A turn then slide
B flip then flip
C flip then slide ______

8.

train taxi bike	rain hail sunshine

Rajiv has to choose one item from each rectangle. How many different pairs could he choose? ______

(Draw a tree diagram to find the answer).

9. The product of 8 and 6. ______

10. 6000 + 300 + 8 + 2 ______

11. 12·5 kg = ______ g

12. Divide or multiply each part by a number to make each question easier to solve.

a 540 ÷ 60
____ ÷ ____ = ____

b 3·6 ÷ 0·9
____ ÷ ____ = ____

36:4 ☐ out of 6 **Extension**

1. The mass of a tub is 1·2 t.
What is the mass, in kilograms, of:
a 3 tubs? ______ **b** 10 tubs? ______

2. How many squares will there be if each side of the rectangle is made twice as long? ______

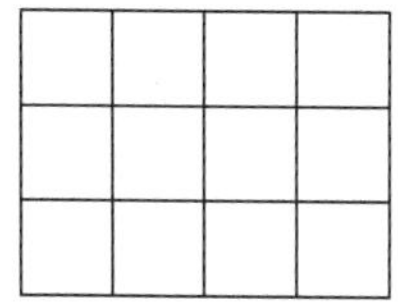

3. To get 31, I double a number and then add 13. What is that number? ______

4. The shaded part has a value of 12. What is the value of the whole?

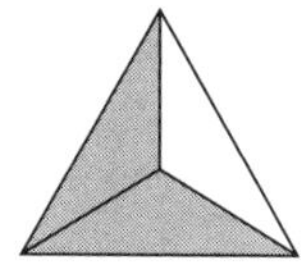

______

5. **a** $\frac{1}{3}$ of 15 ______ **b** $\frac{2}{3}$ of 15 ______
c $\frac{1}{10}$ of 100 ______ **d** $\frac{2}{10}$ of 100 ______

6. There are 4 dogs, 2 cats and a rabbit. How many different ways are there of choosing one of each? ______

Challenge

Write facts about the number 5·231.

______
______
______
______
______

Average speed = distance travelled for each unit of time
Find the average speed if:

a 200 metres is covered in 10 seconds. ______ per second
b 144 kilometres is covered in 3 hours. ______ per hour
c 980 kilometres is covered in 4 days. ______ per day
d 60 millimetres is covered in 5 seconds. ______ per second

37:1 out of 19

1. 7×50 ____
2. $112 - 107$ ____
3. $250 \div 5$ ____
4. $25 + 7$ ____
5. $\begin{array}{r} \$70 \\ \times \quad 9 \\ \hline \end{array}$
6. Divide 180 by 6. ____
7. 8 groups of 40. ____
8. \$120 minus \$9. ____
9. Increase 90 by 40. ____
10. $\begin{array}{r} \$100.00 \\ - \quad \$0.53 \\ \hline \end{array}$
11. Round off the answer to Question 10, correct to the nearest 5c. ____
12. 7 km^2 = ____ ha if 1 km^2 = 100 ha.
13. 100% of \$5 is ____.
14. The next four multiples of 8.

    96, ____, ____, ____, ____
15. Write $\frac{5}{3}$ in words. ____
16. **a** Write this as 24-hour time. ____

    b What will be the 24-hour time in 18 minutes? ____

17. Use am or pm to write:

    a 07:32 ____ **b** 21:32 ____

    c 18:40 ____ **d** 09:47 ____
18. Find an estimate by rounding off each number:

    a 53×19 ____

    b 41×39 ____

    c 22×58 ____
19. 2 ha = ____ m^2

37:2 out of 18

1. 9×80 ____
2. $90 - 90$ ____
3. $210 \div 70$ ____
4. $89 + 15$ ____
5. $\begin{array}{r} 3\cdot85 \\ +91\cdot6 \\ \hline \end{array}$
6. $640 \div 8$ ____
7. $8{\cdot}1 \div 0{\cdot}9$ ____
8. $3{\cdot}6 \div 0{\cdot}6$ ____
9. 7 squared. ____
10. $\begin{array}{r} 410 \\ \times \quad 80 \\ \hline \end{array}$
11. 60 000 m^2 = ____ ha
12. How many outfits can be chosen from 2 shirts and 4 pants?

    ____

    (Draw a tree diagram to find the answer.)
13. Square kilometres in 600 ha. ____
14. The area of:

    a the shaded part? ____

    b the part not shaded? ____

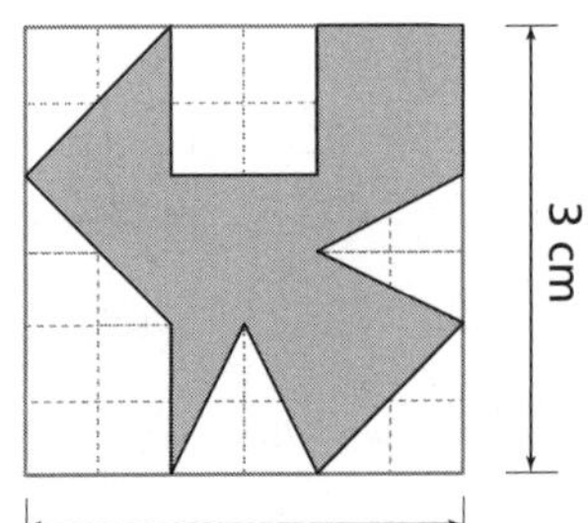

15. 3 squared add 7 squared. ____
16. 50% of \$3.20 is ____.
17. How many square metres in:

    a $\frac{1}{2}$ hectare? ____

    b $\frac{1}{4}$ hectare? ____

18. Grams in 3 kg 497 g. ____

Turn to ID Card C on page 8.
Give the answers for these numbers.

(11) ____ (16) ____
(17) ____ (18) ____
(19) ____ (20) ____
(21) ____ (22) ____
(23) ____ (24) ____

37:3 ☐ out of 11

1
```
  2194031
  1360292
+  843603
```

2
```
  3672000
  2401701
+  517391
```

3
```
  1590000
−  271500
```

4
```
  9872000
−  530120
```

5 A square with 100 m sides has an area of 1 hectare. (100 m × 100 m = 1 ha). Find the area (in ha) of each of these.

a

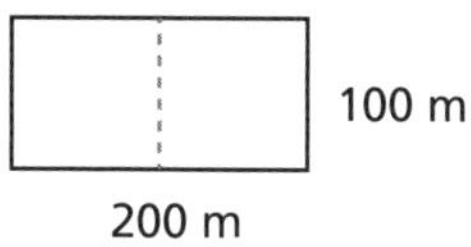

b

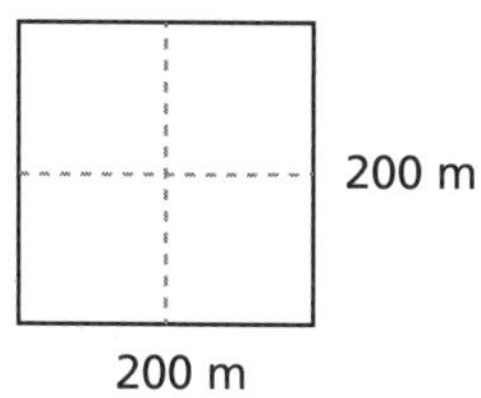

________ ________

6 200 ha = ________ km²

7 Circle the best estimate for 8·14 × 8.

0·65 6·5 65 650

8 The product of 7 and 5. ________

9 50% of \$4.70 is ________.

10 7 km² = ________ ha

11

Each dog has a mass of about 15 kg. Calculate the approximate mass of:

a 5 dogs ________

b 10 dogs ________

37:4 ☐ out of 5 — Extension

1 1 hectare = 10 000 m²

a 1 ha − 8000 m² ________

b 1 ha − 9076 m² ________

2 10% reduction was given on the price of a TV set marked at \$890. How much was paid? ________

3 If the sides of this rectangle are made 4 times as long, how many times as big will its area be? ________

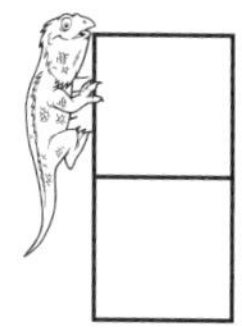

4 Jody started with a number, doubled it, divided by 3 then subtracted 52. She finished with 8. What did she start with? ________

5 How many different choices of a food item and a drink can be made if there are three types of food and two types of drink? ________

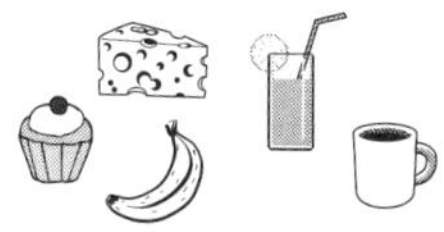

Challenge

Write number sentences that are equal to 24.

____

____

____

____

____

Fill in this table for the person measured in Unit 1.

Name: ________________ **Date:** ________________

Age: ________	Mass: ________ kg	Shoe size: ________
Height: ________ cm	Waist: ________ cm	Neck size: ________ cm

How have these measurements changed since Unit 1? ________________

____

Examples of Measurements

1
- The width of a finger is about 1 cm.
- The length of a place-value tens block is 10 cm.

2
- The height of the girl is a little more than 1 m.

3
- The container of milk holds 2 L.
- The can of softdrink holds 375 mL.
- The teaspoon holds 5 mL.

4
- The boy has a mass of 40 kg.
- The margarine has a mass of 500 g.

5
- A double page of the newspaper has an area of half of 1 m^2.
- The top of a place-value ones block has an area of 1 cm^2.

6
- 30°C is a hot day.
- 3°C is a very cold day.

Use the pictures above to estimate the answers to these questions.

1 **a** How high is the glass?
b How wide is the table?

2 **a** How wide is the clothes line?
b How tall is the woman?

3 **a** How much will the bucket hold?
b How much will the cup hold?

4 **a** What is the mass of the dog?
b What is the mass of 2 L of milk?

5 **a** What is the area of the window?
b What is the area of the top of a matchbox?

6 **a** What is the temperature on a very hot day?
b What is the temperature on a cool day?